Sentimental Rules

Sentimental Rules

On the Natural Foundations
of Moral Judgment

SHAUN NICHOLS

OXFORD
UNIVERSITY PRESS

2004

OXFORD
UNIVERSITY PRESS

Oxford   New York
Auckland   Bangkok   Buenos Aires   Cape Town   Chennai
Dar es Salaam   Delhi   Hong Kong   Istanbul   Karachi   Kolkata
Kuala Lumpur   Madrid   Melbourne   Mexico City   Mumbai   Nairobi
São Paulo   Shanghai   Taipei   Tokyo   Toronto

Published by Oxford University Press, Inc.
198 Madison Avenue, New York, New York 10016

www.oup.com

Oxford is a registered trademark of Oxford University Press

Library of Congress Cataloging-in-Publication Data
Nichols, Shaun.
Sentimental rules : on the natural foundations of moral judgment / Shaun Nichols.
     p. cm.
Includes bibliographical references and index.
ISBN 0-19-531420-4
1. Emotivism.   I. Title
BJ1473 .N53   2004
170′4—dc21   2003056382

9 8 7 6 5 4 3 2 1

Printed in the United States of America
on acid-free paper

For my parents, Gib and Sally Nichols

Preface

A few basic questions about the nature of morality command the attention even of those not steeped in philosophical training. Is morality grounded in rationality or does it depend crucially on the emotions? How did our moral system evolve to its present shape and character? Is morality objective? Would the rejection of moral objectivity have dire consequences for our normative lives? These are the kinds of questions that grab the novice to moral philosophy, and they are the questions that guided the explorations charted in this volume.

My pursuit of these fundamental metaethical issues has been thoroughly interdisciplinary, exploiting resources from philosophy, cognitive psychopathology, developmental psychology, cognitive anthropology, and social history. This interdisciplinary approach was not driven by any principled ecumenism. Rather, in trying to get a purchase on philosophical issues about, say, the role of sentiment in moral judgment or the genealogy of morals, I found myself driven to other disciplines to obtain the kind of information that seemed relevant to the issues. It turns out that there is a great deal of extant empirical work that is philosophically instructive, as I hope to display in this volume. In some instances, the relevant empirical information simply hadn't been sought, though it seemed easy enough to obtain. Initially, I suggested to friends in psychology that they might want to run this or that experiment. Oddly, I found that many psychologists do not particularly like being told which experiments to run. So in some cases I was reduced to running experiments by myself.

These wide-ranging investigations led to an account of the nature of morality in the Humean tradition on which the emotions play a vital role in morality. On the theory I develop, emotions play a critical role in both the psychological and the cultural underpinnings of basic moral judgment. Norms prohibiting harming others are, I argue, associated with a fundamental emotional response, and this connection invests such norms and other "Sentimental Rules" with a distinctive status. Furthermore, I argue that such Sentimental Rules enjoy an advantage in cultural evolution, which partly explains the cultural success and historical development of certain moral norms. The account that emerges, I maintain, has broad ramifications for philosophical ethics.

Given the breadth of the issues taken up, one casualty has been scholarly depth. I have neglected many important works in contemporary metaethics. The situation is rather worse for the other disciplines I plunder. The ground I cover in this slim book is immodestly vast. I am trying to address basic issues that were plumbed by Hume, Kant, and Nietzsche, to name a few of the more intimidating figures. My hope is that naturalistic methods really will shed light on these basic issues. But in attempting to contribute to these hoary debates, this hope has been accompanied by an abiding sentiment of humility.

Acknowledgments

Given the ambitiously interdisciplinary nature of this work, it is perhaps not surprising that my intellectual debts run wide. Many philosophers and psychologists have provided advice and comments on various parts of the book, including James Blair, Deborah Boyle, Bill Casebeer, Jonathan Cohen, Justin D'Arms, Ronald de Sousa, John Doris, Susan Dwyer, Luc Faucher, Owen Flanagan, Trisha Folds-Bennett, Tim German, Todd Grantham, Dan Guevara, Paul Harris, Dan Haybron, Ned Hettinger, Daniel Jacobson, Todd Jones, Christopher Knapp, Larry Krasnoff, Glenn Lesses, Edouard Machery, Ron Mallon, Elizabeth Meny, Aaron Meskin, Adam Morton, Richard Nunan, Marty Perlmutter, Chandra Sripada, Steve Stich, Kyle Swan, and Hugh Wilder. Many thanks to all of these friends and colleagues for their help. Thanks also to my editor, Peter Ohlin, for his support and his speedy work.

Michael Gill and I have discussed the issues and arguments in this book frequently over the last several years. He also provided extensive comments on the entire manuscript. The book is considerably better than it would have been without his input, and I am most grateful for his help.

My greatest intellectual debt is unquestionably to Steve Stich. Before I ever met Steve he was one of my intellectual heroes for his knack at

.

extracting philosophically important conclusions from scientific work. His work has been a model of how to do naturalistic philosophy. Over the last dozen years, Steve has been a frequent collaborator and valued friend. In addition to providing characteristically insightful feedback on the work here, Steve has been a constant source of encouragement and inspiration. I would not have known how to begin, much less finish, this project were it not for Steve.

Finally I am deeply thankful for the love and support of my family, Heather, Sarah, and Julia.

Some portions of the book are drawn from previously published work. I am grateful to the publishers for permission to use material from the following articles: Mindreading and the cognitive architecture under-lying altruistic motivation, *Mind and Language* 16 (2001): 425–55, with permission from Blackwell; Is it irrational to be amoral? How psycho-paths threaten moral rationalism, *The Monist: An International Quarterly Journal of General Philosophical Inquiry* 85 (2002, Peru, Illinois, 61354): 285–304, reprinted by permission; Norms with feeling: Towards a psycho-logical account of moral judgment, *Cognition* 84 (2002): 221–36, with permission from Elsevier; On the genealogy of norms: A case for the role of emotion in cultural evolution, *Philosophy of Science* 69 (2002): 234–55, with permission from the University of Chicago Press.

Contents

Sentimental Rules

I

Norms with Feeling

Toward a Psychological Account
of Moral Judgment

When I am at a loss to know the effects of one body upon
another in any situation, I need only put them in that situation,
and observe what results from it. But should I endeavour to
clear up after the same manner any doubt in moral philosophy,
by placing myself in the same case with that which I consider,
'tis evident this reflection and premeditation would so disturb
the operation of my natural principles, as must render it impossible to form any just conclusion from the phenomenon.
We must, therefore, glean up our experiments in this science
from a cautious observation of human life, and take them as
they appear in the common course of the world, by men's behaviour in company, in affairs, and in their pleasures. Where
experiments of this kind are judiciously collected and compared, we may hope to establish on them a science which will
not be inferior in certainty, and will be much superior in util-
ity, to any other of human comprehension.

—David Hume, *A Treatise on Human Nature*

1. INTRODUCTION

Hume concludes his introduction to the *Treatise* with the above call for a
research program. While naturalistic philosophers of every stripe applaud
Hume's empirical turn, historians of philosophy note that Hume does
not mean "experiment" the way we do today.[1] Rather, for Hume, cautious

---

1. A second qualification concerns his term "moral philosophy" which, in Hume's usage is not
restricted to issues about morality, but rather, refers to the study of humans more generally, or the
"science of human nature" (Hume, *Enquiry Concerning Human Understanding*, 5).

observation of human life primarily consisted in a kind of human ethology. One quietly observes people's behavior in their ordinary environments. Nonetheless, there is no reason to think that Hume would have shrunk from applying the standard experimental method to the study of moral judgment. On the contrary, it is likely that Hume would have championed the use of controlled experiments in moral psychology, had the methodology been readily available in his time. Hume's interests in the nature of moral judgment ranged widely, including issues about the role of sentiment in moral judgment, the role of reason in moral judgment, and the origin of moral judgment. To address these issues adequately requires attention to empirical details. In this volume, I will draw on recent work that attempts to supply such empirical details. Although the bulk of this research has been done by social scientists rather than philosophers, I suspect that were Hume alive today, this research would be high on his reading list.

Many of the deepest issues concerning the nature of morality would be illuminated if we had an adequate account of the nature of moral judgment. So it is scarcely surprising that researchers before and after Hume have invested enormous effort in trying to produce an account of moral judgment. The exploration of moral judgment in psychology stretches back for a century, through Kohlberg and Piaget. The philosophical lineage is much longer and enjoys an even more distinguished cast, including Kant, Hume, and Aristotle.

Throughout the twentieth century, philosophical work in metaethics largely ignored the psychological literature on moral judgment. Part of the explanation for this, I suspect, is simply that much of the best known psychological work seems not to intersect directly with the issues philosophers care about. Much of the psychological work on the nature of morality, for instance, charts developmental changes, gender differences, and cultural variations in moral cognition. But this kind of work seems not to address the core of morality—it does not tell us what is at the heart of moral judgment. As a result, it does not tell us what we want to know in metaethics. Over the last twenty years, a tradition in moral psychology has developed that really does, I will maintain, help us understand the nature of moral judgment. The research explores the ability to appreciate the distinctive status of morality, as reflected by the capacity to distinguish moral from conventional transgressions. In this chapter, I will suggest that this method plausibly reveals a capacity for a kind of core moral judgment. I will also present the prevailing accounts that might explain core moral judgment. There is a long history of perspective-taking accounts of moral capacities. More recently, there is an important proposal that ties moral judgment fairly directly to an affective response. I will maintain that the evidence on core moral judgment indicates that both of these approaches are inadequate. I will argue that the capacity for core moral judgment depends on both a body of information about which actions are prohibited (a "normative theory") and an affective mechanism that confers a special status on the norms.

2. CORE MORAL JUDGMENT

In the psychological literature, the capacity for moral judgment has perhaps been most directly approached empirically by exploring the basic capacity to distinguish moral violations (e.g., pulling another person's hair) from conventional violations (e.g., chewing gum in class). This tradition in psychology began with the work of Elliott Turiel and has flourished over the last two decades (Turiel, Killen, and Helwig 1987; Dunn and Munn 1987; Smetana and Braeges 1990; Nucci 1986; Blair 1993). Turiel explicitly draws on the writings of several philosophers, including Searle, Brandt, and Rawls to draw the moral/conventional distinction. The distinction is characterized as follows: "Conventions are part of constitutive systems and are shared behaviors (uniformities, rules) whose meanings are defined by the constituted system in which they are embedded" (Turiel, Killen, and Helwig 1987, 169). Moral rules, on the other hand, are "unconditionally obligatory, generalizable, and impersonal insofar as they stem from concepts of welfare, justice, and rights" (Turiel, Killen, and Helwig 1987, 169–70). Although Turiel adverts to philosophical precedent for this distinction, the attempt to draw an analytic distinction between morality and convention is fraught with controversy. Fortunately, it is a controversy we can ignore. For we do not need to supply an analysis to see the significance of the data. The research program generated by Turiel's work indicates that people distinguish moral violations from conventional violations along several dimensions.

Rather than embark on an attempt to define the moral and conventional domains, the easiest way to see the import of the data on moral judgment is to consider how subjects distinguish canonical examples of moral violations from canonical examples of conventional violations. Hitting another person is a canonical example of a moral violation used in these studies. Other frequently used examples of moral violations are pulling hair, stealing, and pushing another child. The examples of conventional violations that have been studied are much more varied. Some of the examples are violations of school rules, such as not paying attention during story time or talking out of turn. Some of the examples are violations of etiquette, such as drinking soup out of a bowl. Other examples are violations of family rules, such as not clearing one's dishes. What is striking about this literature is that, from a young age, children distinguish the moral violations from the conventional violations on a number of dimensions. For instance, children tend to think that moral transgressions are generally less permissible and more serious than conventional transgressions. Children are also more likely to maintain that the moral violations are "generalizably" wrong, for example, that pulling hair is wrong in other countries too. And the explanations for why moral transgressions are wrong are given in terms of fairness and harm to victims. For example, children will say that pulling hair is wrong because it hurts the person. By contrast, the explanation for why conventional transgressions are wrong is given in terms of social acceptability—talking out of turn is wrong because it is rude or impolite, or because "you're not supposed to." Further, conventional rules, unlike moral rules, are viewed as dependent on authority. For instance, if at another school the teacher has no rule against chewing gum, children will judge that it is not wrong to chew gum at that school; but even if the teacher at another school has no rule against hitting, children claim that it is still wrong to hit. Indeed, a fascinating study on Amish teenagers indicates that moral judgments are not even regarded as dependent on God's authority. Nucci (1986) found that 100 percent of a group of Amish teenagers said that if God had made no rule against working on Sunday, it would not be wrong to work on Sunday. However, more than 80 percent of these subjects said that even if God had made no rule about hitting, it would still be wrong to hit.

These findings on the moral/conventional distinction are neither fragile nor superficial. On the contrary, the findings are quite robust. They have been replicated numerous times using a wide variety of stimuli (see Smetana 1993 and Tisak 1995 for reviews). Furthermore, the research apparently plumbs a fairly deep feature of moral judgment. For moral violations are treated as distinctive along several different dimensions. Moral violations attract high ratings on seriousness, they are regarded as having wide applicability, they have a status of authority independence, and they invite different kinds of justifications from conventional violations. Finally, this turns out to be a persistent feature of moral judgment. It is found in young and old alike. Thus, it seems that the capacity for drawing the moral/conventional distinction is part of basic moral psychology.

Most of the above research on the moral/conventional distinction has focused on moral violations that involve harming others, and that will be my main focus as well. However, it is clear that harm-centered violations do not exhaust the moral domain. To take one obvious example, we think it is wrong to cheat on one's taxes, but this has little direct bearing on harm. Furthermore, recent evidence indicates that the moral domain may not even be stable across cultures (e.g., Miller, Bersoff, and Harwood 1990; Haidt, Koller, and Diaz 1993). In a clever study by Jonathan Haidt and colleagues, they found that low socioeconomic status (SES) subjects were more likely than high SES subjects to maintain that people engaging in offensive or disrespectful actions (e.g., having sex with a dead chicken or cleaning the toilet with the national flag) should be stopped or punished (Haidt, Koller, and Diaz 1993). Haidt and colleagues conclude that it is parochial to think that harm is central to drawing the moral/conventional distinction (e.g., Haidt, Koller, and Diaz 1993, 625). Although there may be some relativity in the moral domain, the cross-cultural work also indicates that in all cultures, canonical examples of moral violations involve harming others (see, e.g., Hollos, Leis, and Turiel 1986; Nucci, Turiel, and Encarnacion-Gawrych 1983; Song, Smetana, and Kim 1987). Indeed, even Haidt and colleagues found that the subjects in different cultures and different SES groups made similar judgments about violations involving harm—for example, in all groups subjects tended to say that a girl who pushes a boy off a swing should be punished or stopped.

Thus, even though the moral domain is hardly exhausted by harm-based violations, it is plausible that judgments about harm-based violations constitute an important core of moral judgment. For the appreciation of harm-based violations shows up early ontogenetically (as we will see in section 3), and it seems to be cross-culturally universal. Brian Scholl and Alan Leslie make a related point about "theory of mind," the capacity to understand other minds (Scholl and Leslie 1999). They note that, although there are cross-cultural differences in theory of mind, all cultures seem to share a core theory of mind that emerges early ontogenetically (140). Something similar might be said about the findings on moral judgment—despite the cross-cultural differences in moral judgment, the evidence indicates that all cultures share an important basic capacity, what I will call "core moral judgment." The capacity to recognize that harm-based violations have a special status (as compared to conventional violations) is an important indicator of the capacity for core moral judgment. As a first approximation, the capacity for core moral judgment can be thought of as the capacity to recognize that harm-based violations are very serious, authority independent, generalizable and that the actions are wrong because of welfare considerations.

In the remainder of this chapter, I will develop an account of core moral judgment that draws on evidence from developmental psychology and cognitive psychopathology.[2] In contemporary cognitive science, evidence from development and evidence from psychopathologies play particularly central roles in guiding theorizing about the psychological architecture underlying a capacity. For these sources give us a glimpse into which capacities might be independent from one another and which capacities seem to be inextricably linked. In chapters 3 and 4, I will return to the evidence from development and psychopathologies, and I will argue that the evidence poses problems for philosophical accounts of moral judgment from both the rationalist and the sentimentalist traditions. But before we can set out the philosophical ramifications, we would do well to get clear on the psychology. This will require looking closely at the available psychological accounts of the underpinnings of core moral judgment. There are two prominent approaches to the psychological architecture underlying moral judgment that we must consider—the perspective-taking account and Blair's VIM-account. Both accounts, I will argue, are not adequate to the data.

3. PERSPECTIVE: TAKING ACCOUNTS OF MORAL JUDGMENT

The Piagetian tradition in moral psychology ties moral understanding to the capacity for perspective taking, or imagining oneself to have the mental states of another (e.g., Piaget 1932; Kohlberg 1984; Selman 1980; Damon 1977; see also Rawls 1971, chapter 8). The capacity for perspective taking itself has received enormous attention over the last twenty years, in the research on the capacity for understanding other minds, or "mindreading." Researchers in this tradition have explored in detail the capacity for attributing mental states to others and predicting others' behavior (e.g., Baron-Cohen, Leslie, and Frith 1985; Bartsch and Wellman 1995; Goldman 1989; Gopnik and Wellman 1994; Gordon 1986; Harris 1992;

---

2. For the philosophers, I should acknowledge that I am being deliberately ingenuous about some long-standing disputes in metaethics. In particular, I will not engage the noncognitivist view that, despite appearances, moral utterances (e.g., "it is wrong to murder") do not express judgments or beliefs of the speaker but only noncognitive states (like disapproval). Simon Blackburn and other noncognitivists have developed tremendously clever devices for accommodating the apparently cognitivist surface features of moral discourse (e.g., Blackburn 1984, 1985). These noncognitivist pyrotechnics will not be addressed here. For the goal in this volume is to begin by taking commonsense moral thought at face value. On this approach we want to avoid, at least initially, invoking the kinds of subtle reinterpretations of moral discourse that are offered by noncognitivists. In addition, I am independently suspicious of some of the claims that undergird noncognitivism. For instance, noncognitivist accounts typically depend on the view that it is a conceptual truth that moral judgments are motivating, and this claim runs up against serious obstacles (see chapter 5, section 4).

Leslie 1994; Nichols and Stich 2003; Stich and Nichols 1992). This work on mindreading has been carried out largely in isolation from work in moral psychology, but the research on mindreading affords us the opportunity to evaluate perspective-taking accounts of moral judgment much more effectively.

Although the recent mindreading literature boasts no detailed perspective-taking account of core moral judgment, several recent theorists seem to suggest that perspective taking might be required for moral judgment. For instance, Alvin Goldman cites Schopenhauer and Rousseau as advocates of the view that empathy is "the source of moral principles" (1993, 355). And Goldman defines empathy in terms of perspective taking: "Paradigm cases of empathy . . . consist first of taking the perspective of another person, that is, imaginatively assuming one or more of the other person's mental states. . . . The initial "pretend" states are then operated upon (automatically) by psychological processes, which generate further states that (in favorable cases) are similar to, or homologous to, the target person's states. In central cases of empathy the output states are affective or emotional states" (1993, 351). In a similar vein, John Deigh claims that in order to grasp right and wrong in the deeper sense, one needs mature empathy, which involves inter alia, "taking this other person's perspective and imagining the feelings of frustration or anger" (Deigh 1995, 758). Robert Gordon offers a more explicit and sophisticated perspective-taking account of how we determine whether an action is wrong, suggesting that we "imagine being in X's situation, once with the further adjustments required to imagine being X in that X's situation and once without these adjustments. If your response is the same in each case, approve X's conduct; if not, disapprove" (Gordon 1995, 741).

Surely people sometimes use perspective taking in making moral evaluations. And the above authors are not sufficiently precise about which kinds of moral judgments depend on perspective taking to allow us to determine whether they would maintain that the basic capacity to draw the moral/conventional distinction depends on the capacity for perspective taking. There is certainly no systematic argument in the recent mindreading literature for the view that perspective taking is required for drawing the moral/conventional distinction. But the work on the moral/conventional distinction currently provides the clearest way to explore the basic capacity for moral judgment, so it will be of interest to see how a perspective taking account of this capacity fares against the evidence in any case. The evidence suggests that any attempt to defend that position will face some serious obstacles.

The first problem for perspective-taking accounts comes from developmental evidence. Children begin to appreciate features of the moral/

conventional distinction surprisingly early. Smetana and Braeges (1990) found that shortly before the third birthday, children were more likely to judge that moral violations generalized across contexts than conventional violations when they were asked, "At another school, is it OK (or not OK) to X?" (336). Further, according to Smetana and Braeges, after factoring in corrections for language, the results suggest that children generalize moral violations in this way shortly after the second birthday, and they recognize that conventional violations but not moral violations are contingent on authority at two years and ten months (Smetana and Braeges 1990, 342). More conservative estimates put the recognition that moral violations are not authority contingent shortly after the third birthday (Blair 1993). So, apparently young children can make these distinctions in controlled experimental settings. In addition, studies of children in their normal interactions suggest that from a young age, they respond differentially to moral violations and social violations (e.g., Dunn and Munn 1987; Smetana 1989).

The evidence of early success on the moral/conventional distinction sits alongside evidence of a somewhat later trajectory for perspective taking. Although at three years of age, children have some mindreading capacities, their perspective-taking abilities are still quite limited. Most famously, three-year-old children tend to fail the "false belief task." In the classic version of this task, Wimmer and Perner (1983) had children watch a puppet show in which a puppet, Maxi, put chocolate in a box and then went out to play. While Maxi was out, his puppet mother moved the chocolate to the cupboard. Children are asked where Maxi will look for the chocolate. Before the age of four, children tend to give the incorrect answer that Maxi will look in the cupboard, where the chocolate really is. This is another robust finding in developmental psychology. Dozens of studies have replicated the basic findings, and the typical result is that children do not pass the false belief task until after the fourth birthday (for a meta-analysis, see Wellman, Cross, and Watson 2001). As a result, there is reason to doubt that the young children who pass the moral/conventional task are proficient at determining the perspective of another person and then pretending to occupy that perspective.

The evidence on children poses an embarrassment for perspective-taking accounts, and the situation for these accounts is made worse by recent findings on children with autism. Children with autism have serious deficits to their capacity for understanding other minds (see e.g., Baron-Cohen 1995). Perhaps the best known finding is that autistic children fail the false belief task long after their mental age peers pass the task (Baron-Cohen, Leslie, and Frith 1985). They also have difficulty in other tasks that require taking the perspective of others. For instance, they perform poorly when asked to determine which present is appropriate for another person (Dawson and Fernald 1987). In a series of studies on psychopathologies and moral judgment, R. James Blair presented autistic children with the standard moral/conventional task. Despite their deficiencies in perspective taking, Blair found that autistic children were able to make the moral/conventional distinction. Like normally developing children, autistic children treat moral transgressions as more serious and less authority contingent than conventional transgressions. As Blair (1993) points out, this finding poses a significant problem for perspective-taking accounts of moral judgment. For there is no doubt that autistic children have deficits in perspective taking and other sophisticated mindreading capacities. Hence, Blair's data on autistic children suggest that sophisticated mindreading abilities are not required to draw the moral/conventional distinction.

The data from development and psychopathology pose an obstacle for the perspective-taking account of core moral judgment. Arguments in this area are rarely decisive, and the above arguments against perspective-taking accounts are no exception. Nonetheless, the problems facing the perspective-taking account are certainly serious enough to warrant exploring alternative accounts of core moral judgment.

4. BLAIR'S VIM ACCOUNT

Armed with a dazzling series of experiments, Blair has developed the most detailed alternative to the perspective-taking account of moral judgment. Blair maintains that the capacity to draw the moral/conventional distinction derives from the activation of a Violence Inhibition Mechanism (VIM). The idea for VIM comes from Konrad Lorenz's (1966) suggestion that social animals like canines have evolved mechanisms to inhibit intraspecies aggression. When a conspecific displays submission cues, the attacker stops. Blair suggests that there's something analogous in our cognitive systems, the VIM, and that this mechanism is the basis for our capacity to distinguish moral from conventional violations.

Unfortunately, it is not entirely clear how VIM is supposed to produce the moral/conventional distinction, but we do get a broad outline from Blair (1995). It is useful to divide Blair's theory into two parts. The first part of the theory proposes that VIM generates a sense of aversion. VIM is activated by distress cues, but VIM-activation initially simply produces a withdrawal response. This VIM-activation becomes aversive through "meaning analysis": "the withdrawal response following the activation of

VIM is experienced, through meaning analysis, as aversive" (1995, 7). There are important questions about what the meaning analysis comes to, but Blair (1995) does not elaborate this part of his theory.[3] Nonetheless, the important point for our purposes is that the aversive feeling depends on both VIM and meaning analysis. The second part of Blair's theory is that it is this feeling of aversiveness that generates the responses to the moral items on the moral/conventional task. According to Blair, VIM (plus meaning analysis) produces an aversive experience and it is "this sense of aversion to the moral transgression" that results in the act being "judged as bad" (1995, 7). On Blair's account, then, the process seems to go as follows. The VIM is triggered by distress cues or by associations to distress cues; this VIM activation is experienced as aversive through meaning analysis; and events that are experienced as aversive in this way are treated as nonconventional transgressions in the moral/conventional task (Blair 1995, 7; Blair 1993, 83, 88).

Blair's primary evidence for his theory comes from a series of studies on psychopaths. He presented the moral/conventional task to psychopaths in British prisons (Blair 1995; Blair et al. 1995; see also Blair 1997). Since the pool of psychopaths was drawn from a prison population, Blair used nonpsychopathic prison inmates as a control. Blair found that control criminals made a significant moral/conventional distinction on permissibility, seriousness, and authority dependence; psychopaths, on the other hand, did not make a significant moral/conventional distinction on any of these dimensions. Further, although the control criminals tended to appeal to the victim's welfare to explain why the moral transgressions were wrong, psychopaths tended to give conventional-type justifications for both the moral and the conventional transgressions. Apparently, then, the capacity for core moral judgment is compromised in psychopathy.[4]

3. Blair (1993) adverts to Mandler's definition of meaning analysis as "the activation and accessibility of those schematic representations that best fit the available evidence" (Mandler 1984, 126). The meaning analysis seems to supply the agent with certain interpretations about events, and these interpretations then play a crucial role in the generation of conscious emotional states (Blair 1993, 61, 83; Mandler 1984, 46, 126). In the case of VIM, apparently the interpretation of VIM-activation leads to the experience of aversion.

4. There are two important qualifications about the status of Blair's initial data (Blair 1995). The first is a statistical worry. What Blair found was that within the control group, there was a significant distinction between moral and conventional violations on all the dimensions; by contrast, in the psychopath group, he did not find a significant distinction between moral and conventional violations on any of the dimensions. Although this finding is suggestive, there were only ten subjects in each group, and it is possible that with more subjects, the psychopath group would show a distinction between the moral and conventional violations. What would be more statistically compelling is if Blair found group level differences between psychopaths and control criminals across the dimensions. Blair (1995) only found group level differences on one of the criterion dimensions—authority contingency (16). This worry is partly alleviated by the fact that Blair and colleagues largely replicated the null effect with twice as many

Blair and colleagues also found another important difference between psychopaths and control criminals. Nonpsychopathic and psychopathic criminals were shown threatening pictures (e.g., an angry face) and pictures of distressed individuals (e.g., a crying child). Both nonpsychopathic and psychopathic criminals show high physiological response to threatening cues. Nonpsychopathic criminals also show high physiological response to cues of distress in others. By contrast, psychopaths show significantly lower physiological response to distress cues (Blair et al. 1997; Blair 1999b). Blair interprets this as evidence that psychopaths have a defective VIM, and thus that the evidence supports his account of moral judgment.

One important feature of Blair's account is that it proposes that VIM is independent of any capacity for understanding other minds. Hence, on Blair's account, it is possible for the capacity to draw the moral/conventional distinction to be dissociated from the capacity for mindreading. Blair argues that this claim is corroborated by his finding that autistic children were able to make the moral/conventional distinction, despite their difficulties with mindreading (Blair 1996). He suggests that this evidence shows that the capacity for mindreading or "mentalizing" is entirely dissociated from the capacity to draw the moral/conventional distinction: "Children with autism have been demonstrated to be incapable of 'mentalizing'" (e.g., Baron-Cohen, Leslie, and Frith 1985) and so, they are incapable of "forming a representation of the mental state of the other" (Blair 1995, 22). He maintains that his theory explains how autistic children can make the moral/conventional distinction even though they

subjects (Blair et al. 1995). In this study, psychopaths did not draw a moral/conventional distinction on the authority contingency question or on the permissibility question. A difference did, however, show up on the seriousness question.

Another limitation on Blair's (1995) data concerns the response pattern of the psychopaths. Although psychopaths failed to draw the moral/conventional distinction, they did so in a surprising way. Contrary to Blair's predictions, psychopaths rated both moral and conventional transgressions as impermissible, very serious, and not dependent on authority. Thus, it may seem that psychopaths regard all transgressions as moral. Blair (1995) proposes that the real explanation is that because the psychopaths were incarcerated, they were motivated to give answers that they thought would improve their case for release (23). This might be part of an explanation, but it is obviously not entirely satisfying.

Both of the above worries are largely addressed by two important considerations. First, as Blair (1995) notes, the justifications psychopaths offered for why the moral transgressions are wrong were typically consonant with conventional-type justifications, whereas the control criminals tended to appeal to nonconventional (harm or rights-based) justifications for why the moral transgressions were wrong (24). This finding was also replicated with the larger pool of psychopaths (Blair et al. 1995). This suggests that the psychopaths are indeed failing to grasp the distinctive nature of moral violations. Second, perhaps the most interesting criterion category, for philosophical purposes anyway, is authority contingency. And in a subsequent study, Blair found that children with psychopathic tendencies were more likely than other children to treat moral violations as authority contingent (Blair 1997; see also Blair et al. 2001; Nucci and Herman 1982).

cannot mentalize: "While children with autism may not be able to represent a mental state of another's distress, this distress, as a visual or aural cue, will activate their VIM" (Blair 1995, 22).

Blair's argument for a dissociation between the capacity for mindreading and the capacity for drawing the moral/conventional distinction is unconvincing. Claiming that autistic children cannot "mentalize" or that they cannot represent the mental states of others overstates their deficit. There is reason to think that autistic children can represent some mental states. Autistic children are capable of attributing simple desires and emotions (e.g., Tan and Harris 1991; Yirmiya et al. 1992). They understand that people can have different desires and "that someone who gets what he wants will feel happy, and someone else who does not get what he wants will feel sad" (Baron-Cohen 1995, 63). Furthermore, studies of spontaneous language use in autistic children indicate that these children use the term "want" and "hurt" appropriately (Tager-Flusberg 1993). Thus there is good reason to think that a basic capacity for attributing desires is largely intact in autistic children (see Nichols and Stich 2003). As a result, the fact that these children can distinguish moral from conventional violations does not provide evidence that the capacity for making this distinction is entirely independent from the capacity for mindreading.[5]

So, Blair's evidence does not support his hypothesis that mindreading is unnecessary for drawing the moral/conventional distinction. Moreover, there are serious shortcomings in Blair's account itself. Perhaps the easiest way to illustrate the shortcomings is by exploiting the venerable distinction between judging something "bad" and judging something "wrong." Many occurrences that are regarded as bad are not regarded as wrong. Toothaches, for instance, are bad, but they are not wrong. The moral/conventional task gets its interest primarily because it gives us a glimpse into judgments of wrong. This is reflected by the fact that the items in the moral/conventional task are explicitly transgressions, and the first

5. Of course, one of the major themes in recent work on mindreading is that it is important to distinguish among different aspects of mindreading. For instance, the capacity for attributing beliefs might depend on different mechanisms from the capacity for attributing desires and emotions (Nichols and Stich 2003). So Blair's evidence might be taken to support the more restricted claim that some aspects of mindreading are dissociable from the capacity for drawing the moral/conventional distinction. For instance, the evidence on autism might be taken to support the view that the capacity to attribute false beliefs is dissociable from the capacity to draw the moral/conventional distinction. However, Blair's evidence does not support the stronger claim that the capacity for drawing the moral/conventional is dissociable from all mindreading capacities. In particular, the evidence on autism does not support the claim that the capacity for drawing the moral/conventional distinction is dissociable from the capacity to represent the mental states of another's distress. For there is good reason to think that this mindreading capacity is intact in autism.

question in standard moral/conventional tasks checks for the permissibility of the action. As we will see, the problem with Blair's account is that, although the proposal might provide an account of judging something bad (in a certain sense), it does not provide an account of judging something wrong.

If the first part of Blair's theory is right, VIM (plus meaning analysis) produces a distinctive aversive response. As with toothaches, we might regard the stimuli that prompt this aversive response as "bad." Furthermore, it might be important to treat stimuli that produce VIM-based aversion as "bad" in a distinctive way. Now, what is the class of stimuli that are bad in this sense? Well, anything that reliably produces VIM activation. Distress cues will be at the core of this stimulus class (Blair 1995, 1999a). The class of stimuli that will be accordingly aversive will include distress cues from victims of natural disasters and accidents and even superficial distress cues like paintings and drawings. Thus, the class of stimuli that VIM (plus meaning analysis) will lead us to regard as "bad" includes natural disaster victims, accident victims, and superficial distress cues. But it is implausible that these things are regarded as wrong. Natural disasters are, of course, bad. But, barring theological digressions, natural disasters are not regarded as wrong. Indeed, this is clear from the first criterion category in the moral/conventional task—it doesn't even make sense to say that natural disasters are impermissible. Similarly, if a child falls down, skins her knee, and begins to cry, this will produce aversive response in witnesses through VIM. Yet the child's falling down does not count as a moral transgression. It is instructive here to consider a probe that is sometimes used to distinguish between transgressions and nontransgressions. Subjects asked whether punishment is appropriate for certain events tend to say that punishment is appropriate for both conventional and moral transgressions, but not for nontransgressions (cf. Davidson, Turiel, and Black 1983; Zelazo, Helwig, and Lau 1996). Although a child crying after a fall will be "bad" in the VIM sense, it would be rather sadistic to suggest that the child should be punished. This is plausibly because scraping one's knee and crying is not considered wrong—it is not a transgression. As a final example, consider again the fact that superficial distress cues produce aversive response through VIM (plus meaning analysis). This aversive response can be generated whether or not one believes that the other person is in distress. Indeed, this is crucial for Blair's view on autism and moral judgment. According to Blair, even though autistic children cannot represent distress, they have an intact VIM, and this is the basis for their capacity for moral judgment. Artificial distress cues might thus be judged as bad in the VIM sense, but producing such cues (e.g., by creating or playing a tape of simulated crying) would presumably not be judged as nonconventionally wrong. That is, it is unlikely that producing artificial distress cues would be judged to be significantly less permissible, more serious and less authority contingent than standard conventional transgressions (e.g., talking out of turn in class). Indeed, like the cases of natural disasters and accidental injury, producing artificial distress cues is typically not regarded as a transgression at all.

So, although Blair's theory might provide an account of how people come to judge things as bad in a certain sense, it does not provide an adequate account of moral judgments of wrong on the moral/conventional task. Of course, Blair's theory might be developed further to try to exclude all of the problematic cases, but as it stands, the theory has no motivated explanation for why these bad stimuli are not regarded as wrong.

5. THE SENTIMENTAL RULES ACCOUNT OF MORAL JUDGMENT

The central problem for Blair's theory, I've argued, is that it does not provide an adequate account of judgments of wrong. Perhaps the most plausible way to remedy this problem is to maintain that there is a body of information specifying which acts are wrong, that is, which acts are transgressions. On this proposal, in typical moral scenarios presented in the moral/conventional task, people's judgments are guided by an internally represented body of information, a "normative theory," prohibiting behavior that harms others. Important clarifications are in order about my terminology here. "Normative theory" is not intended in any inflated sense. Rather, even a motley set of rules prohibiting certain behaviors will count as a normative theory. Internally represented rules concerning table manners, for instance, will count as a normative theory. The normative theory of central interest to us, however, is the normative theory prohibiting harmful actions. The operative notion of harm also needs to be qualified. Unless otherwise noted, "harm" is restricted to psychological harms like pain and suffering.

Part of what makes such an appeal to a normative theory plausible is that it is widely agreed that all of the populations studied in these tasks have information about normative prohibitions—for all the populations are fluent with the *conventional transgressions,* and the prevailing explanation of this is that subjects have knowledge of the conventional rules.

Of course, this body of information about moral violations cannot be captured by a simple rule like "a behavior is wrong if it causes harm." At least among adults, behavior that is unintentionally harmful is often not regarded as transgressive. Sometimes a person can even intentionally cause suffering without incurring negative moral judgments. For example, applying an anti-infective to a child's scraped knee causes the child sharp pain, but we do not judge this to be morally wrong. Among other things, the normative theory provides the basis for distinguishing wrongful harm from acceptable harm.

The normative theory that prohibits harming others, on the current proposal, does depend on some capacity for mindreading. For it requires some mindreading abilities to properly categorize harm and to recognize the distinction between genuine and superficial distress cues. Nonetheless, the requisite mindreading abilities here are plausibly minimal. As a result, the evidence on autism fits comfortably with the present proposal. For, as noted earlier, despite their deficits in some aspects of mindreading, autistic children are capable of attributing wanting and hurting to others.

Although I am suggesting that the normative theory underlying core moral judgment implicates at least a minimal capacity for mindreading, this does not exclude the possibility that there are important differences between the moral judgments of children with autism and those of other children. Indeed, it is likely that one of the central features of moral development is that the normative theory becomes increasingly sophisticated. Presumably this increasing sophistication will sometimes draw on increasingly sophisticated mindreading abilities. For instance, it is part of the moral normative theory of older children (and adults) that lying is prohibited. But because an understanding of lying depends on fairly sophisticated mindreading capacities, this prohibition may be absent from the normative theories of young children and children with autism.

An adequate account of core moral judgment must also explain Blair's data on psychopaths. Blair finds that psychopaths have a deficit both in moral judgment and in their affective response to others' suffering. Although Blair characterizes the affective deficit as a deficit to VIM, VIM is linked to Lorenz's evolutionary account, which is regarded with considerable suspicion in the contemporary literature (e.g., de Waal 1996). As a result, I'm inclined to adopt a descriptive characterization of the affective system that is neutral about evolutionary function. In the following chapter I will discuss the relevant affective systems in more detail. But for present purposes, it suffices to note that from a young age, children respond with distress and concern to another's suffering (e.g., Batson 1991; Eisenberg et al. 1989; Nichols 2001). These responses seem to be diminished in psychopaths. The affective mechanism underlying these responses need not be characterized as VIM. Rather, we can simply note that Blair's studies indicate that the population that performs abnormally on the moral/conventional task (psychopaths) also shows abnormally low affective response to suffering in others. By contrast, the populations that perform normally on the moral/conventional task (young children, children with autism, children with Down syndrome) apparently do not respond with abnormally low affective response to suffering in others. For current purposes, the precise characterization of the affective mechanism is not really crucial. The important claim is simply that some affective mechanism that is responsive to others' suffering is plausibly implicated in moral judgment.

Core moral judgment depends on two mechanisms, then, a normative theory prohibiting harming others, and some affective mechanism that is activated by suffering in others. Core moral judgment thus implicates what I will call "Sentimental Rules," rules prohibiting actions that are independently likely to elicit strong negative affect.[6] The set of rules or normative theory prohibits actions of a certain type, and actions of that type generate strong affective response.[7] There is reason to think that the two mechanisms underlying core moral judgment are at least partly dissociable. Children exhibit distress and concern at another's suffering well before the second birthday (e.g., Simner 1971; Zahn-Waxler et al. 1992a). But one-year-olds presumably do not make moral judgments, and this can be attributed to the fact that they have not yet acquired the nor-

6. In recent philosophical circles, much attention has been devoted to the view, sometimes called "particularism," that rules or principles play no role in morality (e.g., Hooker and Little 2000). Because I explicitly invoke rules as essential to core moral judgment, my account seems at odds with particularism. However, it is important to note that there are several different ways one might develop a particularist account. One might adopt a kind of metaphysical particularism according to which moral principles are not the source of what is really right and wrong. Or one might promote a prescriptive particularism according to which moral judgment should not be based on rules or principles. It is no part of my project to pronounce on these views. One might, however, advocate a kind of "descriptive particularism," according to which lay moral judgments do not implicate rules in any way. This form of particularism does conflict with my thesis. But it is not clear that any particularists actually endorse descriptive particularism (e.g., Sinnott-Armstrong 1999 and Dancy 1999). To be sure, no particularist has developed a sustained and empirically sensitive case that children have no knowledge of rules or that they do not exploit their knowledge of rules in making moral judgments. So I will not take the time to argue against such a view.

7. I do not mean to suggest that conventional transgressions carry no affective force. People might find it generally upsetting when rules of any sort are broken. But of course, because this applies to all rules, it does not distinguish conventional normative judgment from nonconventional normative judgment. Thus, my claim might be somewhat more carefully cast as the claim that moral violations implicate an affective component that goes beyond whatever affect might attend all transgressions. This still leaves open important questions. For instance, transgressions might come to be treated as nonconventional because of the intensity of the accompanying affect or, alternatively, because of the kind of affect. This interesting question will not be addressed here. For simplicity, I am not restricting the kind of affect that can generate the nonconventional responses. However, future research might well indicate that only certain kinds of emotions can generate the distinctive pattern of nonconventional responses that I am attributing to Sentimental Rules.

mative theory that will guide their moral judgments in the coming years. Psychopaths, on the other hand, might show a dissociation in the other direction. As we have seen, psychopaths apparently have a deficit to an affective mechanism that is essential to moral judgment. Blair does not address whether psychopaths might have a normative theory that prohibits harming others. Nonetheless, it seems plausible that psychopaths do have some such normative theory. Notice first that the difference between psychopaths and control criminals is not that psychopaths do not grasp normative judgments at all. In some sense, psychopaths know the difference between right and wrong. They correctly note that the child should not talk out of turn or hit another child. What they apparently fail to do is distinguish between these two kinds of normative judgments appropriately. [8]

Blair's evidence does indicate, then, that psychopaths have a normative theory prohibiting hitting even if they neglect the distinction between moral and conventional transgressions. Furthermore, it is likely that the notion of harm plays an important role in the psychopath's normative theory. By Blair's reckoning, the telling feature about the psychopaths' performance is that they offer conventional-type justifications for moral violations rather than justifications in terms of harm to the victim (Blair 1995, 24). But presumably psychopaths are well aware of the fact that hitting another falls under the general category of harm-based violations. For instance, if psychopaths were presented with a novel transgression of causing harm to another, they would likely be able to extrapolate and say that it is wrong. So, psychopaths do presumably have a normative theory prohibiting harming others, despite their deficit in affective response to others' distress. Thus, it seems that the normative theory is at least partly dissociable from the affective system.

To be sure, if psychopaths do recognize that actions that are harmful are proscribed, this raises a question about why psychopaths and control criminals provide different explanations for why it is wrong to hit or pull someone's hair. Psychopaths offered conventional-type justifications (e.g., "it's not the done thing" [the subjects were British]), whereas the nonpsychopathic criminals offered justifications based on the victim's welfare.

---

8. It is important to note that I am not making a conceptual claim here. I am not suggesting that it is a conceptual truth that psychopaths fail to make genuine moral judgments. A great deal of work in metaethics focuses on the idea that it is conceptually possible that someone might have mastery of moral concepts without having any concomitant motivation to act morally or any concern for others. I think this is right and of some significance for evaluating certain claims about internalism (see chapters 3 and 5). However, the issue in this chapter is the empirical question—what mechanisms are in fact involved in moral judgment. The claim that it is conceptually possible for an amoralist to be fluent with moral discourse (or to be trained to be so) is a separate issue.

Of course, not only is it the case that psychopaths know that harming others is wrong, control criminals are well aware that harming others is socially discouraged. So both control criminals and psychopaths presumably have available to them both social-convention explanations and harm-based explanations for why it is wrong to hit another. Yet when asked why it is wrong to hit another, control criminals and psychopaths offer different explanations. Why is that? One possibility is that psychopaths regard the conventional justification as primitive, whereas the control criminals treat the harm-based justification as primitive. That is, for control criminals, pulling hair is socially discouraged precisely because it harms the other. For psychopaths, harming others is wrong because it is socially discouraged.[9] All of this is consistent with the independently plausible claim that psychopaths do have a normative theory that prohibits harmful actions.

In this section, I've argued that moral judgment depends on two different psychological components, an affective mechanism and a normative theory. However, none of the foregoing addresses how these mechanisms interact to produce the responses on the moral/conventional task. There isn't enough evidence at this point to draw any firm conclusions on the issue. In section 8, I will consider some possibilities. But first, I will report experimental evidence that helps to corroborate the Sentimental Rules account of core moral judgment.

6. THE DISGUSTING/CONVENTIONAL DISTINCTION

I've claimed that the nonconventional responses to the moral questions derive from two factors, a normative theory prohibiting harming others and an affective system that is sensitive to harm in others. On this ac-

---

9. Although the issue has not been explored as far as I know, it would be interesting to see how psychopaths and nonpsychopaths would respond if asked to elaborate their justifications for why it is wrong to hurt others. One possibility is that the justifications reach the end of the road here. For instance, it seems possible that nonpsychopathic subjects will typically not be able to offer much of an elaboration for why it is wrong to harm others. Recent work by Jonathan Haidt and colleagues is particularly intriguing in this context. They found that when a subject is asked to explain why a particular case of brother-sister incest is wrong, the subject can easily be "dumbfounded," that is, left without a justification for his view. But the subject continues to believe that the case of incest is wrong (Haidt et al. forthcoming). It is possible that people could also be dumbfounded on the basic question "Why is it wrong to hurt people?" Here is an exchange I had with my (then) five-year-old daughter:

    Q: Why is it wrong to hit?
    A: Because it hurts the person.
    Q: Why is it wrong to hurt someone?

count, the moral/conventional task really taps a distinction between a set of norms (harm norms) that are backed by an affective system and a set of norms (conventional norms) that are not backed by an affective system. That is, the pattern of results on the moral/conventional task is explained by the fact that affect-backed norms are treated differently than affect-neutral norms. Thus, the account predicts that transgressions of other (non-harm-based) rules that are backed by affective systems should also be treated as nonconventional. As a result, if we find that other affect-backed norms are also distinguished from conventional norms along the dimensions of permissibility, seriousness, authority contingency, and justification type, then this will provide an independent source of evidence for the Sentimental Rules account. On Blair's account, by contrast, treating transgressions as nonconventional depends on the VIM, so his account does not predict that transgressions implicating other emotional responses will be treated as nonconventional.

To test the prediction we need to exploit a body of (non-harm-based) rules that are backed by an affective system. In a pair of recent experiments, I elected to focus on disgusting transgressions (Nichols 2002b). These experiments explored the extent to which disgusting transgressions would be distinguished from affectively neutral conventional transgressions.

In one experiment, subjects were given a set of transgression scenarios, each of which was followed by questions about permissibility, seriousness, authority contingency and justification. Two of the scenarios were moral transgressions, two were neutral conventional transgressions, and two were disgusting transgressions. In each case, after the transgression is described, the subject is asked four questions, taken from the moral/conventional task (Blair 1995). For instance, in one of the disgust-scenarios, subjects were presented the following scenario and questions:

> Bill is sitting at a dinner party and he snorts loudly and then spits into his water before drinking it.
> 1. Was it OK for Bill to spit in his water?
>
> If it's not OK for Bill to do that, then:

A: Because you might hurt them really bad.
Q: Why would that be wrong?
A: Because you might break their bones.
Q: Why would that be wrong?
A: Because it would hurt really bad.

It would be nice to have some real evidence on this, of course, but the anecdote suggests that the harm-based explanation is the end of the line for children.

TABLE I.I Description of justification categories judgment

Welfare	Any reference to victim's welfare (e.g., "it will hurt her"; "it's not fair")
Rule	Any reference to rules, even if implicit (e.g., "it's not socially acceptable")
Disorder	Any reference to disorder caused by the behavior (e.g., "it will distract others")
Rudeness	Any reference to the rudeness of the behavior (e.g., "it's bad manners")
Health	Any reference to health risks involved with the behavior (e.g., "bad hygiene")
Disgust	Any reference to the disgustingness of the behavior (e.g., "it's gross")
Other	Any other response

2. On a scale of one to ten, how bad was it for Bill to spit in his water?

3. Why was it bad for Bill to spit in his water?

4. Now what if, before Bill went to the party, the hosts had said, "At our dinner table, anyone can spit in their food or drink." Would it be OK for Bill to spit in his water if the hosts say he can?

The hypothesis suggested by the Sentimental Rules account is that subjects will distinguish disgusting transgressions from neutral conventional transgressions on all the criterion judgments (i.e., permissibility, seriousness, authority contingence) and that subjects will tend to give different kinds of justifications for the two classes of violations.

The disgusting violations were indeed distinguished from the conventional violations on all the criterion judgments. The disgusting violations were regarded as less permissible, more serious, and less authority contingent than the neutral violations (Nichols 2002b). In addition, subjects tended not to offer conventional explanations for why the action was wrong (see table 1.1 for justification categories). In the case involving Bill spitting in his glass, which was the most disgusting of the violations, over 60 percent of the subjects explained why the action was wrong by appealing to disgust (e.g., "because that's gross!"). None of the subjects gave this sort of explanation for why it is wrong to drink the soup. Rather, the subjects offered conventional justifications for why drinking the soup was wrong, either adverting to rudeness (e.g., "It's bad manners") or to rules (e.g., "You aren't supposed to do that at social functions"). Of course, the justifications for why the moral transgressions were prohibited were different from either the conventional or disgusting transgressions. Subjects typically offered welfare-based explanations for why pulling hair is wrong.

The preceding experiment shows that disgusting violations, which seem clearly to be affectively charged, are treated as distinct from neutral conventional violations. What the experiment does not address, however, is whether diminished disgust-sensitivity will have an effect on a subject's tendency to treat disgusting violations as impermissible, serious or authority independent. Blair's experiments suggest that the psychopaths' diminished response to suffering underlies a compromised capacity for core moral judgment. A second experiment explored whether something analogous might be the case for disgusting transgressions. Subjects with high disgust sensitivity and subjects with low disgust sensitivity were compared on their responses to the permissibility, seriousness and authority contingency of a disgusting violation. The violation that was used was slightly different and less disgusting than the spitting in the glass case:

> Michael is sitting at a dinner party and he picks up a paper napkin, snorts, and spits into the napkin.

The subjects were asked to judge the permissibility, seriousness, justification, and authority contingence of this action. Subjects then filled out a disgust scale questionnaire (Haidt, McCauley, and Rozin 1994), which generated a disgust rating for each subject. Although there was no statistically significant difference between low and high disgust subjects on the permissibility question, there were significant differences on the other two criterion judgments. The low disgust subjects were more likely than the high disgust subjects to treat the disgusting transgression as authority contingent (see figure 1.1). Further, low disgust subjects judged the transgression as significantly less serious than high disgust subjects (Nichols 2002b) (see figure 1.2).

7. NORMS WITH FEELING: THE DISGUSTING AND THE IMMORAL

The empirical findings thus support the hypothesis that disgust-backed transgressions would be distinguished from affectively neutral transgressions on the classic moral/conventional dimensions. Transgressions that are disgust-backed are judged to be less permissible, more serious, less contingent on authority, and are more likely to elicit nonconventional justifications than affectively neutral conventional transgressions. The findings also indicate that the affective response does play a critical role in

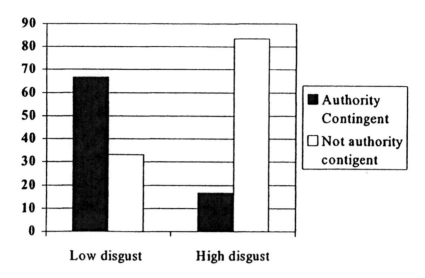

FIGURE 1.1 Judgments of authority contingence in low and high disgust subjects

prompting individuals to treat disgusting violations as nonconventional. For low-disgust subjects were more likely than high-disgust subjects to judge the disgusting violation as contingent on authority and less serious. This suggests that responses to the criterion dimensions are somehow mediated by affective response.

Although affect thus seems to play a crucial role in generating nonconventional judgment, such judgment cannot be wholly explained by appealing to affect, even in the case of "disgust" transgressions. Rather, just as there are norms against harming others, there are norms against disgusting behavior. And, as in the case of harm norms, there isn't a

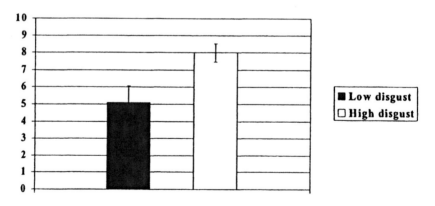

FIGURE 1.2 Judgments of seriousness in low and high disgust subjects

single simple rule that prohibits disgusting behaviors. For clearly some disgusting behaviors, for example, unintentional vomiting, are not prohibited. There are even intentional actions that are disgusting but not prohibited, for example, some parlor tricks (I leave it to the reader to recall or construct his own examples). Thus, there seems to be a body of information, a normative theory, proscribing a class of disgusting behavior. Furthermore, it seems that the normative theory is at least partially independent from the affective system. For even though low disgust subjects were more likely to say that the disgusting action was not wrong if an authority said it wasn't, most of these subjects also maintained that the action was normatively prohibited.

It is worth saying a bit more clearly how the findings on disgusting transgressions help to confirm the Sentimental Rules framework suggested above for moral judgment. Since the experiments indicate that the disgust system provokes nonconventional responses to questions about permissibility, seriousness, authority contingency and justification, we have evidence that nonconventional responses to these questions can be induced by affective response. There is independent reason to think that suffering in others inspires considerable affective response, and that this kind of affective response to others' distress emerges early (see, e.g., Nichols 2001; Zahn-Waxler et al. 1992a). As a result, we have a couple of important pieces in place to corroborate the Sentimental Rules account of moral judgment. Harm-scenarios generate affective response, and affective response can provoke nonconventional answers to the standard moral/conventional questions. So it is reasonable to suppose that the affective response to harm-scenarios does play a crucial role in leading subjects to judge that hitting others and pulling hair is impermissible, very serious, and not authority contingent. More broadly, it is plausible that the norms prohibiting disgusting behavior and the norms prohibiting harmful behavior are part of an important class of norms, Sentimental Rules. Violations of Sentimental Rules are judged as less permissible, more serious, and less dependent on authority than conventional normative violations. In addition, the level of affective response has a significant effect on the extent to which subjects distinguish Sentimental Rules from other rules.

8. PSYCHOLOGICAL MODELS

On the general picture that I've suggested, then, two different mechanisms are implicated in nonconventional normative judgment: a normative theory and an affective system. This proposal leaves open a wide range of possibilities about how these mechanisms work together to produce nonconventional normative judgment. The evidence suggests that affective mechanisms can play a crucial role in generating nonconventional judgments. But what role does affect play? In particular, what role does affect play in leading subjects to judge disgusting violations and moral violations as (i) very serious; (ii) not contingent on authority; and (iii) possessing extraconventional justification? There isn't enough evidence available to answer these questions with any confidence. But one explanation for why disgusting transgressions are judged as less permissible and more serious than affectively neutral transgressions is that disgusting transgressions carry both the aversiveness of being transgressive and an additional aversive component—they provoke disgust. That is, in addition to violating a rule, disgusting transgressions activate an affective mechanism, which makes them more offensive than transgressions that merely violate a rule. This also suggests how disgusting violations might come to be regarded as not authority contingent and as having extraconventional justification. In the case of conventional violations, when we imagine that the rules are suspended, that suffices to undermine any basis for judging the action as an offense. By contrast, when one imagines that certain disgust rules are suspended, as in the case of the host proclaiming that it is okay to spit in one's water glass, imagining the activity still provokes the disgust response and so this activity continues to be regarded as an offense. Indeed, on this proposal, precisely what makes disgust-transgressions especially serious persists even when the rules are suspended. What makes them especially serious is that these violations are disgusting.

This is, of course, a rather crude model for what is surely a rich and complex phenomenon. Furthermore, this model entirely neglects the issue of when this process takes place. The available evidence does not remotely decide between the various options. But I do want to be explicit about some rather dramatically different ways that the capacity for moral judgment might be psychologically realized.

From a developmental vantage, one interesting possibility is that there are important ontogenetic factors in fixing the cognitive mechanisms that subserve judgments surrounding disgusting violations and harmful violations. One useful way to characterize such approaches is as "developmental contingency" models (see Morton 1986; Blair 1993; Leslie and Thaiss 1992) on which we can view some psychological mechanisms as developmentally necessary for the normal acquisition of some capacity. It is possible, for instance, that the affective mechanism and the normative theory are both developmentally necessary for achieving the nonconventional normative theory. For instance, in the case of disgusting violations, the child is provided with (whether by instruction or by innate endowment) a body of rules regarding spitting. The disgust mechanism might then shape this body of rules into a nonconventional normative theory. More generally, it might be that when normative prohibitions are paired with affective response, as is the case with disgust prohibitions, the affect provides a kind of reinforcement for the prohibitions that instills a deeper repugnance for actions that transgress these norms, and this might infuse the norms with a nonconventional status. In the case of core moral judgment, the affective mechanism responsive to suffering in others, in conjunction with information about harm norms, produces the nonconventional normative theory that guides responses on the moral/conventional task (see figure 1.3). This nonconventional normative theory is to be distinguished from the other, conventional normative theories that the child arrives at, like the normative theory about table manners. If the affective mechanism is absent, or, perhaps, if it is absent during some critical developmental period, then the child would not develop a proper nonconventional normative theory. This model might explain the data on psychopathy by proposing that the relevant affective mechanism is defective in psychopaths from an early age and as a result, they do not develop the nonconventional normative theory.

The developmental view can also be cast in a more extreme fashion. It might be that the affective mechanism is not only developmentally necessary for developing the nonconventional normative theory, but that the affective mechanism is unnecessary after some critical period. On this model, the affective mechanism is the equivalent of Wittgenstein's ladder—it can be kicked away once it has played its critical role.

A quite different kind of psychological model of how the normative theory and the affective system interact is to appeal only to on-line pro-

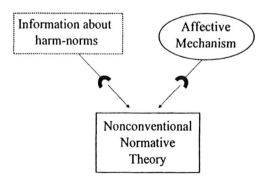

FIGURE 1.3 Developmental contingency model of affect and moral judgment

cessing. One might claim that, when one is presented with moral violations, the affective mechanism works on-line, in conjunction with the
normative theory prohibiting harmful actions, to generate the nonconventional answers that subjects give in response to cases of moral transgressions (see figure 1.4). That is, when one is asked whether a particular
transgression is serious, if one simultaneously experiences negative affect
on hearing about the transgression, that transgression is judged to be
especially serious. Since the description of a harm-based transgression is
likely to elicit negative affect, this might explain performance on the
moral/conventional task. On this account, one might maintain that psychopaths have basically the same normative theory that the rest of us do,
but their responses to the moral-violation probes are not influenced by
the relevant affective mechanism, because that mechanism is defective in
psychopaths. That explains their abnormal performance on the moral/
conventional task.

The latter two views mark out extremist positions. The extremist developmental story maintains that after some critical period, affect plays
no important role in producing the nonconventional responses. The extremist on-line processing account maintains that at any given point, the
affective response is sufficient to make a subject treat a transgression as
nonconventional. Although we lack the evidence to reject either theory, I
think it would be surprising if either of these extreme views were right.
The extremist on-line theory makes the prediction that if we managed to
activate an agent's affective system while the agent was evaluating some
conventional transgression (e.g., it's wrong to put the fork on the right),
then the subject should treat that transgression as nonconventional. Although this kind of prediction hasn't been tested, it would be startling
indeed if it turned out that conventional judgment was so easily trans-
formed into nonconventional judgment. On the other hand, the extremist

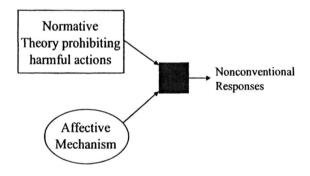

FIGURE 1.4 On-line model of affect and moral
judgment

developmental position also makes a surprising prediction. On this account, after subjects have developed the nonconventional normative theory, the subjects' affective system could be entirely eradicated and yet they would continue to treat the same violations as nonconventional. It would be striking if affect played no role in sustaining the subjects' judgment that certain of these transgressions are nonconventionally wrong.

Of course, one needn't take an extremist view at all. It is possible, for instance, that the affective system plays both a developmental and an online role in generating and preserving the nonconventional normative judgments. The point I wish to emphasize is simply that even if nonconventional normative judgment does involve both a normative theory and an affective mechanism, it remains to be seen exactly how those different mechanisms interact to enable the distinctive kinds of judgments subjects make about disgusting violations and moral violations.

9. CONCLUSION

Psychologists have generated a fascinating array of findings on the basic capacity to treat moral violations as distinctively wrong. This capacity for core moral judgment has been robustly confirmed in the empirical literature over the last two decades. In this chapter, I have argued that core moral judgment implicates both an affective mechanism and an internally represented set of rules, a normative theory. The normative theory and the affective system are independent mechanisms, but they somehow conspire to produce the distinctive responses tapped by the moral/conventional task. Affective response infuses the harm-norms with a special nonconventional status, and this status seems to be shared by other Sentimental Rules, like norms prohibiting disgusting behavior.

The idea that affect is essential to moral judgment has extremely distinguished origins in intellectual history, tracing back to the philosophical musings of Hume and Shaftesbury. The ensuing centuries have seen philosophers feverishly debate whether moral judgment really does depend on the emotions. This philosophical debate has not, to say the least, produced consensus. A more empirically oriented approach might offer greater promise of producing consensus. Although the psychological account sketched in this chapter is vastly underdescribed, it contains enough substance to generate significant philosophical coin. It can, I will argue over the course of this volume, provide the beginnings of an empirical case that might vindicate the Humean speculation that morality derives from the sentiments.

2

Sparks of Benevolence

*The Varied Emotional Responses
to Suffering in Others*

Look Rev, I hate to see a man cry. So shove off out the office;
there's a good chap.

        —From Monty Python's "Motor Insurance Sketch"

1. INTRODUCTION

In the last chapter, I argued that core moral judgment depends on both
a normative theory and an affective mechanism that is sensitive to suffering in others. Because core moral judgment emerges so early, and, in
particular, because it can be present in the absence of sophisticated mindreading capacities, we need to determine which affective systems are also
available in young children. Thus, in this chapter I want to explore in
detail the nature of the affective response to suffering in others. As it
happens, the human response to suffering in others is complex and interesting. There are different kinds of response, each of which apparently
emerges fairly early in development. Most of this chapter will be devoted
to delineating the emotional responses to suffering and the mechanisms
underlying these responses. But at the end of the chapter, I will explicate
more fully the relation between these emotional responses and core moral
judgment.

What kind of emotional responses to suffering are available? This
issue has been explored most systematically in the literature on prosocial
behavior, that is, behavior that benefits others. The familiar saw is that
"empathy" is the emotional response underlying prosocial behavior. But
research over the last two decades suggests that the unqualified appeal to
empathy blurs importantly different kinds of emotional responses. More-

over, the appeal to empathy might even neglect important categories of response to harm in others. For it might turn out that some affective responses to suffering are not plausibly viewed as empathic. Much of the task of the present chapter will be to sort this out. As we will see, some of the sorting can be done fairly quickly. One kind of response, "emotional contagion," is by now familiar in the empathy literature. An apparently different emotional response, "personal distress" is fairly easy to depict. A third kind of response, "concern," presents a much more complicated set of issues. As a result, the bulk of this chapter will be devoted to setting out the underpinnings of concern.

2. EMOTIONAL CONTAGION AND PERSONAL DISTRESS

As noted above, it is often held that an empathic response provides the motivation for prosocial behavior.[1] Most generally, empathy is regarded as a "vicarious sharing of affect" or an emotional response in which the emotion is "congruent with the other's emotional state or situation" (Eisenberg and Strayer 1987, 3, 5). This definition itself encompasses vastly different ways of attaining the vicarious sharing of affect. For we might share in another affective response by perspective taking, that is, by imagining oneself to have the other person's mental states.[2] But a different way that we arrive at the same affect is by emotional contagion, when we "catch" another's affect. This phenomenon is familiar in everyday life—it's the reason for laugh tracks in lame sitcoms. More to our purposes, we can be brought to tears by seeing or hearing another person cry. This kind of "reactive crying" is present at birth. In a famous study, Simner presented newborn infants with tapes of a range of auditory stimuli, including spontaneous crying by a newborn infant, spontaneous crying by a five-month-old infant, a computer generated crying sound, and white noise of equivalent sound intensity (Simner 1971). Simner found that the newborns cried significantly more in reaction to the tape of the newborn crying than in the other conditions. These findings have been replicated by separate laboratories (Sagi and Hoffman 1976; Martin and Clark 1982). The standard interpretation of these results is that the infants are experiencing emotional contagion (e.g., Thompson 1987). Because the

---

1. Altruistic behavior is one form of prosocial behavior, but prosocial behavior also encompasses selfishly motivated behavior that helps others. For example, intentionally helping a stranger merely to impress onlookers counts as prosocial, though presumably not altruistic.

2. I will delay discussion of perspective taking until section 5.

emotion felt is distress, we might regard the infant's response as "contagious distress."

The notion of "personal distress," which has gained prominence largely as a result of work by C. Daniel Batson, is cast as a "self-oriented" feeling that is caused by distress in others. Personal distress is sometimes interpreted as equivalent to contagious distress (e.g., Preston and de Waal 2002). However, it is not obvious that personal distress felt by the observer is homologous to the distress felt by the victim. On Batson's account, personal distress is characterized by "feelings such as upset, alarm, anxiety, and distress" (1991, 117). And when people feel such upset, alarm or anxiety, it is by no means clear that they are feeling anything that mimics what the victim feels. Consider, for instance, the following items, which are supposed to reflect personal distress on a standard questionnaire designed to track individual differences in empathy:

> In emergency situations, I feel apprehensive and ill-at-ease.
>
> I sometimes feel helpless when I am in the middle of a very emotional situation.
>
> Being in a tense emotional situation scares me.
>
> I tend to lose control during emergencies.
>
> When I see someone who badly needs help in an emergency, I go to pieces. (Davis 1980)

At least often in emergency situations, the victim does not go to pieces. In some emergency contexts, badly injured victims are found unconscious and hence not experiencing any distress. But people can still experience upset, alarm and anxiety upon witnessing such victims. Indeed, it seems plausible that people might have these distress reactions on finding an accident victim who is obviously dead. In these cases, then, personal distress cannot be assimilated to any form of emotional contagion. Nancy Eisenberg and Janet Strayer explicitly depict personal distress as a nonempathic response to others' distress: "When perceiving cues related to another's distress, some people may experience an aversive state such as anxiety or worry that is not congruent with the other's state" (Eisenberg and Strayer 1987, 7). On this construal, personal distress does not count as empathy, because it is not a vicarious sharing of homologous affect.

Although contagious distress and personal distress might have important differences, they share important characteristics as well—they are both self-oriented and they are both rather closely tied to situational cues. For our purposes, these shared features will often be more important than the apparent differences between contagious distress and personal distress. Furthermore, although it is evident that infants experience either contagious distress or personal distress, it is not entirely clear which category best characterizes infant responses to distress in others. In light of this, I will use the term "reactive distress" as a broader category that includes both contagious distress and personal distress. As we will see shortly, it is plausible that there is another kind of emotional response available as well—one that is not so situation dependent as reactive distress. The nature of this kind of response emerges from a consideration of work on altruism. As a result, it will be important, and of independent interest, to take a close look at accounts of the underpinnings of altruistic motivation.

3. CORE CASES OF ALTRUISTIC MOTIVATION

Because most of the remainder of this chapter will focus on the underpinnings of altruistic motivation, it will be useful to provide an overview of what's to come. The literature on altruism is simply enormous, and it spans several disciplines including philosophy, social psychology, developmental psychology, and evolutionary biology. Although I will draw on work from all of these areas, my goal is restricted to the project of determining the cognitive and affective mechanisms underlying basic altruistic motivation. Since numerous cognitive mechanisms play an essential role in generating altruistic behavior—for example, perceptual input systems, attentional mechanisms, motor control systems—it will be important to be a bit more explicit about my explanatory goals. I want to sketch an account of altruistic motivation that addresses two different questions. One question asks which mechanism produces the motivational state itself. In keeping with the prevailing views, I will argue that the motivational state is an affective state, produced by an affective system, the "Concern Mechanism." The other question asks which mindreading mechanisms are required to activate the affective mechanism. For the most part, I will defer discussion of the affective component of altruistic motivation until section 9. Until then, the focus will be on the extent to which mindreading is required for altruistic motivation. I will consider in some detail recent proposals about the mindreading mechanisms underlying altruistic motivation. I will argue against the radical view that mindreading capacities are unnecessary for altruistic motivation. Then I will sketch the more prevalent proposal, that altruistic motivation depends on the capacity for perspective taking. I will maintain that none of the arguments for the perspective-taking account is convincing and that there is considerable evidence that altruistic motivation does not depend on such sophisticated mindreading capacities. Rather, I will suggest that altruistic motivation depends on a Concern Mechanism that requires only minimal mindreading capacities, for example, the capacity to attribute distress to another. This will be rather important for our purposes, because it will mean that by the time children succeed on the moral/conventional tasks, they have the mindreading abilities required for altruistic motivation.

To begin a discussion of altruistic motivation, it will be helpful to set out some core cases of altruistic behavior. In science in general, it is not always clear at the outset what the core cases are, and new evidence and arguments might alter our conception of what should be included as core cases. The situation is no different in studying altruism, and we may want to revise our view about what the core cases are. Philosophical discussions in this area tend to rely on hypothetical cases of altruism. But because the present goal is to give an account of the psychological mechanisms implicated in actual cases of altruistic behavior, it is important to begin with real cases. To his credit, philosopher Lawrence Blum takes this strategy and offers real examples of helping behaviors that he suggests need to be accommodated by an adequate theory of altruism (Blum 1994). Blum's cases all come from young children. For present purposes, it will suffice to recount just a few of the examples:

1. Sarah at twelve months retrieves a cup for a crying friend. (Blum 1994, 186)
2. Michael at fifteen months brings his teddy bear and security blanket to a crying friend. (Blum 1994, 187)
3. A two-year-old accidentally harms his friend (another two-year-old) who begins to cry. The first child looks concerned and offers the other child a toy. (Blum 1994, 187)

The clearest real-life examples of altruistic behavior in adults come from work on helping behavior in social psychology. Perhaps the best known research on adults' helping behavior is the work on the "bystander effect" by Bibb Latané and John Darley (1968). They found that when there are numerous bystanders, subjects are relatively unlikely to offer assistance to those in need. This finding is often used to draw a rather bleak picture of human altruism (e.g., Campbell 1999). However, focusing on these studies obscures the pervasiveness of human altruism. For it turns out that if subjects perceive unambiguously serious distress cues and there are no bystanders, virtually everyone helps. For instance, in one study, Clark and Word (1974) had each subject engage in a distracter task and as the subject left the experiment, he passed a room in which a man (the experimenter's accomplice) made a sharp cry of pain and then feigned unconsciousness apparently as a result of being shocked by an electronic probe. The researchers found that when the accomplice was no longer touching any of the electronic equipment, all of the subjects offered help. And even when the accomplice was still touching electronic equipment (thus presenting potential danger to the helper), over 90 percent of the subjects offered help (Clark and Word 1974, 282). An adequate account of altruistic motivation should explain the underpinnings of these kinds of helping behaviors.

This list of core cases is, admittedly, rather short. It excludes possible cases of altruistic motivation that do not involve helping others in need. Sometimes people are generous to strangers who are not in need, and I do not mean to suggest that such behaviors cannot be altruistically motivated. However, I think that by focusing on a more limited range of cases, we are more likely to make progress on a psychological account of altruistic motivation. The cases of comforting or helping others in distress form a plausible core because such cases emerge so early in children and they appear to be pervasive among adults. Furthermore, although I'm focusing on a very short list of core cases, these cases already present a fairly daunting task. Devising an account of altruistic motivation that would capture both the child cases and the adult cases would be a considerable advance. Of course, it is possible that the examples from children and the examples from adults cannot be captured by a single account. But all else being equal, an account of altruistic motivation that can capture both of these cases would be preferable to an account that captures only one. I will argue that a close look at the role of mindreading in these cases will provide us with a unified account.

4. ALTRUISM WITHOUT MINDREADING?

In recent attempts to characterize the psychological mechanisms underlying altruistic motivation, one central question is the extent to which the capacity for altruism depends on the capacity for mindreading. We will engage this issue in some detail over the next several sections. To begin, I want to consider the radical view that the capacity for altruism is entirely independent of any capacity for mindreading. There are two versions of the view that are discussed in the recent literature. However, as we will see, neither account fits the evidence well.

4.1. Emotional Contagion

Just as empathy is frequently invoked to explain prosocial behavior in general, it is also invoked to explain altruistic motivation. For instance, Goldman writes, "empathy . . . seems to be a prime mechanism that disposes us toward altruistic behavior" (1993, 358). However, we need to keep clear the distinction between perspective-taking empathy and emotional-contagion empathy. I will postpone discussion of perspective-taking accounts of prosocial motivation until section 5. For now, I want to consider whether emotional contagion might explain altruistic behavior. The standard view, as noted earlier, is that some capacity for emotional contagion is present at birth as evidenced by the fact that infants will cry when they hear the cries of another infant (Simner 1971; Martin and Clark 1982). If emotional contagion appears this early, it is clear that the capacity for emotional contagion does not require the capacity for perspective taking. Indeed, if the capacity for emotional contagion is present at birth, this capacity is presumably completely independent of mindreading capacities. There is some dispute about when mindreading capacities become available, but all sides agree that newborn babies cannot engage in mindreading.

The capacity for emotional contagion suggests a natural and simple account of altruistic motivation. If the distress of another causes oneself to feel distress, this may provide a motivation to relieve the distress of the other—it will thereby relieve one's own distress. This view has a certain elegance, but it is not easy to find a prominent advocate for the view. Although Goldman maintains that altruistic behavior is generated by empathy, Goldman also maintains that emotional contagion is not genuine empathy (1993). Indeed Goldman's simulation account of empathy (described below in section 5) is implausible as an account of emotional contagion (see Nichols et al. 1996), so it is unlikely that Goldman thinks that altruism derives from emotional contagion. Martin Hoffman, one of the most influential figures in empathy research, has been read as proposing something like the simple emotional contagion view in the following passage: "Empathic distress is unpleasant and helping the victim is usually the best way to get rid of the source. One can also accomplish this by directing one's attention elsewhere and avoiding the expressive and situational cues from the victim" (Hoffman 1981, 52, quoted in Batson 1991, 48). It is not clear that Hoffman is really committed to the simple emotional contagion view, but it is instructive to consider the account in any case.

Notice that on the emotional contagion account of altruistic motivation, mindreading is not essential to altruistic motivation. For emotional contagion need not implicate mindreading processes at all. The distress cues are like bad music that you try to turn off. It requires no knowledge of electronics to be motivated to figure out how to stop the offensive stimuli coming from a stereo—one simply experiments with the various knobs and switches. Failing that, one can just leave the room. Similarly, then, one might find the cries of an infant offensive, so one might try to figure out how to stop the stimuli. To be sure, mindreading can provide useful tools for stopping the unpleasant stimuli. But on this account, mindreading needn't be essential to triggering the motivation to stop the crying.

This story has a prima facie virtue—emotional contagion is thought to be well within the repertoire of young children who provide some of our core cases of altruistic motivation. So, the emotional contagion account provides an extremely simple explanation of altruistic motivation, and it extends to children in an unproblematic way. Hence, it would seem that our problem is solved. Altruistic motivation does not depend on mindreading at all. Rather, it depends on the rather primitive capacity for emotional contagion.

Things are not so simple, however. For consider that, at least in the core cases of altruism from adults, one way to rid oneself of the unpleasant cues is to leave the situation. But this is not what happened in the core cases noted above. Although the subjects could have eliminated contagious distress by fleeing the situation, almost none of them did so (Clark and Word 1974). The fact that adults often help when they could perfectly well escape has now been extensively explored in the work of Batson and his colleagues (Batson et al. 1981; Batson et al. 1983; Batson 1990, 1991). This research provides powerful evidence that some core cases of altruistic motivation cannot be accommodated by the simple emotional contagion account.

Batson has the broader agenda of defending a perspective-taking account of altruism, which we will consider in section 5, but for present purposes, it will suffice to see how his data undermine the emotional contagion account. In classic social psychological fashion, Batson and his colleagues set up a mock shock methodology. Subjects were told that they would be in a study with another person and that one of them would be picked at random to be the worker and the other would be the observer. The worker would perform tasks while being given electric shock at irregular intervals, and the observer would watch the person performing the task under these aversive conditions. Of course, the real subjects always ended up in the observer condition, and the "worker" was really a confederate. The subjects were then told that they would view the "worker" via closed-circuit television (though it was really a videotape). The experiment manipulated the *ease of escape* for the subjects. In the easy-escape condition, subjects read "Although the worker will be completing between two and ten trials, it will be necessary for you to observe only the first two"; in the difficult escape condition, subjects read "The worker will be completing between two and ten trials, all of which you will observe" (Batson 1991, 114). The subjects subsequently viewed the worker endure two trials (of the ten trials that the worker had agreed to) in which the worker exhibited considerable discomfort. Subjects were given the opportunity to help out the worker by taking over some of her trials. Using this framework, Batson and colleagues also manipulated the degree of "empathy" in the subjects (see section 7 for details). Across a wide range of studies, they found that subjects in low empathy conditions were much less likely to help when escape was easy. By contrast, subjects in the high empathy condition were equally likely to help whether it was easy to escape or not.

For our purposes, the crucial point is the following. On the emotional contagion model, one should only help when it is harder to escape than it is to help. However, the evidence from Batson and his colleagues suggests that there is an important kind of altruistic motivation that cannot be satisfied by escaping the situation. Hence, this kind of motivation cannot be captured by the emotional contagion model (see also Batson et al. 1981; Batson et al. 1983; Miller et al. 1996, Eisenberg and Fabes 1990). More generally, largely as a result of Batson's work, it is now clear that an adequate account of altruistic motivation needs to accommodate the fact that in core cases of altruism, people often prefer to help even when it is easy to escape.

4.2. Sober and Wilson on Altruistic "Sympathy"

In Sober and Wilson's recent book (1998), they propose an alternative path to altruism that does not rely on mindreading or emotional contagion, but rather on a certain kind of sympathy. They suggest that both sympathy and empathy may motivate altruistic behavior (e.g., 1998, 232). They then try to distinguish sympathy from empathy in two ways.

First, Sober and Wilson maintain that there is a crucial difference between empathy and sympathy because in sympathy,

> your heart can go out to someone without your experiencing anything like a similar emotion. This is clearest when people react to the situations of individuals who are not experiencing emotions at all. Suppose Walter discovers that Wendy is being deceived by her sexually promiscuous husband. Walter may sympathize with Wendy, but this is not because Wendy feels hurt and betrayed. Wendy feels nothing of the kind, because she is not aware of her husband's behavior. It might be replied that Walter's sympathy is based on his imaginative rehearsal of how Wendy would feel if she were to discover her husband's infidelity. Perhaps so—but the fact remains that Walter and Wendy do not feel the same (or similar) emotions. Walter sympathizes; he does not empathize. (1998, 234-35)

But this example does not really distinguish sympathy from empathy. As Sober and Wilson seem to anticipate, a sophisticated empathy account can easily accommodate their case by claiming that we use our imagination to empathize with what Wendy would feel if she were to discover the infidelity. Hence, as far as this example is concerned, "sympathy" might merely be a special form of empathy.

The second, and more important, feature of their account is their claim that "sympathy" does not require mindreading. Sober and Wilson maintain that empathy requires that one be a psychologist, but that sympathy does not: "Empathy entails a belief about the emotions experienced by another person. Empathic individuals are 'psychologists' . . . ; they have beliefs about the mental states of others. Sympathy does not require this. You can sympathize with someone just by being moved by their objective situation; you need not consider their subjective state. Sympathetic individuals have minds, of course; but it is not part of our definition that sympathetic individuals must be psychologists" (1998, 236). Thus, Sober and Wilson apparently maintain that "sympathy" does not require any capacity for mindreading.

Of course, Sober and Wilson are welcome to define a notion of "sympathy" on which mindreading is not required for sympathy. However, they provide no evidence that this kind of sympathy exists. If we rely on traditional signs of sympathy, the evidence suggests that children only begin to exhibit the characteristic signs of sympathy after the first birthday (see section 9) and at this age, children probably have some rudimentary mindreading skills (see, e.g., Gergely et al. 1995; Woodward 1998). So, it may well turn out that the capacity for sympathy exists only in creatures that have mindreading capacities and that the capacity for sympathy depends crucially on the capacity for mindreading. Furthermore, even if Sober and Wilson's "sympathy" does exist, they provide no reason to think that it explains anything like the core cases of altruism with which we began. Again, as we will see, children only begin exhibiting comforting behaviors after the first birthday, by which time they probably have some rudimentary mindreading skills. So, if we take Sober and Wilson's suggestion as an empirical claim about the cognitive underpinnings of core cases of altruistic motivation, it is utterly unsupported.

In sum, then, neither emotional contagion nor Sober and Wilson's sympathy provides a promising explanation of altruistic motivation. It is particularly clear that neither proposal offers a unified account of the core cases of altruistic motivation with which we began. Hence, if we are to have a model of altruistic motivation that can accommodate our core cases, it cannot be one of these models that rejects outright the role of mindreading.

5. PERSPECTIVE-TAKING ACCOUNTS OF ALTRUISTIC MOTIVATION

In the Piaget-Kohlberg tradition, the capacity for perspective taking is thought to be essential to a wide range of moral capacities, including altruistic behavior. Unlike the no-mindreading accounts of altruistic motivation, there is no shortage of advocates for the perspective-taking account of mindreading and altruism. In the recent literature, the most prevalent account of mindreading and altruism continues to be that altruistic motivation depends on perspective taking. This view is suggested by several figures including Batson (1991), Blum (1994), Darwall (1998b), and Goldman (1993).

Goldman (1992; 1993) is by far the most explicit about the cognitive architecture underlying perspective taking, so his work provides a useful starting point. As we've seen, Goldman maintains that empathy is central to altruism, and he maintains that genuine cases of empathy depend on perspective taking. His account of perspective taking draws on his earlier work on the off-line simulation account of folk psychology (Goldman 1989; see also Gordon 1986). Goldman maintains that the process of perspective taking is subserved by off-line simulation in the following way: "Paradigm cases of empathy . . . consist first of taking the perspective of another person, that is, imaginatively assuming one or more of the other person's mental states. . . . The initial 'pretend' states are then operated upon (automatically) by psychological processes, which generate further states that (in favorable cases) are similar to, or homologous to, the target person's states. In central cases of empathy the output states are affective or emotional states" (1993, 351). Now, if we try to incorporate this account of empathy into an account of altruistic motivation, we get the following account of the processes underlying altruistic motivation when the agent sees another in distress. First, the agent determines the beliefs and desires of the person in distress. Then the agent pretends to have those beliefs and desires. These pretend-states are then operated on automatically, leading to affective states that are similar to the target's state, namely distress. These unpleasant affective states then motivate the agent to eliminate the problem at its source—the other person's distress.

Batson's picture is less architecturally explicit, but is still clearly dependent on perspective taking. Batson claims that altruistic motivation derives from "empathy" (1991, 83), and as Batson defines it, empathy requires perspective taking. He writes, "Perception of the other as in need and perspective taking are both necessary for empathy to occur at all" (1991, 85). The empathic response to perceived need "is a result of the perceiver adopting the perspective of the person in need" (1991, 83) and this involves "imagining how that person is affected by his or her situation" (1991, 83).

Blum's (1994) view is somewhat more difficult to interpret. He maintains that altruistic behavior, or "responsiveness" requires "that the child understand the other child's state" (1994 , 197). He rejects the idea that this understanding is limited to cases in which the subject infers "the other's state of mind from a feeling the subject herself has, or has had, in similar circumstances" (1994, 192). Blum rejects this account because it is too "egocentered" (1994, 193), and he argues that this cannot be the sole cognitive process because "such inference would not account for understanding states of mind different from those one is experiencing or has experienced oneself" (1994, 192). Rather, Blum maintains that "understanding others means understanding them precisely *as other* than oneself—as having feelings and thoughts that might be different from what oneself would feel in the same situation" (1994, 193; emphasis in original). So Blum apparently maintains that altruistic motivation depends on the understanding of others as potentially having different beliefs, desires, and emotions. But he does not offer an explicit explanation about how this understanding is achieved.

Although these accounts have important differences, they all share an assumption that altruistic motivation depends on some fairly sophisticated mindreading capacities. First, on Blum's account, and possibly Batson and Goldman's as well, the subject must be able to recognize that the other person might have different mental states than the subject herself would have in a similar situation. Second, for Goldman and Batson, perspective taking requires using the imagination to figure out someone else's mental states. As a result, in sharp contrast to the emotional contagion account, the perspective-taking accounts of altruistic motivation invoke complex mindreading capacities.

6. A MINIMAL MINDREADING ACCOUNT OF ALTRUISTIC MOTIVATION

The accounts of altruistic motivation that make no appeal to mindreading have difficulty accommodating the psychological evidence and capturing the core cases of altruistic motivation. However, I think that we can accommodate the data with a much more austere proposal about the role of mindreading than the perspective-taking accounts. I want to sketch an account of altruistic motivation that draws on as little mindreading as necessary to accommodate the core cases of altruism. Then in the subsequent sections, we will consider the relative merits of the minimalist account and the perspective-taking account.

The crucial finding on altruistic motivation from social psychology is the fact that people often help even when it would be easy to escape (e.g., Batson 1991). If the motivation is caused strictly by an aversive response to immediate situational cues, as proposed by the simple emotional contagion model, then escape is a good alternative. For one can simply remove oneself from the source of discomfort. However, escape is not an adequate alternative if the motivation comes from an enduring internal cause. As a result, a natural first move is to suppose that subjects elect to help rather than escape because some aspect of the situation is preserved in an enduring mental representation, and this mental representation produces the motivation. One could conceivably try to use this move to extend the emotional contagion account. An emotional contagion theorist might continue to deny any role for mindreading and maintain that altruistic motivation comes from an enduring representation of the behavioral, acoustic, or physiognomic cues that cause contagious distress. On this modified emotional contagion account, the reason subjects do not escape in the experiments is that the motivation comes not simply from the immediate situational cues, but also from the enduring representation of those cues. So, on this story, the subjects help because the emotional contagion can only be alleviated by eliminating the aversive cues. However, even this extended emotional contagion account is still inadequate. The problem is that superficial cues can produce emotional contagion, and if one knows that the cues leading to emotional contagion are merely superficial, this typically does not prevent one from experiencing emotional contagion, but it does undermine altruistic motivation.[3] In the present context, the best way to see the problem is by considering what the account predicts about behavior in Batson-style scenarios with superficial distress cues. The extended emotional contagion account predicts that in these situations, subjects will be motivated to eliminate superficial distress cues rather than escape, and, although the relevant experiments have not been conducted, this prediction seems most implausible. For instance, if a subject found herself in an empty classroom with a projector

---

3. The notion of emotional contagion is defined as involving a "vicarious sharing of affect." As a result, the definition technically precludes merely superficial cues from producing emotional contagion, because one cannot share affect with something that does not have that affect. But obviously the mechanisms underlying emotional contagion can be activated by merely superficial cues, because one can synthetically produce many of the cues that lead to "real" emotional contagion. Since the issue at hand is what mechanisms are in play, it is appropriate to use a broader category of response that also includes instances of "ersatz" emotional contagion in which the affect is produced by merely superficial cues.

showing a computer-generated hologram of a baby crying convulsively, this stimulus would likely produce a negative affective response, and presumably the subject would have enduring representations of the cues that lead to this negative response. But in this case, so long as the subject realizes that the stimulus is a hologram and not a real crying baby, her aversive response will likely be relieved about equally well whether she turns off the projector or leaves the room. As a result, the extended emotional contagion account does not accurately predict when escape will be an adequate solution for the subject.

Rather than opt for this implausible attempt to rescue the emotional contagion view, I think that we need to appeal to some capacity for mindreading to obtain an adequate account of altruistic motivation. A rough first proposal here is that altruistic motivation depends, not on a representation of superficial cues, but on a representation of the target's pain (or some other negative affective or hedonic mental state). Appealing to these kinds of representations will provide at least a partial explanation for why subjects help rather than escape in Batson-style scenarios. If altruistic motivation is triggered by a representation that the target is in pain, escape is not an effective solution to the motivational problem because merely escaping the perceptual cues of pain will not eliminate the consequences of the enduring representation that another is in pain. Thus, this account provides some explanation for why escaping the situation is not an adequate solution. Further, the account explains why the extended emotional contagion account is inadequate—if, in a Batson-scenario, you know that the aversive cues are merely superficial, then you do not have a representation that the target is in pain, so escape is an adequate solution. This account also fits well with Batson's finding that the motivation to help is relieved when the subject comes to think that the target's pain has been alleviated, regardless of whether the target's pain was alleviated by the subject or someone else (Batson 1991).

I suggest, then, that altruistic motivation depends on the minimal mindreading capacity to attribute negative affective or hedonic states to others. On this view, a person can have the capacity for altruistic motivation even if the person does not have or does not exploit the capacity for imagining himself in the other's place and having different beliefs, desires or emotions than he himself would have in that situation. However, a person cannot have the capacity for altruistic motivation without some capacity to attribute negative affective or hedonic states to another. For the remainder of the chapter, I will focus on distress as the exemplar mental state, but this is merely for ease of exposition. I do not mean to exclude the possibility that representations of other negative affective and hedonic states (e.g., grief, fear, sorrow) will produce altruistic motivation.

Appealing to the capacity to attribute distress helps explain why subjects are motivated to help even when they could more easily escape. Thus, the account seems, at least at this point, to accommodate the important cases promoted by social psychologists. However, I have thus far neglected to consider whether the account fits with the other class of core cases—comforting behaviors in young children. Is there reason to think that young children attribute distress? And are such attributions plausibly connected with their comforting behaviors? The answer to both questions is "Yes." Henry Wellman and colleagues have explored emotion and pain attribution in the spontaneous speech of young children, using transcripts of children's speech from the CHILDES (Children's Language Data Exchange System) database (MacWhinney and Snow 1990). Though this database was initially established to study children's language it has been an extremely valuable resource for studying the young child's understanding of the mind (see especially Bartsch and Wellman 1995). Wellman and colleagues examined the spontaneous speech of five children, focusing on the transcripts collected for each child from the age of two until the age of five. The researchers found that already at the age of two, the children frequently make attributions of pain, usually using the word "hurt" (Wellman et al. 1995, 130). Furthermore, in the cases analyzed by Bartsch and Wellman (1995), there are transcripts available for four children before the age of two, and in each of these cases, the child is attributing pain well before the second birthday (Sachs 1983; Bloom 1970; Bloom 1973). So pain attribution apparently emerges very early indeed.

Not only do young children make pain attributions, but in the work on comforting behavior, we find that young children respond to a variety of distress cues, and they direct their comforting behavior in ways that are appropriate to the target's distress. As we saw in the examples from Blum (1994), children exhibit comforting behavior in response to another's crying. In experimental studies on one-year-olds, crying also elicited comforting behaviors; so did coughing and gagging (Zahn-Waxler and Radke-Yarrow 1982, 116); and Zahn-Waxler and colleagues (1992a) found that children exhibited comforting behaviors in response to the target bumping her head, saying "ow" and rubbing the injured part. Furthermore, in these studies, the children often comfort the target in appropriate ways. Zahn-Waxler and Radke-Yarrow (1982) conducted a longitudinal study in which a group of fifteen-month-olds and twenty-month-olds were each studied for nine months. The researchers report that during this period, every single child in these groups exhibited an instance of "prosocial actions that focus on the specific distress cue" (124). For example, they describe one instance in which the mother of a nineteen-month-old child hurts her foot and the child witnesses the event. The child exhibited concern, ran over, said "hurt foot" and rubbed the mother's hurt foot (124). In addition to showing that young children direct their comforting behaviors in appropriate ways, this example also indicates that young children actually make pain attributions in conjunction with their comforting behavior, and they seem to recognize what the target is distressed about.[4] Thus, there is good reason to think that the minimal mindreading account I've proposed to explain the core cases of altruistic motivation in adults can also be extended to explain the comforting behaviors of young children.

As noted in section 3, this account is not intended to capture all instances of what we would consider altruistic motivation. We can be motivated to be altruistic to someone without attributing any negative affective states to them. For a dramatic example, we might be motivated to prevent the painless death of a peacefully sleeping stranger. However, one of the aims here is to develop an account of altruistic motivation that does not exceed the cognitive abilities of young children who exhibit comforting behavior. And although children display comforting behavior before the age of two, they do not have an understanding of death until much later (see, e.g., Carey 1985). So if we try to develop an account of altruistic motivation that will capture cases like preventing painless death, the account might no longer be able to accommodate young children. As a result, I think that a promising initial strategy in developing a cognitive account of altruistic motivation is to focus on cases of altruistic motivation that are clearly within the repertoire of young children. This will leave

---

4. One interesting question for future research concerns the extent to which altruistic motivation depends on the child's appreciation that distress is an intentional mental state, a state that is (or can be) directed towards some object. For example, is the altruistic motivation mechanism (the "Concern Mechanism" to be discussed below) activated by the attribution that Mommy is "sad that she hit her foot"? The evidence from Radke-Yarrow and Zahn-Waxler (1982) suggests that children often do appreciate what the target's distress is about, and I mean for the minimalist account to be consistent with the possibility that the motivational system can be activated by attributions of distress as an intentional state. However, it is possible that one might try to develop an even more minimalist account on which altruistic motivation is activated by a general attribution that the target is in distress, with no specification of what the distress is about. (I am indebted to Paul Harris for raising this issue.)

Much of the available evidence seems to be compatible with both of these minimalist alternatives. Consider, for instance, the case from Blum in which the child retrieves a cup for a crying child. One possibility is that the child's belief that the target is "sad that she lost her cup" activates the altruistic motivation system which then produces the motivation to relieve the target's lost-cup distress. An ultraminimalist might maintain rather that the child's motivation comes from the general attribution that the target is in distress. That is, the attribution that the target is sad (simpliciter) activates the motivation system which produces the motivation to relieve the target's sadness. The child then uses other resources to determine a course of action for relieving the target's sadness, and these resources might include the fuller intentional attribution of the target's specific distress states. It is an open empirical matter which of these stories is right about the requisite mindreading underlying altruistic motivation, and of course it is possible that the altruistic motivation system can process both kinds of distress attribution.

open a number of interesting issues about the relation between "early" altruistic motivation and "mature" altruistic motivation. One possibility is that mature altruistic motivation develops out of the core system that I am attempting to sketch in this chapter. Another possibility is that there are independent systems subserving what we commonly group together as mature altruistic motivation, and the early emerging core system is just one of these independent systems. I will not try to address those issues here. There is, however, another fundamental way in which this account is only a partial account of altruistic motivation. Like the perspective-taking account, the minimal mindreading account does not yet explain the process that goes from mindreading to motivation. As will be discussed below (section 9), on both the perspective-taking account and the minimalist account, a natural assumption is that the representations generated by mindreading produce an affective response that motivates the agent to behavior altruistically. But first, we need to consider the relative merits of the minimal mindreading account and the perspective-taking account.

7. ARGUMENTS FOR PERSPECTIVE TAKING: BATSON'S EVIDENCE

Now that the two proposals are on the table, we can consider the arguments for each account. Although it is widely thought that altruistic motivation depends on perspective taking, it is not easy to find an argument for the view in the recent literature. The only systematic argument comes from Batson's data. Batson used various methods to manipulate the "empathy" of subjects, creating conditions in which subjects would have either high empathy or low empathy. Batson is less architecturally explicit than one would like. But according to Batson, his evidence indicates that perspective taking is required for altruistic motivation because in the experiments high empathy subjects were much more likely than low empathy subjects to help in easy-escape conditions (e.g., Batson 1991, 87; see also Darwall 1998b, 273). Batson's data do, I think, provide an important source of evidence against emotional contagion accounts, but they fall far short of establishing that perspective taking is required for altruistic motivation.

To begin, it is important to note that Batson's experiments cannot be decisive evidence for the perspective-taking account. For the evidence does not show that altruistic motivation is absent among those with low empathy. A substantial minority of subjects in the low empathy conditions do help—averaging across studies, nearly a third of the low empathy subjects helped (Batson 1991, chapter 8). And it is possible that most of the other low empathy subjects had some altruistic motivation, but not enough to outweigh the competing motivation to avoid the pain of electric shock. Submitting to painful electric shock to relieve a stranger is a rather high cost action, and it seems likely that if the altruistic option were low cost (e.g., returning an elderly person's books to the campus library), then the difference between high empathy and low empathy subjects might largely disappear.

Although Batson's evidence hardly counts as a decisive argument for the perspective-taking account, it does seem that the perspective-taking account provides a natural explanation for why high empathy would lead to higher altruistic motivation. For if altruistic motivation depends on taking the perspective of others, then increased perspective taking might increase the motivation. However, I think that the minimalist account can provide equally good explanations for Batson's findings. To see why, we need to consider in a bit more detail Batson's two central empathy manipulations: the perspective-taking manipulation (Batson 1991, 120) and the similarity manipulation (Batson 1991, 114). In the perspective-taking manipulation, subjects watched a videotape of a student with broken legs. The subjects were either told to "attend carefully to the information presented on the tape" or to "imagine how the person interviewed felt about what happened." Subjects who were told to imagine the other's feelings were more likely than subjects in the other group to help in the easy-escape condition. Although the perspective-taking account can explain these results, the minimalist account can explain the results equally well. For in the high perspective-taking conditions, subjects are more likely to focus on the other's distress, and they are more likely to develop elaborate representations of the other's distress. Thus, on the minimalist account, it is hardly surprising that the perspective-taking manipulation facilitates altruistic motivation, because perspective taking implicates representations of the other's distress. In principle, it will be hard to undermine a minimalist account using this kind of manipulation because if you increase a subject's perspective taking of a distressed target, you will also typically increase the subject's representations of the target's distress.

In Batson's other important "empathy" manipulation, subjects were shown a questionnaire purportedly filled out by the person who would later need help. One group of subjects saw questionnaires that expressed similar views to those expressed on the subject's own questionnaires. The other group saw questionnaires that expressed dissimilar views. Batson and colleagues found that subjects in the high-similarity group were more likely than subjects in the low-similarity group to help in the easy-escape condition. Batson notes that previous research by Stotland (1969) and

Krebs (1975) shows that subjects in high-similarity conditions display increased empathy. But there is a crucial hedge on "empathy" here. What Stotland (1969) and Krebs (1975) found was that subjects in high-similarity conditions showed heightened physiological response and expressed more concern for the other person. The level of perspective taking in these tasks was not measured. Nor do the researchers suggest that perspective taking is the crucial mechanism underlying the response of subjects in high-similarity conditions. There is, in fact, a large literature in social psychology suggesting that subjects are more attracted to people they think have similar attitudes (e.g., Newcombe 1961; Byrne 1971), and even that people are repulsed by those that they think have different attitudes (Rosenbaum 1986). In light of this, it is hard to see how Batson's similarity manipulation could support the perspective-taking account. What his findings do show is that we are more likely to help people who we think have similar attitudes (for a disturbing variation on this, see Tajfel 1981). Coupled with the data on similarity and attraction, we might conclude from this that we are more prone to help people that we like. But this is quite irrelevant to whether altruistic motivation requires perspective taking.

8. DEVELOPMENTAL EVIDENCE AND PERSPECTIVE TAKING

Thus far, we have no reason to think that altruistic motivation depends on the kind of sophisticated mindreading suggested by perspective-taking accounts. In this section, I will argue that the empirical evidence actually weighs against the perspective-taking account. As we saw in the first chapter, in trying to determine the core architecture underlying a capacity, cognitive scientists pay close attention to evidence from development and evidence from psychopathologies. I will argue that evidence from development indicates that altruistic motivation is independent of sophisticated mindreading abilities like perspective taking. In section 10, I will take up evidence from psychopathologies and argue for a similar conclusion.

The discussion of altruism began with Blum's cases of altruism in young children. Nor are his examples atypical. Blum draws some of his examples from a large body of literature in developmental psychology. This research claims that we start seeing the kind of behavior exemplified in Blum's cases early in the second year. Radke-Yarrow and colleagues (1983) found that at ten to twelve months, children did not respond like the kids in Blum's examples, but "Over the next six to eight months the behavior changed. General agitation began to wane, concerned attention remained prominent, and positive initiations to others in distress began to appear" (Radke-Yarrow, Zahn-Wexler, and Chapman 1983, 481). And, as noted earlier, in Zahn-Waxler and Radke-Yarrow's (1982) study, they found that every single one of their young subjects performed a prosocial act directed at a specific distress cue.

Despite this impressive capacity for altruistic motivation, children under the age of two have severely limited mindreading abilities. Of particular significance, young children have severe deficiencies in their capacity to take the perspective of others. As noted earlier, children under the age of four fail the standard false belief task and similar tasks (see also Wellman 1990; Bartsch and Wellman 1995). Furthermore, although children begin to pretend by around eighteen months, they seem unable to use the imagination to understand other minds until much later (see, e.g., Nichols and Stich 2000, 2003). Thus, since toddlers provide core cases of altruistic motivation and they lack the requisite perspective taking capacities, this provides a serious prima facie argument against the perspective-taking accounts.[5]

In fact, young children's comforting behaviors offer a striking picture of both altruistic motivation and limited perspective taking. The comforting behaviors of young children tend to be "egocentric." Hoffman notes that young children's helping behaviors "consist chiefly of giving the other person what they themselves find most comforting" (1982, 287). For instance, young children will offer their own blanket to a person in distress. Hoffman offers an example of a thirteen-month-old who "responded with a distressed look to an adult who looked sad and then offered the adult his beloved doll" (1982, 287; see also Zahn-Waxler and Radke-Yarrow 1982; Dunn 1988, 97). Thus, toddlers' comforting behavior seems to be simultaneously altruistic in motivation and egocentric in perspective.

Although much early altruistic behavior is guided by "egocentric" considerations, this is perfectly compatible with the minimalist account. A common interpretation of the fact that toddlers offer their own comfort objects is that it shows that children do not really understand that it is the other person who is in distress. For instance, Hoffman (1982) claims that the fact that children tend to give their own comfort objects to help others indicates that "Children cannot yet fully distinguish between their

---

5. Of course, one might deny that toddler comforting behaviors count as core cases of altruism. Rather, one might claim that such cases should be construed as ersatz altruism. However, one would need an argument for excluding these cases. For if we focus on the underlying motivation, the evidence suggests that altruistic concern in toddlers is continuous with altruistic concern in later childhood and adulthood (e.g., Zahn-Waxler et al., 1992a; Eisenberg and Fabes, 1990; Eisenberg et al., 1989).

own and the other person's inner states . . . and are apt to confuse them with their own" (1982, 287). However, the examples of "egocentric" comforting responses provide no reason to think that the child fails to distinguish her own states from the states of others. On the contrary, these responses provide evidence that the child recognizes that the other is in distress. After all, the child is offering the comfort object to the *other* person. Further, the fact that the child offers a comfort object suggests that the child does understand that *distress* is involved. Children do not try to relieve the other's distress by completely bizarre behavior like pretending that a banana is a telephone. And there's no reason to think that before eighteen months, the child experimented with various means of eliminating crying in others (as one might experiment with an unfamiliar piece of electronics). However, the young child has limited mindreading resources at hand and thus relies on egocentric mindreading strategies. As a result, the child's knowledge of how his distress is relieved guides his thinking about how to relieve the other person's distress. Thus, the toddler's egocentric comforting cases are not only consistent with the minimalist account, the cases provide further evidence that the child attributes distress to the other person.

Although there is strong evidence against the perspective-taking model, it would be derelict to claim a quick victory for the minimalist account that I have proposed. For there is a less austere alternative that is not excluded by the evidence. By the time toddlers exhibit comforting behaviors, they probably have the capacity to attribute desires that they do not have (see, e.g., Repacholi and Gopnik 1997). So one might maintain that it is this mindreading capacity, the capacity to attribute discrepant desires, that is essential for altruistic motivation. This view has not been elaborated and defended in the literature, but it is possible that the view is close to Blum's (1994) account. Recall that Blum maintains that the understanding of others required for altruistic motivation depends on understanding that others might have thoughts and feelings that are "different from what oneself would feel in the same situation." He rejects more austere accounts as too "egocentered" (193).

Although this moderate "discrepant desire" position does not contravene any of the data, it is unclear why the capacity to attribute discrepant desires should be essential to altruistic motivation. To see this, it is important to distinguish between three different kinds of egocentrism. One kind of egocentrism is just the view that an individual's basic motivations derive solely from that individual's own affective or hedonic states. We might call this view "psychological egoism." Psychological egoism might be wrong, but the issue belongs primarily to the foundations of psychological science, not to moral psychology. On the second kind of egocentrism—let's call it "ethical egocentrism"—a person is egocentric if none of the individual's desires are directed at another person's needs, except insofar as the individual thinks that addressing the other person's needs will help him.[6] What is crucial about ethical egocentrism (and what distinguishes it from simple psychological egoism) is that if a person is ethically egocentric, he must go through a process of instrumental reasoning before arriving at a motivation to help another. For he must think that helping another will benefit himself. Both of these kinds of egocentrism need to be distinguished from a third kind of egocentrism—mindreading egocentrism. To say that someone is egocentric in this sense is to claim that the individual either cannot or tends not to grasp that others have different likes and dislikes, different judgments, and different feelings than the individual himself. Notice that ethical egocentrism and mindreading egocentrism make independent claims. A person can perfectly well be ethically egocentric without being an egocentric mindreader. That is, a person might know that others have different interests and beliefs than he does, but at the same time, he might not care in the least about the interests of others, except insofar as he thinks it will affect him. Psychopaths seem to fit this characterization fairly well. Conversely, a person could be an egocentric mindreader without being ethically egocentric. That is, a person might be oblivious to the fact that others have different desires and thoughts than she does, but she might care about trying to help others in need, even if she does not think that doing so will serve her own interests. Of course, if she is an egocentric mindreader, she may not be very effective at helping others, because she will not be sensitive to the variation in desires, feelings, and thoughts that actually exists among those she tries to help. Now, finally, we can get to the point of drawing these distinctions—if someone is an egocentric mindreader, that provides no reason to conclude that she lacks altruistic motivation. The kind of egocentrism that undermines the claim for altruistic motivation is *ethical* egocentrism, not *mindreading* egocentrism. As we've seen, when toddlers offer comfort, they often offer their own comfort objects to others. The fact that these children are using egocentric mindreading strategies does not undermine the claim that these children are altruistically motivated. Even if children turned out to be completely egocentric mindreaders, I see no reason to conclude that their attempts to comfort adults with their dolls and blankets would not be the product of altruistic motivation. Thus, although the discrepant desire view fits with the available evi-

---

6. Ethical egocentrism is, like psychological egoism, a descriptive claim. Thus, this notion should not be confused with ethical egoism, which is a normative theory according to which the moral worth of a person's action depends only on the consequences of the act for the actor himself.

dence, it is not at all clear why we should prefer this account to the simpler minimalist theory.

9. AFFECT AND ALTRUISTIC MOTIVATION

I have argued that altruistic motivation requires only the minimal mindreading capacity for distress attribution, but I have said nothing about how attributing distress to another leads to altruistic motivation. In keeping with most other accounts, I will assume that altruistic motivation is mediated by an affective response (see, e.g., Eisenberg 1992; Goldman 1993; Hoffman 1991). In this section, I will try to characterize the affective response underlying altruistic motivation.

Before continuing, I should acknowledge that it is possible that affect plays no role in altruistic motivation. Rather, perhaps altruistic motivation follows directly from an attribution of distress. Something like this might be Sober and Wilson's ultimate view (1998, 312ff.). They suggest that evolution built a mechanism for altruistic motivation that does not rely on hedonic or affective states. However, they do not explain how that mechanism might have evolved in the existing motivational systems of our ancestors. Furthermore, there is some evidence suggesting important correlations between affect and altruistic behavior. As I will elaborate shortly, the developmental data suggest a correlation between affective response and helping behavior in children, and the social psychological data suggest a similar correlation in adults. In addition, as we will see in section 10, evidence on psychopathy indicates that psychopaths' lack of helping behavior might be correlated with a deficit to their affective response to others' distress.

If altruistic motivation does depend on affect, what is the character of this affective response? In section 2, I distinguished between personal distress and contagious distress. We have already seen that contagious distress seems an inadequate model for altruistic motivation. Batson also provides intriguing evidence that neither is personal distress the predominant emotion that drives altruistic behavior. There are two manipulations of his basic experimental procedure that provide evidence for this. As detailed in section 4, Batson's basic experimental design has subjects watch the "worker" (actually a confederate) endure some trials of shocks in which the worker exhibits discomfort. In the difficult escape condition, subjects were required to watch the remaining trials; in the easy escape condition, subjects were not required to watch the remaining trials. Subjects were then given the opportunity to help out the worker by taking over some of her trials. In one experiment, after viewing the worker endure the two trials (and before they were given the opportunity to help), subjects were asked to report their feelings in reaction to observing the worker. Subjects' self reports were classed into two groups: (i) those who reported feeling predominantly "personal distress," that is, "self-oriented feelings such as upset, alarm, anxiety, and distress" (117) and (ii) those who reported feeling predominantly "other-oriented feelings" for the victims, like compassion, tenderness, and softheartedness (117).[7] Now for the results: In the difficult escape condition, subjects who reported feeling personally distressed were equally likely to help as subjects who reported feeling compassion. However, when escape was easy, subjects that reported feeling personally distressed were significantly less likely to help than subjects who reported feeling compassion (Batson et al. 1983; Batson 1991, 124).

The other relevant manipulation of Batson's exploits the venerable but invariably surprising misattribution methodology. Batson suggests that for most people, witnessing another in distress likely produces both personal distress and compassion. Hence, Batson reasoned, if subjects could be led to misattribute one of these feelings to a drug, then those subjects would discount this feeling and regard the other feeling as their predominant response. In an experiment designed along these lines, all subjects took a drug called "Millentana" (actually a placebo) before they observed the worker endure any shocks. Half of the subjects were told, "Millentana produces a clear feeling of warmth and sensitivity, a feeling similar to that you might experience while reading a particularly touching novel." Subjects in this condition were expected to regard personal distress as their predominant emotion. The other half of the subjects were told "Millentana produces a clear feeling of uneasiness and discomfort, a feeling similar to that you might experience while reading a particularly distressing novel" (Batson et al. 1981, 298–99). Subjects in this condition were expected to regard compassion as their predominant emotion, because they would misattribute their genuine personal distress to the drug. After observing the worker go through two trials of shocks, subjects were given the opportunity to help. The results came out as predicted. In the easy escape condition, subjects who were led to attribute their personal distress to the drug were more likely to help than subjects who were led to attribute their compassion to the drug (Batson et al. 1981).

These data indicate, then, that the affective response underlying altruistic motivation is not personal distress. However, there remain a couple of importantly different possibilities for the character of the affective re-

---

7. Batson actually uses the term "empathy" to describe the emotional response of the second group. Obviously, that term only muddies our waters.

sponse. I have suggested that the attribution of another's distress produces an affective response that underlies altruistic motivation. One possibility is that the representation of the other's distress produces a distinctive emotion of sympathy for the other person and this emotion is not homologous to the emotion of the person in need. The sympathy view has some support from an emerging body of research which ties altruistic behavior to a distinctive facial expression (Roberts and Strayer 1996, 456; Eisenberg et al. 1989, 58; Miller et al. 1996, 213). There is also a bit of evidence that sympathy might have distinctive physiological characteristics (Eisenberg and Fabes 1990, 140; Miller et al. 1996). Facial expression and physiological signs are two of the central features that have been used to delineate "basic emotions" (e.g., Ekman 1992). The exciting possibility here is that sympathy is a genuine, distinctive basic emotion with a characteristic facial expression and physiological profile and that this emotion is the motivation behind altruistic behavior. Darwin himself actually made a similar suggestion: "Sympathy with the distresses of others, even with the imaginary distresses of a heroine in a pathetic story, for whom we feel no affection, readily excites tears. . . . Sympathy appears to constitute a separate or distinct emotion" (Darwin [1872] 1965, 215). But Darwin seems to have had a somewhat different notion of sympathy in mind because he thinks that we can sympathize with the happiness of others.

The possibility that altruistic motivation derives from a distinctive basic emotion of sympathy is theoretically appealing, but it has turned out to be difficult to get unequivocal data correlating the postulated features of sympathy with altruistic behavior. There are several different measures, including self-report, facial expressions, and physiological measures. The findings suggest that some of these features are correlated with altruistic behavior some of the time. For example, Eisenberg and Fabes (1990) showed preschoolers a film of children who were injured and in the hospital, and the preschoolers were given the chance to help the hospitalized children by packing crayons for them rather than playing. Although children's self-reports were unrelated to their helping behavior, the physiological measure of sympathy (heart-rate deceleration) was positively correlated with higher levels of helping (Eisenberg and Fabes 1990, 140–41). Further, facial expressions of concerned attention have been significantly correlated with greater helping in boys, but the findings are much weaker for girls (Eisenberg and Fabes 1990, 141). And there is a bit of evidence that there is a correlation between these emotions and helping behavior in Batson-style experiments (Eisenberg et al. 1989).

Notice that the above account suggests that sympathetic motivation for altruism does not count as empathy at all. Rather, on the sympathy view, altruistic behavior is motivated by a distinctive emotion that is not homologous to the emotion felt by the person in need, or indeed homologous to any other emotion.[8] This would entail that a certain class of empathy-based accounts is thoroughly mistaken. If empathy is a vicarious feeling of the emotion that the target is feeling (caused by perspective taking or emotional contagion), then the empathy account is wrong not just about the mindreading required for altruistic motivation but also about the affect. For on the sympathy account, the emotion driving altruistic behavior does not parallel any other emotion. So, except in the iterative case of empathizing with someone feeling sympathy, empathy will not produce the emotion that generates altruistic behavior.

Although the idea that a distinctive emotion of sympathy underlies altruism is theoretically appealing, there is another possibility. The distress attribution might produce a kind of second order contagious distress in the subject. For example, representing the sorrow of the target might lead one to feel sorrow. This would provide a kind of empathic motivation for helping. And the motivation would be effective even when escape is easy. For the cause of the emotion is still the representation of the other's mental state and as a result, one is motivated not simply to escape the situation because that would not rid one of the representation. As a result, this story would provide an equally effective explanation of the fact that subjects help even in easy escape conditions. And some of the above research on sympathy actually provides support for this alternative story. For instance, Eisenberg and colleagues (1989) found that the strongest predictor of helping in adults was not facial sympathy, but facial sadness (Eisenberg et al. 1989, 61). The available evidence does not really decide between these two accounts of the affect underlying altruistic motivation. Indeed, perhaps both affective mechanisms are operative.[9]

8. As we saw in section 3, Sober and Wilson (1998, 234–5) maintain that sympathy does not require that the sympathizer and the target feel the same emotion simultaneously. But that does not really distinguish sympathy from sophisticated accounts of empathy. The psychological work, however, raises the possibility of a profound distinction. Feelings of sympathy may not parallel any other feeling.

9. As Paul Harris has reminded me, there is a great deal of individual variation among young children in their response to distress in others (e.g., Cummings et al. 1986; Zahn-Waxler et al. 1979). This might be thought to undermine the suggestion that a basic emotion underlies altruistic behavior. However even in emotions that are widely accepted to be basic emotions, one finds considerable individual variation (e.g., Haidt, McCauley, and Rozin 1994 on individual variations in disgust). More importantly, as is often the case in cognitive science, it is difficult to know what to make of the individual variation in behaviors. There is an abundance of factors that seem to contribute to the individual variation in children's responses to another's distress. Some of the variation is attributed to differences in child-rearing practices (Zahn-Waxler et al. 1979); some of it is attributed to other family environmental features (e.g., Klimes-Dougan and Kistner 1990); some of the variation seems to be genetically based (Zahn-Waxler et al. 1992b); and, in older children, some of the variation might be due to differences in perspective-taking abilities (Stewart and Marvin 1984). In light of the complex interaction of these and other

TABLE 2.1 Responses to suffering

	Reactive Distress	Concern
Empathic	Contagious Distress	2nd-order Contagious Distress
Non-empathic	Personal Distress	Sympathy

In section 2, I introduced the term 'reactive distress' to enfold both contagious distress and personal distress. Here I want to make a parallel terminological grouping. I will use the term 'concern' to pick out the class of affective responses that includes both sympathy and second-order contagious distress. For, as we have seen, it is plausible that at least one of these responses explains altruistic motivation, which distinguishes the class crucially from reactive distress. However, it is not yet clear whether altruistic motivation derives from sympathy, second-order contagious distress, or both, so it is useful to lump the responses together under a single heading, 'concern.'

Both contagious distress and second-order contagious distress are empathic. For in both cases, the subject feels an emotion homologous to that of the sufferer. By contrast, neither personal distress nor sympathy is empathic. For in cases of personal distress and sympathy, while the subject's emotion is triggered by suffering (or cues of suffering), the subject's emotion itself is not homologous to that of the sufferer. Hence, these four candidate responses can be slotted neatly into a table (see table 2.1).

It is clear that at least one form of reactive distress is present in earliest infancy. It is also plausible that at least one form of concern is present by the second birthday. In adults, both forms of reactive distress are present; in the case of concern, it is less clear whether both forms are present. But that need not prevent us from trying to characterize more fully the underpinnings of concern.

10. THE CONCERN MECHANISM

We are now in a position to state the proposal about the core architecture a bit more precisely. Altruistic motivation depends on a mechanism that takes as input representations that attribute distress, for example, "John

---

features, the individual variation seems consistent with the proposal that altruistic motivation depends on a basic affective mechanism.

is experiencing painful shock," and produces as output affect that, inter alia, motivates altruistic behavior. Following the terminology introduced above, I will call this system the Concern Mechanism. In this section, I want to provide a somewhat fuller characterization of the Concern Mechanism, and I will begin by revisiting the perspective-taking account. For there seems to be a double dissociation between the capacity for perspective taking and the capacity for concern.

First, let us return to the developmental evidence. The comforting behaviors of toddlers suggest that the Concern Mechanism is intact and functioning in young children. This is corroborated by a study in which Zahn-Waxler and colleagues traced the development of concern and comforting behaviors in one year old children. They trained mothers to record their child's emotional and behavioral responses to distress in others. Mothers were also trained to simulate various distress situations. Between thirteen and fifteen months, children were reported to respond with "empathic concern" (sad facial expressions or sympathetic remarks) to 9 percent of the natural distress situations and 8 percent of the simulated distress situations. Between eighteen and twenty months, children responded with empathic concern to 10 percent and 23 percent of natural and simulated distress situations. And by twenty-three to twenty-five months, children responded this way to 25 percent and 27 percent of natural and simulated distress situations (Zahn-Waxler et al. 1992a, 131). So it certainly appears that the capacity for concern emerges before the age of two. Furthermore, between eighteen and twenty months, there is a marginally significant correlation between concern and comforting behavior, and by twenty-three to twenty-five months, there is a significant correlation between concern and comforting behavior. The developmental pattern charted by these results suggests, perhaps not surprisingly, that the coordination of the concern response and altruistic behavior is a complicated developmental process. This developmental process no doubt depends on a suite of conditions, environmental and otherwise, that we do not understand. Nonetheless, the broad pattern indicates that the Concern Mechanism is up and running well before the capacity for perspective taking has developed, which suggests that the Concern Mechanism is dissociable from the capacity for perspective taking.

The possibility of a dissociation between the Concern Mechanism and the capacity for perspective taking is further suggested by evidence on children with autism. As discussed in chapter 1, researchers in the mindreading tradition have explored in some detail the capacities of people with autism, and on a wide range of mindreading and perspective-taking tasks, children with autism tend to perform much worse than their mental age peers (see, e.g., Baron-Cohen 1995; Frith 1989; Dawson and Fernald 1987). Further, one of the central characteristics of autism is lack of imaginative activities and spontaneous pretend play (Wing and Gould 1979). Thus, there is considerable evidence that the capacity for perspective taking is seriously compromised in autism.

Despite their difficulties with perspective taking and imagination, recent studies show that autistic children *are* responsive to distress in others (Bacon et al. 1998; Blair 1999a; Yirmiya et al., 1992). For instance, in one recent experiment, autistic children were shown pictures of threatening faces and distressed faces, and the autistic children showed the normal pattern of heightened physiological response to both sets of stimuli (Blair 1999a). Thus, although autistic children have a deficit in perspective taking, they do respond to the distress of others. In addition, a recent study suggests that autistic individuals engage in comforting behaviors. Sigman and colleagues (1992) explored responses to distress in autistic, Down syndrome, and normally developing children. In one task, the distress was made as salient as possible. The parent was seated next to her child at a small table, and while showing the child how to use a hammer with a pounding toy, the parent pretended to hurt her finger by hitting it with the hammer. The parent then made facial and vocal expressions of distress but did not utter any words (Sigman et al. 1992, 798). Researchers found that autistic children were much less likely than other children to attend to the distress. This fits with a broader pattern of inattentiveness to social cues in autism. For instance, autistic children are much less likely than Down Syndrome children to orient to someone clapping or calling their name (Dawson et al. 1998). Despite the fact that autistic children were less likely to notice or attend to the distress, several autistic children provided comfort to the parent in this experiment. Overall, few children helped, but autistic children helped as often as the children in the other groups.[10]

The fact that autistic children show normal physiological response to distress in others and the finding that autistic children do engage in comforting behaviors suggests that the core architecture for altruistic motivation may be intact in autism. This would pose a serious problem for the perspective-taking account because that account predicts that individuals with serious deficits to imagination and perspective taking would show corollary deficits to altruistic motivation.[11]

10. Six out of twenty-nine autistic children helped; seven out of thirty mentally retarded children helped; and three out of thirty normally developing children helped (Sigman et al. 1992, 800).

11. Although the evidence on autistic children might pose a serious problem for perspective-taking accounts, it is perfectly compatible with the minimal mindreading account. For as noted in chapter 1,

So, even though autistic children have a profound deficit in perspective taking, the available evidence indicates no correspondingly serious deficit to the Concern Mechanism. The complementary question is whether there are individuals who show a deficit to the Concern Mechanism but no serious deficit to perspective taking. There's some reason to think that psychopaths fit this description. The standard diagnostic tool used in the United States, the fourth edition of the *Diagnostic and Statistical Manual of Mental Disorders* (*DSM-IV*), uses the diagnostic category of Antisocial Personality Disorder, and the *DSM-IV* suggests that psychopathy is the same condition (645). People with Antisocial Personality Disorder "frequently . . . tend to be callous, cynical, and contemptuous of the feelings, rights, and sufferings of others" (647). "Persons with this disorder disregard the wishes, rights, or feelings of others. They are frequently deceitful and manipulative in order to gain personal profit or pleasure (e.g., to obtain money, sex, or power). . . . They may believe that everyone is out to 'help number one' and that one should stop at nothing to avoid being pushed around" (646). A number of researchers characterize psychopathy somewhat differently from the Antisocial Personality Disorder (e.g., Hare 1991), but the alternative diagnostic criteria tend to present a similarly disturbing portrait of psychopaths. For instance, psychopathy is characterized by a lack of remorse and empathy, being deceitful and manipulative, and a tendency to adult antisocial behavior (Hare 1991). These characterizations certainly suggest that psychopaths are significantly less likely than nonpsychopaths to exhibit altruistic behavior. Of course, we have already seen that psychopaths show abnormally low physiological response to suffering in others.[12] Coupled with their apparent lack of altruistic behavior, this suggests that the Concern Mechanism is defective in psychopathy. Nonetheless, evidence indicates that psychopaths are capable of perspective taking, and that they perform as well as normal adults on standard perspective-taking tasks (Blair et al. 1996).

Hence, although the evidence is still preliminary, there seems to be a double dissociation between perspective taking and the Concern Mechanism. Young children and autistic children have immature or impaired perspective-taking abilities, yet young children and perhaps even autistic children have an intact and functioning Concern Mechanism. Psycho-

---

despite their deficits in perspective taking, children with autism are capable of attributing simple negative emotions (e.g., Yirmiya et al. 1992; Baron-Cohen 1995; Tager-Flusberg 1993).

12. It remains to be seen exactly how the affective deficits in psychopathy map onto the different responses to suffering in others that we have been exploring in this chapter. But one story is that both the system for contagious distress and the Concern Mechanism are defective, perhaps because the system for contagious distress is developmentally necessary for acquiring a normal Concern Mechanism.

paths, by contrast, seem to have a normal capacity for perspective taking but a deficit to the Concern Mechanism. The evidence from development and psychopathologies thus counts heavily against the perspective-taking account. It seems that altruistic motivation does not require sophisticated mindreading or perspective-taking abilities. And it doesn't take any imagination to be an altruist.[13]

11. EVOLUTIONARY PRECURSORS

Thus far in this chapter, I have characterized two different classes of responses to suffering in others: reactive distress and concern. Neither reactive distress nor concern requires sophisticated mindreading abilities. Reactive distress can apparently be triggered by rather low-level cues like crying. Concern, I have argued, does require mindreading, but only the minimal mindreading capacity to attribute pain to others. There is reason to think that at least some of these emotional responses are present in our evolutionary forebears.

First, it is important to note that if the basic story about mindreading and the Concern Mechanism is right, this has interesting implications for the possibility of altruism in nonhuman animals. For if human altruism requires so little mindreading, it becomes possible that the mechanisms underlying helping-behavior in some nonhuman animals are analogous to the mechanisms underlying altruistic motivation in humans. Although it is hotly debated at present, some nonhuman animals may well have the mindreading capacity to attribute distress to another. There is some evidence, for instance, that chimpanzees can attribute goals (Premack and Woodruff 1978; Call and Tomasello 1998).[14]

13. The Concern Mechanism has many of the features of modules as set out by Fodor (1983). The evidence on development and psychopathology indicates that the Concern Mechanism has a characteristic ontogeny and a characteristic pattern of breakdown. It is also plausible that the mechanism is fast. It is somewhat more difficult to evaluate whether the Concern Mechanism is "encapsulated" (Fodor 1983, 2000) because the relationship between affective systems and encapsulation is far from clear in the current literature. But the Concern Mechanism plausibly possesses at least one feature of encapsulated systems. A cognitive mechanism is encapsulated if it has little or no access to information outside of its own proprietary database, and one of the central features of an encapsulated system is that such systems resist our preferences (Fodor 2000, 63): You cannot make the Müller-Lyer illusion disappear by wanting it to go away. It is likely that the Concern Mechanism is similarly resistant to our preferences and to the dictates of practical reason. For instance, I might think it best, all things considered, not to feel concern when my daughter gets inoculated because any show of concern on my part might intensify her anxiety about inoculations. Nonetheless, it can be extremely difficult to suppress concern in these circumstances. In this sense at least, the Concern Mechanism resembles encapsulated systems.

14. Apart from its intrinsic interest, the possibility that the psychological underpinnings of altruism might be present in nonhumans is of some importance to an evolutionary approach to altruism. If

Research on nonhuman primates does indicate that at least some nonhuman primates are sensitive to a conspecific's distress signals (e.g., Miller et al. 1963). Preston and de Waal (2002) provide a fascinating review of the experimental literature on the response to another's distress in nonhuman animals. They note that several species have been shown to be upset when witnessing the distress of a conspecific. One particularly striking finding comes from research on rhesus monkeys by Masserman and colleagues (1964). The researchers trained the monkeys to get a food pellet by pulling one chain in response to a red light and a different chain in response to a blue light. After the training session, one of the food-chains was rigged so that it would also administer a sharp shock to a conspecific on the other side of a plexiglas divider. There were fifteen animals in the experiment. Ten of these showed a statistically significant preference for the nonshock chain. Two additional animals stopped pulling either chain for a number of days. The researchers conclude that it seems that the monkeys "will consistently suffer hunger rather than secure food at the expense of electroshock to a conspecific" (Masserman, Wechkin, and Terris 1964, 585; see also Wechkin, Masserman, and Terris 1964).

Thus, there is some evidence showing that some animals are sensitive to the suffering of conspecifics. Nonetheless, it is unclear from the available data which mechanism is operative in the nonhuman primates, whether it is a form of reactive distress or a form of concern. But what is clear and important is that there are powerful evolutionary precursors for responding to suffering in conspecifics.

Although there are evidently evolutionary precursors, I demur from embracing an account of the evolutionary function of these mechanisms. The familiar problem with developing such accounts is a lack of adequate comparative data (see, e.g., Grantham and Nichols 1999; Nichols and Grantham 2000). It is difficult to evaluate, let alone defend, proposals about the evolutionary function of a mechanism in the absence of comparative evidence, including evidence of which animals lack the mechanism. So although we have evidence that many species do respond to distress, it is hard to know the function of the underlying mechanisms

---

altruistic motivation in humans is an adaptation that depends on sophisticated mindreading abilities like perspective taking, then the altruistic motivation system must have been shaped after the evolution of our sophisticated mindreading abilities. If so, the mechanisms for altruistic motivation presumably emerged relatively recently in evolutionary time because, by most accounts, humans are the only primates with sophisticated mindreading abilities. The Concern Mechanism account of altruistic motivation, on the other hand, need not be committed to the view that altruistic motivation is a recent adaptation because on this view the requisite mindreading mechanisms are minimal and may well have been present in our more distant phylogenetic ancestors.

without knowing which species lack the mechanisms. Experimental questions leap to mind. Do asocial species respond to distress in nonkin? Does the level of response vary with the degree of sociality? Are there gender differences in the response to distress in some species? These questions are much easier to ask than to answer. But without some answers, it is hard to evaluate proposals about evolutionary function in any remotely rigorous fashion. It is for this reason that I have opted to take a descriptive approach to characterizing the mechanisms, rather than an evolutionary psychological approach.

12. SENTIMENTAL RULES AND THE MORAL SENSE

Now that we have a sharper picture of the human responses to suffering, we can provide a more articulate rendering of the Sentimental Rules proposal. According to the Sentimental Rules account, norms that prohibit emotionally upsetting actions receive a special status. Such norms are distinguished from emotionally neutral conventional rules. This chapter makes clear that actions that cause suffering in others are indeed emotionally upsetting in multiple ways. For suffering in others itself is upsetting in multiple ways—suffering or indications of suffering trigger contagious distress, personal distress, and concern. As a result, norms prohibiting harm will, for normal people, be central instances of Sentimental Rules.

With the characterization of the candidate affective mechanisms in hand, it is clear that the Sentimental Rules account differs in important ways from the more traditional sentimentalist view that moral judgment derives from a moral sense. Traditional moral sense theorists, like Hutcheson, promoted the moral sense as the source of distinctive feelings of approval and disapproval which are triggered by the perception of virtue and vice. This moral sense produces a pain of disapproval when we perceive an action that is vicious or morally wrong. Furthermore, when an action prompts the moral sense to deliver the pain of disapproval, we condemn the action as wrong.

None of the affective mechanisms explored in this chapter counts as a moral sense. For none of these mechanisms tracks vice (or virtue). Rather, each of the emotions we have explored—personal distress, contagious distress, and some form of concern—can be activated in the absence of any moral judgment. Eighteen-month-old human infants can probably respond with reactive distress and concern; yet it would be a stretch to say that such infants have the capacity for core moral judgment. More importantly, in adults with a mature capacity for moral judgment, forms of reactive distress and concern can be activated in the conspicuous absence of any judgment that a transgression has occurred. Indeed, the emotions can be activated in the absence of any judgment that an *action* has occurred. When we come upon accident victims, we exhibit characteristic emotional responses of concern and reactive distress. Yet at least often, this is not accompanied by any judgment of wrongdoing or viciousness.

On the Sentimental Rules account, reactive distress or concern plays a crucial role in leading people to treat harmful transgressions as wrong in a distinctive way. Thus, these relatively simple, primitive emotions supply the sentiment to moral judgment. No further moral feeling is invoked as a necessary part of core moral judgment. Perhaps there is a further special feeling, but it is not posited by the Sentimental Rules account. Rather, on this account, the relatively primitive emotions of reactive distress and concern lead us to treat harm norms as distinctive. But again, these emotions can be activated in the absence of a judgment of vice. So none of them can be identified with a moral sense.

13. CONCLUSION

The human response to suffering is impressively multifaceted. Contagious distress, personal distress, and some form of concern each constitute distinctive emotional responses elicited by suffering in others. Some of these responses emerge early ontogenetically, perhaps even by the time of birth. But all of them are plausibly present in the young child, including the elements of altruistic motivation. The evidence suggests that basic altruistic motivation requires only a minimal capacity for mindreading, the capacity to attribute negative affective or hedonic mental states like distress. These attributions, I have suggested, produce altruistic motivation by activating an affective system, the Concern Mechanism. Of course, the account of altruistic motivation I have offered in this chapter is hardly a full account of the psychological mechanisms implicated in mature altruistic behavior, for the altruistic capacities of adult humans far outstrip those provided by the primitive mindreading and Concern mechanisms. Nonetheless, the empirical work suggests that the Concern Mechanism and a minimal capacity for mindreading form the core of our capacity for altruism. By the age of two years, this capacity is in place in normal humans, along with the capacity for reactive distress, which is in place much earlier.

The emotions set out in this chapter allow us to fill out the Sentimental Rules account of core moral judgment. On that account, norms prohibiting actions that are likely to elicit strong negative affect will be treated as distinctively wrong. Suffering in others triggers strong negative affect in the form of contagious distress, personal distress, and concern. As a result, norms prohibiting actions that cause suffering in others will count as Sentimental Rules. Furthermore, the responses to suffering are present in children by two years of age. Hence, children have these emotional responses well in place by the time they treat harm-based violations as distinctively wrong.

3

Is It Irrational to Be Amoral?

How Psychopaths Threaten Moral Rationalism

It was almost as if he [I] said it was wrong for all these things
to happen. "It is wrong for me to jaywalk. It is wrong to rob a
bank. It is wrong to break into other people's houses. It is
wrong for me to drive without a driver's license. It is wrong
not to pay your parking tickets. It is wrong not to vote in elections. It is wrong to intentionally embarrass people."

—Presumed psychopath Ted Bundy, quoted in
S. Michaud and H. Aynesworth,
Ted Bundy: Conversations with a Killer

1. INTRODUCTION

In this chapter, I will consider how the empirical findings in moral psychology fit with moral rationalism, the idea that morality is founded on
reason or rationality. This rich metaethical tradition stretches back
through Kant and Cudworth, and over the last twenty years, a number of
central figures in moral philosophy have defended some version of moral
rationalism (e.g., Gewirth 1978; Darwall 1983; Nagel 1970, 1986; Korsgaard 1986; Singer 1995; Smith 1994, 1997). The view has been attractive
to many because rationalism seems like the most promising way to secure
moral objectivism. If morality derives from reason, then morality might
enjoy an objective basis. Nonetheless, in this chapter I will argue that

Epigraph. A note is in order about Bundy's use of the third person at the beginning of the quota-
tion. In his interviews with Michaud and Aynesworth (1989), Bundy initially refused to talk about
the murders he was accused of committing. The interviewers suggested that, to avoid incriminating himself,
Bundy use the third person to talk about the murders. Bundy agreed to this arrangement, and as a result,
many of his statements are presented in the third person, even though they are presumably about Bundy
himself.

moral rationalism is threatened by thought experiments concerning psychopaths and by real experiments on psychopaths. The argument will depend on drawing a distinction between two different rationalist claims, a conceptual claim and an empirical claim. The conceptual claim is that it is a conceptual truth that moral requirements are rational requirements, and the empirical claim is that human moral judgment is produced by rational cognitive mechanisms. I will argue that these claims are independent, but that each claim faces serious problems. I will maintain that the conceptual claim is threatened by the conceptual possibility of a rational amoralist. I will go on to argue that while the empirical claim is independent of the conceptual claim, the evidence on moral development and psychopathologies indicate that the empirical rationalist claim is false as well.

2. RATIONALISM AND OBJECTIVISM

The broadly Humean view that moral judgment is based on sentiments or emotions has been defended by a wide range of theorists (e.g., Stevenson 1944; Gibbard 1990; Wiggins 1991). However, according to a familiar line of argument (e.g., Hume [1739] 1964, 469), the Humean view is often thought to undercut moral objectivism. For if moral judgment derives from the emotions, then, were our emotions different, our moral judgments would be different as well. So, according to this line of reasoning, the moral judgments that we do make are not objectively true, apart from any perspective.[1] This consequence has seemed repugnant to a number of ethical theorists, and the most prominent alternative to Humean accounts is moral rationalism.

Moral rationalism can be traced back before Hume, at least as far as Cambridge Platonists like Cudworth and Whichcote (see, e.g., Darwall 1995; Gill 1999), however, the view is most visibly associated with Kant. According to rationalism, morality is grounded in reason or rationality rather than the emotions or cultural idiosyncrasies, and this has seemed to many to be the best way of securing a kind of objectivism about moral claims. Consider the following representative statements:

> 1. Just as there are rational requirements on thought, there are rational requirements on action, and altruism is one of them. . . . If the requirements of ethics are rational requirements, it follows that the mo-

---

1. This is obviously a vastly oversimplified sketch of an anti-objectivist argument. A somewhat fuller sketch will be discussed in chapter 8.

tive for submitting to them must be one which it would be contrary to reason to ignore. (Nagel 1970, 3)

2. The objective badness of pain . . . is . . . just the fact that there is reason for anyone capable of viewing the world objectively to want it to stop. The view that values are real is . . . that our claims about value and about what people have reason to do may be true or false independently of our beliefs and inclinations. (Nagel 1986, 144)

3. The Kantian approach to moral philosophy is to try to show that ethics is based on practical reason: that is, that our ethical judgments can be explained in terms of rational standards that apply directly to conduct or to deliberation. Part of the appeal of this approach lies in the way that it avoids certain sources of skepticism that some other approaches meet with inevitably. If ethically good action is simply rational action, we do not need to postulate special ethical properties in the world or faculties in the mind in order to provide ethics with a foundation. (Korsgaard 1986, 311)

4. If our concept of rightness is the concept of what we would desire ourselves to do if we were fully rational, where this is a desire for something of the appropriate substantive kind, then it does indeed follow that our moral judgements are expressions of our beliefs about an objective matter of fact. (Smith 1994, 185)

As these passages indicate, the consequences are profound and reassuring if moral rationalism is true. So it is no wonder that the view has drawn such a distinguished following. However, I will argue that despite its appeal, rationalism is an implausible view.

3. CONCEPTUAL AND EMPIRICAL RATIONALISM

Before we can begin to evaluate moral rationalism it is crucial to recognize two different rationalist claims, a conceptual claim and an empirical claim. They might be put as follows:

Conceptual rationalist claim: It is a conceptual truth that a moral requirement is a reason for action.

Empirical rationalist claim: It is an empirical fact that moral judgment in humans is a kind of rational judgment; that is, our moral judgments derive from our rational faculties or capacities.

In this section, I want to stress the fact that each of these claims is independent of the other.

We can find both kinds of rationalist claims in the recent literature. Michael Smith (1994) is especially clear about the conceptual claim. He writes that the rationalist's conceptual claim is that "our concept of a moral requirement is the concept of a reason for action; a requirement of rationality or reason" (64). The idea here is that it is a conceptual truth that it is contrary to reason to be amoral. This claim is taken to depend only on a close a priori inspection of our moral concepts and not on any empirical observations.

In recent years, Peter Singer has developed a version of empirical rationalism in the context of the evolutionary problem of how to explain the sense of responsibility:

> How can evolutionary theory explain a sense of responsibility to make the entire world a better place? How could those who have such a sense avoid leaving fewer descendants, and thus, over time, being eliminated by the normal workings of the evolutionary process?
>
> Here is one possible answer. Human beings lack the strength of the gorilla, the sharp teeth of the lion, the speed of the cheetah. Brain power is our specialty. The brain is a tool for reasoning, and a capacity to reason helps us to survive, to feed ourselves, and to safeguard our children . . . the ability to reason is a peculiar ability . . . it can take us to conclusions that we had no desire to reach. For reason is like an escalator, leading upwards and out of sight.
> (Singer 1995, 226–27)

Singer suggests that this natural capacity for reason enables us to "distance ourselves from our own point of view and take on, instead, a wider perspective, ultimately even the point of view of the universe" (229).

Although few other writers develop empirical rationalism in an evolutionary framework, there is reason to think that other rationalists also find empirical rationalism attractive. For instance, Thomas Nagel (1997) is concerned to dispel subjectivism, which he regards as an empirical hypothesis (110–11). And Smith tries to explain the behavior of actual miscreants, like the successful criminal, by appealing to failures in the criminal's rational processes (1994, 194–96). In effect, Smith suggests that those who actually exhibit persistent failings in moral judgment suffer from rational failings.

More broadly, rationalists often remark on the amount of actual agreement that is found in moral discourse, and they take this to support a rationalist claim. In discussing values, Nagel (1986) writes that "the degree to which agreement can be achieved and social prejudices transcended in the face of strong pressures suggests that something real is being investigated" (148). Similarly, Smith (1994) writes, "the empirical fact that moral argument tends to elicit the agreement of our fellows gives us reason to believe that there will be a convergence in our desires under conditions of full rationality. For the best explanation of that tendency is our convergence upon a set of extremely unobvious *a priori* moral truths" (187). These observations about actual agreement on moral issues are not about our concept of moral requirements; rather, they are claims about our actual and predicted moral judgments. Coming to agreement about moral issues is supposed to count as evidence that we arrive at our moral judgments through rational means. In this context, the analogy with mathematics is especially appealing. Smith exploits this analogy:

> Why not think . . . that if such a convergence emerged in moral practice then that would itself suggest that these particular moral beliefs, and the corresponding desires, *do* enjoy a privileged rational status? After all, something like such a convergence in mathematical practice lies behind our conviction that mathematical claims enjoy a privileged rational status. So why not think that a like convergence in moral practice would show that moral judgements enjoy the same privileged rational status? . . . . It remains to be seen whether sustained moral argument can elicit the requisite convergence in our moral beliefs, and corresponding desires to make the idea of a moral fact look plausible. . . . Only time will tell. (Smith 1993, 408–9; emphasis in original)

By exploiting this analogy between moral judgment and mathematical judgment, we can offer a somewhat sharper characterization of empirical rationalism:

> The psychological capacities underlying moral judgment are, like the psychological capacities underlying mathematical judgment, rational mechanisms.

If this is right, then all rational creatures should eventually reach agreement about moral claims, as they do about mathematical claims.

Rationalists thus make both the conceptual and the empirical claims, and what I want to stress for present purposes is that the claims are independent. Either of the claims could be true while the other claim is false. Rationalists have noted that conceptual rationalism might be true even if we humans do not attain true moral judgment. For instance, Smith distinguishes between conceptual and substantive rationalist claims. As noted above, Smith (1994) writes that the rationalist's conceptual claim is that "our concept of a moral requirement is the concept of a reason for action" (64). The rationalist's substantive claim is that "there are requirements of rationality or reason corresponding to the various moral requirements (64–65). Smith goes on to note that the conceptual claim might be true even if the substantive claim is false: "Even if we accept the rationalists' conceptual claim, we must still go on to defend the rationalist's substantive claim. And conversely, even if we deny the rationalists' substantive claim, we must still engage with the rationalists' conceptual claim" (65).[2] Indeed, Smith ultimately maintains that conceptual rationalism is true but that it is still an open question whether substantive rationalism is true, partly because we do not know whether agreement will be achieved on moral issues (189). So, the arguments for the conceptual claim do not show that the empirical claim is true; nor do the arguments against the empirical claim impugn the conceptual claim. It is possible that our concept of moral requirement is that moral requirements are reasons for action, but that our actual moral judgments are not rational in this sense. For instance, it is possible that our moral judgments are the product of affective mechanisms rather than rational cognitive mechanisms. But even if that is the case, it does not show that the conceptual rationalist claim is false.

Although rationalists recognize that conceptual rationalism does not entail that humans have a correspondingly rational moral psychology, what seems to go unnoticed is that even if conceptual rationalism is false, humans might have a psychological make-up on which moral judgment is rational (whether or not it corresponds to "rational" in the conceptual rationalist sense). Indeed, as Smith (1994) sets up the distinction between the conceptual claim and the substantive claim, the truth of the substantive claim depends on the truth of the conceptual claim (64). However, it might turn out that our actual moral psychology really is akin in the relevant respects to our actual mathematical psychology, and this might be the case even if it is not part of our concept of moral requirement that moral requirements are reasons for action. Similarly, it might turn out that all humans will eventually come to widespread moral agreement, as Nagel and Smith suggest, and this agreement might be the result of rational argumentation. At the same time, it might be the case that it is not part of our concept of a moral requirement that they be reasons for action. That is, it is possible that the commonsense notion of morality includes no conceptual connection to rationality and yet that human moral judgment in fact universally is a product of rational cognitive mechanisms.

Although conceptual rationalism and empirical rationalism are distinct claims, both claims are of interest and importance, and if either claim is true, then some form of moral objectivism follows. If conceptual rationalism is true, then it is a conceptual truth that morality is objective. According to empirical rationalism, on the other hand, human moral judgment is a product of reason. That would provide ample justification for thinking that human morality is in fact objective. Because if human

---

2. Similarly, Korsgaard writes, " . . . if we are rational, we will act as the categorical imperative directs. But we are not necessarily rational" (1986, 331).

moral judgment derives from our rational faculties, then creatures who have all of the rational faculties that we do (including aliens) should arrive at the same moral views that we do, just as such creatures should arrive at the same mathematical views that we do. This might be true without it being the case that the rationality of morality can be shown by conceptual analysis.

Once this distinction between conceptual and empirical rationalism is clear, it is also clear that the arguments for and against each claim are largely independent. The arguments used for and against the conceptual claim are largely irrelevant to the empirical claim. And the arguments for and against the empirical claim are largely irrelevant to the conceptual claim. So the claims and arguments really need to be treated independently.

I will argue that each of these claims is threatened by considerations about psychopaths, but in radically different ways. Conceptual rationalism claims that it is part of our concept of morality that moral requirements are requirements of reason. The problem with this proposal is that common views about psychopaths suggest that conceptual rationalism does not capture our concept of moral requirements. Empirical rationalism is immune to these criticisms, for it claims only that it is an empirical fact about human psychology that moral judgment derives from our rational capacities. However, empirical rationalism is seriously threatened by empirical evidence on the psychology of psychopathy. For the evidence on psychopathy indicates that the capacity for moral judgment is in fact seriously disrupted in psychopaths, but this seems to be the result of an emotional deficit rather than any rational shortcomings.

4. CONCEPTUAL RATIONALISM AND AMORALISM

The basic idea of conceptual rationalism is that it is a conceptual truth that a moral requirement is a reason for action (Nagel 1970; Korsgaard 1986; Smith 1994). For instance, Michael Smith (1994) writes that the rationalist's conceptual claim is that "our concept of a moral requirement is the concept of a reason for action; a requirement of rationality or reason" (64). He goes on to say, "according to the rationalist, it is a conceptual truth that claims about what we are morally required to do are claims about our reasons" (84). I will focus on Smith's version of this position, because his approach is largely insulated from empirical problems raised against classical conceptual analysis (e.g., Stich 1992). Smith adopts David Lewis's (1970, 1972) view that the terms of commonsense theories are defined by the set of platitudes in which they occur. So, as Smith

(1994) envisions the project of conceptual analysis, "an analysis of a concept is successful just in case it gives us knowledge of all and only the platitudes which are such that, by coming to treat those platitudes as platitudinous, we come to have mastery of that concept" (31). This approach elegantly sidesteps empirical problems about the way that concepts are mentally represented. It is clearly the case that lay people know a number of platitudes about morality (e.g., "It's wrong to hit a person without a good reason"). The project of charting those platitudes is both practicable and interesting.

For current purposes, the crucial feature of conceptual rationalism is its account of the link between moral judgment and motivation. Smith maintains that conceptual rationalism entails the Practicality Requirement, according to which "It is supposed to be a conceptual truth that agents who make moral judgments are motivated accordingly, at least absent weakness of the will and the like" (Smith 1994, 66). Thus, conceptual rationalism is committed to the claim that it is a conceptual truth that people who make moral judgments are motivated by them.[3] It is at this point that considerations about psychopaths start to raise trouble.

Psychopaths pose a familiar problem for conceptual rationalism because, contrary to the Practicality Requirement, it seems possible that a psychopath can be fully rational and judge that some action is morally required without being motivated to do it. This sort of rational amoralist is suggested in a number of different places. David Brink (1989) cites Plato's Thrasymachus and Hobbes's Fool as early examples. Hume's example of the sensible knave also seems to raise the possibility of a rational amoralist. Hume sets up the case as follows:

> according to the imperfect way in which human affairs are conducted, a sensible knave, in particular incidents, may think that an act of iniquity or infidelity will make a considerable addition to his fortune, without causing any considerable breach in the social union and confederacy. That *honesty is the best policy,* may be a good general rule, but is liable to many exceptions; and he, it may perhaps be thought, conducts himself with most wisdom, who observes the general rule, and takes advantage of all the exceptions.
>
> I must confess that, if a man think that this reasoning much requires an answer, it will be a little difficult to find any which will to him appear satisfactory and convincing. If his heart rebel not

---

3. One might try to defend conceptual rationalism without committing oneself to the Practicality Requirement. However, the most prominent and influential versions of conceptual rationalism are tied to the Practicality Requirement, and I will simply assume in what follows that conceptual rationalism is committed to the Practicality Requirement.

against such pernicious maxims, if he feel no reluctance to the thoughts of villainy or baseness, he has indeed lost a considerable motive to virtue; and we may expect that his practice will be answerable to his speculation. (Hume [1777] 1975, 282–83; emphasis in original)[4]

In the contemporary literature, Brink develops the amoralist challenge and argues that these sorts of cases show that it is conceptually possible for a rational amoralist to make moral judgments without being appropriately motivated by them (e.g., Brink 1989). Although he ultimately tries to defend conceptual rationalism against Brink, Smith himself suggests that such apparent cases of rational amoralists are not "confined to the world of make-believe. There are, after all, real-life sociopaths" (Smith 1994, 67).

The standard conceptual rationalist response to this problem is to maintain that supposed amoralists like sociopaths or psychopaths do not "*really* make moral judgments at all" (Smith 1994, 67; emphasis in original). When psychopaths say that it is wrong to hurt people, they are not expressing the same thing that normal people do with the same sentence, because psychopaths are not motivated in the right way and thus their words mean something else. Rather, psychopaths use moral terms in an "inverted-commas" sense (Hare 1952). This inverted-commas response has been defended most vigorously by Smith, and it has generated a spirited debate (e.g., Brink 1997; Miller 1996; Smith 1994, 1996, 1997). I want to skirt most of the debate to consider a point at which the inverted-commas response joins an empirical issue.

It is important to be clear about exactly what the inverted-commas claim comes to. If the inverted-commas response is to insulate conceptual rationalism from the rational amoralist, then the claim cannot be that it is an empirical fact about psychopaths that they use moral terms in an inverted-commas sense. Rather, the claim must be that it is part of our concept of moral judgment that psychopaths do not really make moral judgments, but only "moral" judgments. Conceptual rationalism is, after all, supposed to characterize our ordinary moral concepts and intuitions. Indeed, as Smith develops it, conceptual rationalism is supposed to be a

---

4. Hume's example is actually a bit problematic. For Hume is often interpreted as an internalist about moral judgment, so that for Hume, to make a moral judgment requires having the motivation. In this case, one might worry about whether Hume can really maintain that the sensible knave both lacks the motivation and has genuine moral understanding. Hence, one interpretative gambit would be to claim that Hume is not committed to the knave actually having the moral understanding. But these sort of exegetical worries do not subvert the point here. Hume's example nicely brings out the amoralist problem. For Hume's example suggests that a knave can be fully rational, understand what is moral, and yet not be motivated to be moral if it is in his interest to do otherwise.

systematized set of platitudes that characterize the folk concept of morality. Although the project of systematizing the platitudes will presumably require serious analytic resources, the project also has substantive empirical checks because the platitudes themselves are supposed to be claims that most people would accept. Hence, an important initial question is, what *do* people think about moral judgment in psychopaths? Because both conceptual rationalists and their opponents are heavily invested in the debate, we should be wary of relying on their intuitions about what people think about psychopathic moral judgment. A less loaded alternative is to simply ask people who have not been trained in the debate. In light of this, I carried out a small study in which I presented philosophically unsophisticated undergraduates with questions about whether a given person really understands moral claims. Subjects were given the following probes:

> John is a psychopathic criminal. He is an adult of normal intelligence, but he has no emotional reaction to hurting other people. John has hurt and indeed killed other people when he has wanted to steal their money. He says that he knows that hurting others is wrong, but that he just doesn't care if he does things that are wrong. Does John really understand that hurting others is morally wrong?

> Bill is a mathematician. He is an adult of normal intelligence, but he has no emotional reaction to hurting other people. Nonetheless, Bill never hurts other people simply because he thinks that it is irrational to hurt others. He thinks that any rational person would be like him and not hurt other people. Does Bill really understand that hurting others is morally wrong?

The responses to these questions were striking—and they ran in exactly the opposite pattern that conceptual rationalism would suggest. Most subjects maintained that the psychopath did really understand that hurting others is morally wrong, despite the absence of motivation. Neither was this due to an insipid reluctance to deny genuine moral judgment, for, surprisingly, a majority of subjects denied that the mathematician really understood that hurting others is morally wrong.[5] These responses suggest that, at least in some populations, the common conception of psychopaths is precisely that they really know the difference between right and wrong, but they do not care about doing what's right. Prima facie, this counts as evidence against the conceptual rationalist's inverted-commas gambit. For it seems to be a *platitude* that psychopaths really make moral

---

5. Subjects were actually significantly more likely to say that the psychopath understood than that the mathematician did (Nichols 2002a).

judgments. And if it is a platitude that psychopaths really make moral judgments, it will be difficult to prove that conceptual rationalism captures the folk platitudes surrounding moral judgment. This is not to say that there are no responses available to the inverted-commas enthusiast. One might, for instance, maintain that a process of reflective equilibrium would lead people to reject the platitude about psychopathic moral judgment. However, it is important to note that this sort of response is yet another substantive empirical claim, which will not be persuasive without empirical evidence.

There is a more far reaching empirical threat to conceptual rationalism from recent work on philosophical intuitions. Jonathan Weinberg, Steve Stich, and I explored epistemic intuitions in different cultures and socioeconomic groups. We found that there is considerable and surprising variation (both within and across cultures) in folk intuitions about standard epistemological thought experiments (Weinberg, Nichols, and Stich 2001).[6] Although there is not as yet any cross-cultural data on intuitions about metaethics, the findings on epistemic intuitions obviously raise the possibility that there might also be considerable variation in intuitions about moral requirements. Thus, not only is it a substantive empirical assumption that the folk platitudes, when systematized, will exclude the platitude about psychopathic moral judgment, it is also a substantive empirical assumption that there is a stable and cross-culturally uniform set of intuitions or platitudes that comprise *the* folk concept of morality.

It is, I have argued, empirically dubious that there is a single, universal folk concept of morality according to which psychopaths do not make genuine moral judgment. As we saw in chapter 1 and will consider further below, the evidence on psychopathy indicates that the capacity for moral judgment is seriously disturbed in psychopaths, and they might plausibly be regarded as using moral terms in an inverted-commas sense. However, this empirical evidence is of no help to the conceptual rationalist. The problem psychopaths pose for conceptual rationalism concerns only the facts about our concept of psychopaths, not the facts about psychopaths themselves.

None of the above problems raised against conceptual rationalism threaten the empirical rationalist claim. For empirical rationalism offers a substantive version of rationalism that might be maintained even if conceptual analysis is bankrupt. And the conceivability of a rational amoralist does not prove that the empirical rationalist is mistaken. The empiri-

---

6. More recently, Edouard Machery, Ron Mallon, Steve Stich, and I found striking cross-cultural differences in the semantic intuitions of East Asian and Western students (Machery et al. 2004).

cal rationalist appeals to the facts, not the concepts or the platitudes. Thus, nothing that has passed so far poses the slightest objection to the empirical rationalist claim that human morality derives from rational cognitive mechanisms and not from affective mechanisms. Rather, empirical rationalism is the most promising contender for securing moral objectivism.

5. EMPIRICAL RATIONALISM AND THE PSYCHOLOGY OF PSYCHOPATHS

Contrary to the conceptual rationalist claim, it is apparently a platitude that psychopaths understand that it is morally wrong to hurt others but don't care. However, the evidence discussed in chapter 1 suggests that psychopaths really do have a defective understanding of moral violations. But this offers no solace to the rationalist. Ironically, this will actually pose a serious problem for the empirical rationalist. For psychopaths' moral judgment making is deeply disturbed, but this seems not to be the result of a defect in their rational capacities. So, while conceptual rationalism is at odds with our concept of psychopathy, empirical rationalism is at odds with the psychology of psychopathy.

Let us begin by reviewing briefly some of the relevant findings discussed in chapter 1. Blair compared psychopathic and nonpsychopathic subjects on the moral/conventional task. He found that psychopaths were significantly less likely than nonpsychopaths to treat moral violations as distinctive (Blair 1995, 1997; Blair et al. 1995). Nonpsychopathic criminals, like normal adults and children, made a significant moral/conventional distinction on permissibility, seriousness, and authority contingence; psychopaths, on the other hand, didn't make a significant moral/conventional distinction on any of these dimensions (Blair 1995). More importantly, children with psychopathic tendencies were more likely to judge moral transgressions as authority contingent. Furthermore, psychopaths were less likely than the control criminals to justify rules with reference to the victim's welfare. Rather, psychopaths typically gave conventional-type justifications for all transgressions. This failure to distinguish moral and conventional violations is illustrated in the remark taken from Ted Bundy at the beginning of this chapter, when he notes that it is wrong to jaywalk, wrong to rob a bank, wrong to break into other people's houses, and wrong to drive without a license (Michaud and Aynesworth 1989, 116). Bundy does not seem to distinguish between the radically different kinds of wrongs involved here, mixing moral and conventional violations indiscriminately. It seems then, that although there is a sense in which psychopaths do know right from wrong, they don't know (con-

ventional) wrong from (moral) wrong. We would, in fact, have some justification in maintaining that they use the term 'morally wrong' only in an
inverted-commas sense.

6. WHAT IS WRONG WITH PSYCHOPATHS?

The fact that the most celebrated class of amoralists have a defective capacity for moral judgment provides some support to the claim that moral
judgment is closely linked with motivation. For we know that psychopaths
are not motivated by moral prohibitions the way normal people are. But
one then needs to ask what the cognitive mechanisms are that produce
this correlation between moral judgment and moral motivation, and what
cognitive mechanisms are disrupted in psychopathy. It is at that point
that we begin to see the problem posed for the empirical rationalist. For
there is no easy way for empirical rationalists to explain the psychopath's
deficit, but there is a nonrationalist explanation that has some independent support. In this section, I will consider a range of possible explanations that the empirical rationalist might offer for the moral deficit in
psychopathy. I will argue that none of these explanations looks promising.

6.1. Psychopaths Have Not Been Exposed to the Right Arguments

One simple rationalist explanation of the problem with psychopaths would
be that although psychopaths have the relevant psychological faculties,
they have not been exposed to the right reasoning patterns. They just
need to be convinced, presumably by argument, of the claims of morality.
However, this option looks particularly unpromising, for it turns out that
psychopathy is remarkably recalcitrant. Robert Hare, who devised the
standard diagnostic measure for psychopathy, notes that "many writers
on the subject have commented that the shortest chapter in any book on
psychopathy should be the one on treatment. A one-sentence conclusion
such as, 'No effective treatment has been found,' or, 'Nothing works,' is
the common wrap-up to scholarly reviews of the literature" (Hare 1993,
194). As a result, it would seem unduly optimistic to think that a course
in moral philosophy would do the trick.

6.2. Performance Limitations

Obviously the empirical rationalist does not maintain that the actual
moral judgment of a person depends only on rational processes. Rather,

the idea is that reason provides the basic moral competence. But to get from this competence to performance involves a number of other processes like attention, language reception, language production. Perhaps, then, psychopaths have intact moral reasoning, but defects in other mechanisms impede their performance. Perhaps psychopaths show deficient performance on the moral/conventional task because of performance limitations rather than any defect in moral competence.

As far as I know, no one has suggested a performance limitation account of moral deficits in psychopathy. And it would be an uphill fight to develop and defend such an account. For the psychopathic subjects are quite capable of answering questions about rule violations in general, which suggests that they are adequate to many demands of the task, including the linguistic demands. Furthermore, as I will discuss more thoroughly below, some populations with severe cognitive deficits exhibit normal performance on the moral/conventional task. So any attempt to explain the psychopath's deficit as a performance limitation would need to accommodate the fact that success on the moral/conventional task is within the capacities of individuals with serious cognitive deficiencies.

6.3. Rational Defect Hypotheses

A more interesting line of rationalist response is that psychopaths really do lack some crucial faculty of reason that is intact in those who perform normally on the moral judgment task. In order for the empirical rationalist to make this option plausible, he would need some principled account of what kind of rational abilities underlie the capacity for making the moral/conventional distinction, then show that those rational abilities are missing in the psychopath. The rationalist would also need to show that this rational defect is not present in groups that can make the moral/ conventional distinction. This makes the rationalist's project particularly challenging, for the moral/conventional distinction is made by individuals with a wide range of cognitive abilities and disabilities. As we have seen, from a surprisingly young age, children are able to distinguish between moral and conventional violations. Smetana and Braeges (1990) claim that children appreciate the distinction around the third birthday. Children with autism and children with Down syndrome have also been found to make the moral/conventional distinction along the standard dimensions (Blair 1996). Further, nonpsychopathic criminals make the moral/conventional distinction (Blair 1995).

The project of characterizing a rational deficit in psychopaths that might underlie a moral deficit has seldom been addressed directly, and there are few detailed proposals for a rational defect in psychopaths. However, there are some suggestions in the literature that might be interpreted as rationalist hypotheses. I will consider three possibilities.

PERSPECTIVE-TAKING ABILITIES. One possibility is that moral understanding depends on perspective-taking abilities, which are commonly construed as rational cognitive abilities (e.g., Piaget 1965). Nagel (1970) seems to suggest something along these lines: "The principle of altruism . . . is connected with the conception of oneself as merely one person among others. It arises from the capacity to view oneself simultaneously as 'I' and as *someone*—an impersonally specifiable individual" (19; emphasis in original). Elsewhere, he writes, "once the objective step is taken, the possibility is also open for the recognition of values and reasons that are independent of one's personal perspective and have force for anyone who can view the world impersonally, as a place that contains him" (1986, 140). So, perhaps the rationalist can maintain that the problem with psychopaths is that they have a defect in their ability to take a perspective that is not their own. However, there is no reason to think that psychopaths have such a deficit. Indeed, psychopaths seem to be capable of taking the perspective of others (e.g., Blair et al. 1996). That is presumably part of what makes them so successful at manipulating others. Furthermore, the fact that autistic children can make the moral/conventional distinction poses a further obstacle for the perspective-taking proposal. As we have seen, autistic children have an impaired capacity for perspective taking. Yet autistic children do not have the deficit in moral understanding found in psychopaths. So it seems that appealing to the capacity for perspective taking does not provide a good explanation for the psychopath's deficit in moral judgment.

GENERAL RATIONAL ABILITIES. Another possible account of the problem with psychopaths is that they suffer from some general deficit in rationality. It is notoriously difficult to characterize rationality adequately, but in the literature in ethics, several writers have appealed to the idealization of a fully rational individual. Smith (1994) largely adopts Williams's (1981) account, according to which a fully rational agent must have no false beliefs, all relevant true beliefs and the agent must deliberate correctly (Smith 1994, 156). Smith adds that correct deliberation must include the capacity to determine "whether our desires are *systematically justifiable*. . . . we can try to decide whether or not some particular underived desire that we have or might have is a desire to do something that is itself nonderivatively desirable" (158–59; emphasis in original). So, perhaps the rationalist might say that psychopaths deviate too far from the fully rational agent to understand morality.

Although it is possible that psychopaths have a general deficit in reasoning, to make this proposal plausible, one would need to characterize the general deficit in psychopathy and explain how this general deficit in reasoning is responsible for psychopaths' deficiencies in moral judgment. Again, presumably this general rational deficit should be absent in the groups that can draw the moral/conventional distinction. And it seems unlikely that psychopaths diverge from the ideal of the fully rational individual more than three-year-old children, children with autism, and children with Down syndrome.

INTELLECTUAL ARROGANCE. Smith does offer a more specific explanation of the rational defect in the successful criminal, which might be extended into a rationalist account of psychopathy. His suggestion is that the successful criminal suffers from "intellectual arrogance." Smith writes:

> the successful criminal thinks that he has a normative reason to gain wealth no matter what the cost to others, and he sticks with this opinion despite the fact that virtually everyone disagrees with him. Moreover, he does so without good reason. For he can give no account of why his own opinion about what fully rational creatures would want should be privileged over the opinion of others; he can give no account of why his opinion should be right, others' opinions should be wrong. He can give no such account because he rejects the very idea that the folk possess between them a stock of wisdom about such matters against which each person's opinions should be tested. And yet, ultimately, this is the only court of appeal there is for claims about what we have normative reason to do. The successful criminal thus seems to me to suffer from the all too common vice of *intellectual arrogance.* He therefore does indeed suffer from a "failure to consider or appreciate certain arguments," for he doesn't feel the force of arguments that come from *others* at all. (1994, 195–96; emphasis in original)

The claim that the successful criminal suffers from intellectual arrogance is a perfectly sensible hypothesis, but if this hypothesis is supposed to explain why psychopaths do not grasp the moral/conventional distinction, one would need to provide evidence that this kind of intellectual arrogance distinguishes psychopaths from nonpsychopathic criminals, who do make the moral/conventional distinction. And there is little evidence on the issue. Certainly, there is no reason to think that psychopaths are intellectually arrogant in the sense that they will not rely on the knowledge of others. Psychopaths are perfectly willing to believe from their peers that arsenic is poison, that eating too much fat will make you overweight, and so on. So to appeal to intellectual arrogance generally looks unprincipled. Furthermore, Blair's data themselves suggest that psychopaths do recognize that some things are right and some things are wrong. What psychopaths apparently fail to appreciate is that some prohibited actions (e.g., hitting another) have a different status than other prohibited actions (e.g., speaking out of turn). So, they do seem to be capable of learning from their peers, and hence do not exhibit a general intellectual arrogance that would explain their deficit in moral judgment.

These are just three examples of rationalist explanations for the psychopath's deficit in moral understanding. No doubt several other explanations might be generated. However, there is good reason to be skeptical that an adequate explanation is forthcoming from rationalists, especially since moral judgment is intact in humans who have clear limitations in their rational capacities—young children, and children with Down syndrome and autism. Finding a rational deficit in psychopaths that might explain their performance on the moral/conventional task *and* that is not present in any of these other groups seems unlikely.

6.4. Affective Defect Hypotheses

The point of the foregoing was not to provide a knockdown argument against the possibility of finding a rational deficit in psychopaths that would explain their deficit in moral understanding. Rather, the point is to bring out the difficulty of such a project. The empirical rationalist needs to find a rational defect in psychopaths that explains their deficit in moral judgment; and this deficit should not be present in autistic individuals, young children, control criminals, and a host of other rationally idiosyncratic humans who do not share the psychopaths' deficit in moral judgment. But the problem is even worse for the empirical rationalist.

It is difficult to find a rational defect that is present in psychopaths but absent in the groups of individuals that do draw the moral/conventional distinction. There *is* a salient psychological difference between psychopaths and the other groups, but it is not a difference in rational capacities. Rather, it is a difference in affective response. As discussed in chapter 1, Blair and colleagues showed pictures of distressed faces and pictures of threatening faces to a wide range of subject populations. Over a series of studies, they found that normal children, autistic children and nonpsychopathic criminals all show considerably heightened physiological response both to threatening stimuli and to cues that another is in distress; psychopaths, on the other hand, show heightened physiological response to threatening stimuli, but show abnormally low responsiveness to distress cues (Blair et al. 1997; Blair 1999a, 1999b; see also Bacon et al. 1998; Yirmiya et al. 1992). This finding of a distinctive affective deficit in psychopathy provides a promising basis for explaining the psychopath's difficulties with the moral/conventional task.

In chapter 1, I went to some effort to set out Blair's affect-based account and to develop a more plausible affect-based alternative. There are serious questions about the relative merits of these two accounts of the capacities underlying moral judgment. However, for purposes of evaluating empirical rationalism, these issues do not need to be resolved. The important point is that on both Blair's VIM-account and the Sentimental Rules account, an affective mechanism plays a critical role in the capacity for moral judgment. If anything much like these affect-based accounts is right, then it looks like we have a nonrationalist explanation of the psychopath's deficit in moral judgment. For on these accounts, the psychopath's deficit in moral judgment depends on a deficit in an affective mechanism, not on deficits in rationality. Nor is it plausible that this affective deficit can itself be attributed to a failure in rationality. For the operations of the affective mechanisms that respond to distress seem to be extremely quick, unconscious, and largely involuntary.[7] Thus, the evidence on psychopaths seems not to support empirical rationalism at all, but rather, rationalism's rival, sentimentalism. For apparently emotional responsiveness plays a key role in moral judgment after all.

7. CONCLUSION

Moral rationalism has seemed the most promising way to secure moral objectivism. I have suggested that rationalism can be developed in two quite different ways, as a conceptual claim or as an empirical claim, and psychopaths threaten both claims. Contrary to conceptual rationalist claims, psychopaths are commonly regarded as rational individuals who really make moral judgments but are not motivated by them. Blair's evidence provides good reason to think that the common conception of psychopaths is wrong, for the capacity for moral judgment is apparently disturbed in psychopathy. However, this provides no help to the conceptual rationalist and in fact seriously undermines empirical rationalism. For the defective capacity for moral judgment in psychopathy seems not to derive from a rational deficit, but rather from a deficit to an affective system.

---

7. The actual measurement of the physiological response in Blair's studies (1999a, 1999b; Blair et al. 1997) was taken between one and five seconds after showing the stimulus. So the response is certainly present within a few seconds. No doubt studies that were designed to detect initial onset would cut this time down even more.

4

Philosophical Sentimentalism

1. INTRODUCTION

In the previous chapter, I argued that the empirical evidence weighs against one prominent philosophical metaethical position, moral rationalism. The other most prominent philosophical metaethics, sentimentalism, seems a much better fit for the data. According to sentimentalists, moral judgment is grounded in affective response. This tradition begins in the eighteenth century with Shaftesbury, Hutcheson and Hume, but it continues to thrive in contemporary metaethics (e.g., Blackburn 1998; Gibbard 1990; Wiggins 1991). Although my own view obviously has natural affinities and profound debts to this tradition, in this chapter I will argue that contemporary philosophical versions of sentimentalism face a serious empirical problem, though a different one from rationalism. The problem, in brief, is that prevailing sentimentalist accounts propose a sophisticated analysis of what is involved in moral judgment, and it seems that people can make moral judgments without having the kind of sophistication that sentimentalism would require.

On what is perhaps the most prominent contemporary version of sentimentalism, to judge an action wrong is to judge that it would be appropriate to feel guilt on doing the action (e.g., Gibbard 1990). I argue that evidence from developmental psychology seriously threatens this view. As we have seen, a great deal of work in developmental psychology charts a basic capacity for moral judgment in children. This capacity for moral judgment emerges early, apparently well before the capacity to attribute guilt or other moral emotions. The evidence thus suggests that this capacity for moral judgment cannot be captured by accounts which identify the capacity for moral judgment with the capacity to judge that guilt is normatively appropriate. That's the heart of the argument that I will develop in this chapter, but only after putting some of the intellectual background in place.

2. CONSTRAINTS ON AN ADEQUATE SENTIMENTALISM

Before sketching contemporary sentimentalist accounts, I want to review three constraints that sentimentalists have come to regard as central to providing an account of moral judgment. This sketch will be important both in this chapter for setting out how contemporary sentimentalist accounts address these features and later, in chapter 5, where I will argue that the Sentimental Rules account might accommodate these constraints as well.

The one absolutely essential feature of any sentimentalist account, obviously, is that it must maintain that emotion is implicated in moral judgment. Perhaps the oldest and most enduringly influential argument for this thesis appeals to the fact that moral judgments are tied to motivation. If a person judges that it is wrong to perform some action, then the person typically has some concomitant motivation not to perform that action. For instance, if John thinks that it is wrong for him to steal a stranger's money, this will typically provide John with some motivation not to steal the money. This feature of moral judgment has led sentimentalists, from the eighteenth century to the present, to maintain that moral judgment must somehow implicate the sentiments. This argument receives its most famous formulations in Hume. For instance, in the *Enquiry*, he writes, "The final sentence, it is probable, which pronounces characters and actions amiable or odious, praise-worthy or blameable; . . . that which renders morality an active principle . . . depends on some internal sense or feeling, which nature has made universal in the whole species. For what else can have an influence of this nature?" (Hume [1777] 1975, 173).

All sentimentalist accounts appeal to the sentiments as essential to explain features of moral motivation. The other two constraints on an adequate sentimentalism emerged in the middle of the twentieth century as problems for extant sentimentalist accounts. It will be important to see how the problems arose for sentimentalist accounts, but because this bit of the history of metaethics is well known (see, e.g., Rachels 1993), I will be brief.

Under the hands of Stevenson (1944) and Ayer (1936), "emotivism" became the most influential sentimentalist theory in the first half of the twentieth century. According to this view, moral judgments are really expressions of one's feelings. So, when we say that it is wrong to hit, what we are really saying is something like "I disapprove of hitting; do so as well" (see, e.g., Stevenson 1944). One problem that arose for these accounts was that they require that you actually have the emotion that you are expressing when you utter a moral condemnation. However, as Darwall, Gibbard, and Railton ([1992] 1997) put it in a recent review, it seems that "a person can judge something wrong even if he has lost all disposition to feelings about it" (17–18). This suggests a new constraint on an adequate sentimentalist account—a sentimentalist account must accommodate the possibility that a person can judge an action wrong even if he has lost all feelings about the action.

The above problem for emotivism was raised early in the discourse (e.g., Brandt 1946; Ewing 1947). A more vexing problem for emotivism was soon raised as well. Several philosophers challenged emotivism by drawing attention to the role of reasoning in moral judgment (e.g., Toulmin 1950; Brandt 1950; Falk 1953; Baier 1958; Geach 1965). Most crudely, the problem is that we typically think that our moral judgments are supported by moral reasoning, and if moral judgment is simply reporting or expressing one's feeling, it is hard to see how reasoning can play such a central role in moral judgment. The critical literature that arose in the wake of emotivism often illustrated these points with relatively simple examples of moral reasoning. For instance, it is plausible that in making moral judgments, we rely on moral principles, and Toulmin offers the following bit of ordinary moral reasoning from principles:

> Suppose that I say, "I feel that I ought to take this book and give it back to Jones." . . . You may ask me, "But ought you really to do so?" . . . and it is up to me to produce my "reasons." . . . I may reply . . . "I ought to, because I promised to let him have it back." And if you continue to ask, "But why ought you really?," I can answer . . . "Because anyone ought to do whatever he promises anyone else that he will do" or "Because it was a promise." (Toulmin 1950, 146)

In addition to justifying our moral claims by appeal to principle, we also weigh our moral reasons to determine the appropriate course of action.

Baier makes the point as follows: "Having ascertained all the relevant facts, all the moral pros and cons, I just proceed to weigh them in order to determine which course of action is supported by the weightiest moral reasons. . . . We do this by applying the rules of superiority, such as . . . 'It is better to inflict a small amount of harm on one, than a great amount on another, innocent person,' and so on" (Baier 1958, 170).

The examples from Baier and Toulmin are plausibly cases that an adequate account of moral judgment, sentimentalist or otherwise, must accommodate. Geach (1965) offers a more focused attack on emotivism, maintaining that emotivism bungles the logic of moral discourse, since it is difficult to see how an emotivist will explain conditionals that have embedded moral statements. For instance, consider the following conditional: "If spanking children is wrong, then spanking other people's children is wrong." One can agree with the conditional without ever feeling any disapproval for spanking children. Geach maintained that, as a consequence of this deficit, emotivists cannot even capture simple instances of moral reasoning like the following:

> If doing a thing is bad, getting your little brother to do it is bad.
>
> Tormenting the cat is bad.
>
> Ergo, getting your little brother to torment the cat is bad. (Geach 1965, 463)

Predictably, these sorts of examples prompted extensive and sophisticated rejoinders from sentimentalists (see, e.g., Blackburn 1984). But the thrust of the examples should be clear enough. Sentimentalists were confronted with the task of offering some account of how reasoning can play a central role in a sentimentalist account of moral judgment. In their recent article, Justin D'Arms and Daniel Jacobson (2000) make clear that this feature of moral judgment continues to exercise sentimentalists: "Philosophers who take inspiration from Hume must allow reasoning, as well as feeling, to play a role in evaluative judgment. The central challenge for sentimentalism is to preserve the idea that values are somehow grounded in the sentiments, while at the same time making sense of the rational aspects of evaluation" (2000, 722; see also Smith 1998).

Thus, an adequate sentimentalist account needs to accommodate the following claims:

1. Emotion plays a crucial role in moral judgment.
2. A person can judge something wrong even if he has lost all feelings about it.
3. Reasoning plays a crucial role in moral judgment.

Given the disparate nature of these constraints, a sentimentalist theory that manages to meet all the constraints would be an impressive achievement indeed.

3. NEOSENTIMENTALISM: MEETING THE CONSTRAINTS

The sentimentalist accounts developed in the latter half of the twentieth century differ widely (e.g., Blackburn 1998; Gibbard 1990; Wiggins 1991). But despite extensive disagreement on some issues, sentimentalists in the latter half of the twentieth century largely converged on a solution that meets the constraints set out in the previous section. The general structure of the theory is set out by D'Arms and Jacobson (2000). Indeed, this basic structure is so crucial to recent accounts that D'Arms and Jacobson identify it as the heart of "neosentimentalism."

> The crucial idea, which we take to be the defining characteristic of neosentimentalism, is that an important set of evaluative concepts (or terms or properties) is best understood as invoking a normative assessment of the *appropriateness* (or merit or rationality) of some associated emotional response. Hence,
>> (RDT) To think that X has some evaluative property Φ is to think it appropriate to feel F in response to X.
> For the neosentimentalist, to think a sentiment appropriate in the relevant sense is a normative judgment . . . in favor of feeling it.
> (D'Arms and Jacobson 2000, 729; emphasis in original)

As formulated above, neosentimentalism is supposed to provide a general theory of evaluative judgment. But the interest of the theory comes largely from its promise in delivering an account of moral judgment, and the initial impetus for neosentimentalism was as an account of moral judgment. Darwall, Gibbard, and Railton ([1992] 1997) attribute the innovation at the heart of neosentimentalism to Ewing and Brandt: "As Ewing and Brandt had suggested . . . moral judgments seem not to be moral sentiments or dispositions to certain moral sentiments, but judgments of what moral sentiments are fitting or justified" (18). Because our interests are restricted to narrowly moral judgment, this chapter will focus exclusively on neosentimentalist accounts of moral judgment.

Unfortunately, neosentimentalists have often been less than clear about which emotion is supposed to play the crucial role when the neosentimentalist schema is applied to moral judgment. According to neosentimentalism, to think that X is morally wrong is to think it appropriate to feel some emotion (or suite of emotions) in response to X. But what emotion? It is clear enough that the operative emotion cannot be anything as simple as sadness, happiness, or anger, because there will be many occasions on which one will think it appropriate to feel one of those emotions in response to X, without thinking that X is wrong. The central substantive proposal about which emotion plays the role in moral judgment comes from Allan Gibbard (1990). He writes, "what a person does is *morally wrong* if and only if it is rational for him to feel guilty for doing it, and for others to resent him for doing it" (Gibbard 1990, 42; emphasis in original). Elsewhere, he writes "to think an act *morally reprehensible* is to accept norms that prescribe, for such a situation, guilt on the part of the agent and resentment on the part of others" (1990, 47; emphasis in original). Because Gibbard is the most visible advocate of a specific proposal here, the discussion will focus on his theory. Gibbard invokes both guilt and resentment in his account of moral judgment, but for ease of exposition, I will focus only on the proposed role of guilt in moral judgment.[1] According to Gibbard, to think X is morally wrong is to think it appropriate to feel guilty for doing X.

Although metaethics is not an area that generates anything like consensus, neosentimentalism has attracted an impressive following in contemporary metaethics (Blackburn 1998; D'Arms and Jacobson 1994, 2000; Gibbard 1990; McDowell 1985; Wiggins 1991). And for good reason. Neosentimentalism promises to meet all the central constraints on an adequate sentimentalism in an elegant fashion. By appealing to a crucial role for the sentiments in moral judgment, neosentimentalism can explain why there is such a close connection between moral judgment and motivation. Moral judgments are judgments about the appropriateness of certain emotions; so they are judgments about states that are motivating. But these judgments about emotions can occur even if one is not disposed to have the emotion. Neosentimentalism also provides an account of the role of reasoning in moral judgment. When we disagree and argue about moral matters, we are arguing about the appropriateness of feeling certain emotions in response to certain situations. Neosentimentalism is an impressive achievement indeed for offering a unified account of moral judgment that can address the disparate constraints on an adequate sentimentalist theory. Despite these considerable virtues, I will argue that neosentimentalism fits poorly with the available evidence on moral judgment.

---

1. This simplification does not vitiate the critique I will offer of neosentimentalism. Indeed, as will be apparent, the problem I raise for neosentimentalism is only exacerbated if we include resentment as well as guilt in the neosentimentalist account of moral judgment.

4. NATURALISTIC COMMITMENTS

Many neosentimentalists take an explicitly naturalistic approach. For instance, Gibbard (1990) writes: "The ways we see norms should cohere with our best naturalistic accounts of normative life" (8); "Normative judgments are to be explained psychologically, and so I need a psychology" (26). Similarly, Blackburn writes, "the reconciliation of the normative and the natural must be carried out somehow" (1998, 49; see also D'Arms and Jacobson 1994, 2000). More generally, the tradition of sentimentalism since Hume is typically accompanied by broadly naturalistic sympathies.

For all the naturalistic enthusiasm surrounding neosentimentalism, this cluster of views is notoriously difficult to evaluate empirically, and researchers in this tradition seldom consider what empirical evidence could confirm or disconfirm neosentimentalism. However, there is one crucial place where the theory does seem to have an empirical commitment. If moral judgments are judgments of the normative appropriateness of certain emotions, then there cannot be dissociations between these capacities. There should be no cases in which an individual has the capacity to make moral judgments but lacks the capacity to make judgments about the appropriateness of the relevant emotion. More specifically, if moral judgments are judgments of the appropriateness of guilt, then an individual cannot have the capacity to make moral judgments unless she also has the capacity to make judgments about the appropriateness of guilt.

In the next section, I will argue that there are such dissociations between the capacity for moral judgment and the capacity for normative assessment of the appropriateness of guilt. This, I will argue, presents a serious problem for naturalistic neosentimentalism.

5. DISSOCIATIONS

If there are populations in which subjects have the capacity for moral judgment but lack the capacity for normatively assessing the appropriateness of guilt, then the capacity for moral judgment cannot be identified with the capacity for normatively assessing the appropriateness of guilt. Indeed, if there are these dissociations, it seems to follow that the capacity for normative assessments of guilt is not essential for the capacity for moral judgment. In chapter 1, I argued that a basic capacity for moral judgment is reflected by passing the moral/conventional task. That is, distinguishing moral from conventional violations indicates a capacity for "core moral judgment." This provides us with an opportunity to see whether core moral judgment can be dissociated from the capacity to judge the appropriateness of guilt. There are two populations that seem to exhibit this kind of dissociation: young children and people with autism.

5.1. Young Children

Children begin to appreciate features of the moral/conventional distinction surprisingly early. As discussed in chapter 1 (section 3), Smetana and Braeges found that children distinguished moral from conventional violations on some dimensions before the third birthday. The full range of distinctions is found among three-and-a-half-year-olds. The evidence thus suggests that from a young age, children can make these distinctions in controlled experimental settings. In naturalistic settings, research also indicates that well before the fourth birthday, children respond differentially to moral violations and social-conventional violations (e.g., Dunn and Munn 1987; Smetana 1989).

Although children have a strikingly early grasp of core moral judgment, their understanding of guilt seems to emerge significantly later. According to developmental psychologists, children do not understand complex emotions like guilt, pride and shame until around age seven (Harris 1989, 1993; Harris et al. 1987; Nunner-Winkler and Sodian 1988; see also Thompson and Hoffman 1980). Young children are actually good at attributing simple emotions like sadness and happiness. Indeed, if someone unintentionally harms another person, preschool children expect the harmer to be sad (Nunner-Winkler and Sodian 1988). However, young children do not show this pattern with actions that are intentionally harmful. Gertrude Nunner-Winkler and Beate Sodian asked children to predict how someone would feel after intentionally pushing another child off of a swing. Children under the age of six tended to say that the pusher would feel happy. Unlike the young children, children over the age of six tended to say that the person who intentionally hurt the other would have negative affect. In another study, the experimenters showed the subjects images of two individuals, each of whom had committed a moral violation. One of the children had a happy expression and the other had a sad expression. The subjects were asked to rate how "bad" the children were. While most four-year old children judged the happy and sad transgressors as equally bad, "the majority of 6-year-olds and almost all 8-year-olds judged the person who displayed joy to be worse than the one who displayed remorse" (Nunner-Winkler and Sodian 1988, 1329). So, between the ages of four and eight, children are gradually developing the idea that moral transgressions are and should be accompanied by some negative affect. But the findings make it seem unlikely that three- and four-year-old children are capable of "invoking a normative assessment of the *appropriateness*" of feeling guilty in a range of situations. As a result, the understanding of core moral judgment seems to be present in young children well before the capacity for judging when it is appropriate to feel guilt.

5.2. Autism

As we saw in chapter 1, Blair presented autistic children with the standard moral/conventional task. Blair found that autistic children were able to make the moral/conventional distinction, treating moral violations as less permissible, more serious and less authority contingent than conventional violations (Blair 1996). Thus it seems that core moral judgment is intact in autism. However, despite competence with core moral judgment, autistic individuals have great difficulty understanding complex emotions. This comes out vividly in a famous passage from Oliver Sacks, discussing Temple Grandin, a high-functioning autistic adult:

> She was bewildered, she said, by *Romeo and Juliet* ("I never knew what they were up to"), and with *Hamlet* she got lost with the back-and-forth of the play. Though she ascribed these problems to "sequencing difficulties," they seemed to arise from her failure to empathize with the characters, to follow the intricate play of motive and intention. She said that she could understand "simple, strong, universal" emotions but was stumped by more complex emotions and the games people play. "Much of the time," she said, "I feel like an anthropologist on Mars." (Sacks 1995, 259)

Grandin herself writes: "My emotions are simpler than those of most people. I don't know what complex emotion in a human relationship is. I only understand simple emotions, such as fear, anger, happiness, and sadness" (Grandin 1995, 89).

Experimental studies confirm the impression given by Grandin. Sigman and Capps (1997) report recent work that shows, for instance, that people with autism lack an understanding of pride. "Like adolescents in the normally developing comparison group, adolescents with autism frequently mentioned feeling happy about receiving a desirable gift and feeling sad about the death of a pet. But they had difficulty comprehending complex emotions, such as pride and embarrassment" (121; see also Baron-Cohen 1995, Capps, Yirmiya, and Sigman 1992). Of course, it will be important to look more closely at the understanding of guilt in individuals with autism. But because the understanding of guilt in nonautistic children seems to emerge at about the same time as the understanding of pride and shame (Harris 1989), there is good reason to expect that the understanding of guilt is deficient in autism.

Thus, it seems that young children and individuals with autism have the capacity for core moral judgment but lack the capacity to attribute guilt. This dissociation seriously threatens the neosentimentalist view that for S to think that X is morally wrong is for S to think that it would be appropriate to feel guilty for having done X. For young children and people with autism apparently make moral judgments but lack the capacity to judge whether guilt is normatively appropriate for a situation.

In light of the dissociation problem, the developmental sequence that neosentimentalism suggests begins to look implausibly demanding. To make moral judgments, one must be able to

1. Attribute guilt.
2. Make normative judgments about the appropriateness of emotions.
3. Exploit both of these capacities to judge the normative appropriateness of guilt.

It is somewhat perverse to think that the child's understanding of morality would hang on all of this. Indeed, if one is inclined to give constructive accounts of concepts, a prima facie more plausible story is that children learn first to determine what is moral, then they use their concept of the moral to develop an understanding of moral emotions like guilt. Perhaps older children and adults do come to see that the actions that they judge as morally wrong are those for which guilt is appropriate, but the dissociation argument suggests that this is likely a peripheral feature, not a necessary component of moral judgment.

6. THE DISSOCIATION ARGUMENT: OBJECTIONS AND REPLIES

The dissociation argument is utterly simple in structure: According to neosentimentalism, the capacity for moral judgment depends on the capacity for judging the appropriateness of guilt. However, there are large populations of individuals who have the capacity for moral judgment and lack the capacity for judging the appropriateness of guilt. The simplicity of the argument invites two classes of responses: (i) core moral judgment is not genuine moral judgment and (ii) the populations in question *do* have the capacity to attribute guilt. I will consider these responses and a third objection in turn.

6.1. "Core" Moral Judgment Is Not Genuine Moral Judgment

OBJECTION. If children and autistic individuals do not make judgments about the normative appropriateness of guilt, then they do not make moral judgments. That is, "core moral judgment" is not genuine moral judgment, but rather ersatz moral judgment. The capacity for genuine moral judgment is not present in young children and people with autism. Genuine moral judgment is properly restricted to nonautistic adults who are engaged in a process of reflection about which moral emotions are appropriate to a situation.

REPLY. There are several costs associated with maintaining that "core moral judgment" is not real moral judgment and hence not the phenomenon that neosentimentalism seeks to explain. First, everyday normative life is supposed to be what neosentimentalism explains (Gibbard 1990, 26; Blackburn 1998, 13), and it is an empirical assumption that most adult moral judgment is radically different from core moral judgment. That is, it might well be that the kind of moral judgment we see in preschool children is preserved in a great deal of adult moral judgment. There is an influential and distinguished tradition in current developmental science according to which the "core knowledge" of folk physics and folk psychology emerges early. Although the core knowledge might be "enriched" throughout development, the early core knowledge is thought to persist unrevised into adulthood, and to continue to guide adult judgment (e.g., Spelke 1994; Carey and Spelke 1996). Something similar might well be the case about core moral judgment. That is, the basic understanding of moral wrong might be preserved without revision into adulthood and it might well guide a great deal of adult moral judgment. As a result, if neosentimentalists ignore core moral judgment, they risk neglecting a central part of our everyday normative lives.

To restrict neosentimentalism to more sophisticated forms of moral judgment runs an additional empirical risk. Although the psychological work suggests that core moral judgment is cross-culturally stable, the studies also suggest that more sophisticated forms of moral judgment are not cross-culturally stable (see Miller, in press, for a review). The most extensive cross-cultural research on moral judgment has been conducted under Kohlberg's familiar stage approach. The results show a striking degree of cross-cultural variability in the moral reasoning of adults. In some cultures, adults apparently tend to reason at Kohlberg's stage 2 (reciprocal needs); in other cultures, adults reason at Kohlberg's stage 3 (interpersonal harmony and concern); in other cultures, adults reason at

Kohlberg's stage 4 (social harmony and order); and in other cultures, like our own, adults tend to reason in terms of a social contract, individual rights, or universal moral principles (stages 5 and 6). Apparently in several of the cultures studied, none of the subjects exhibited the kind of sophisticated moral reasoning (stages 5 and 6) that we find common in our culture (see Snarey 1985 for a review). So if neosentimentalists focus on sophisticated moral judgment, they may be focusing on features of moral judgment that are idiosyncratic to our own culture, in which case, the project is really a project in ethnometaethics.

In addition to these risks, there is a more serious and immediate problem for neosentimentalists who respond to the dissociation problem by excluding moral judgment in young children from the domain of "genuine" moral judgment. As noted above, perhaps the central impetus for sentimentalism is the fact that moral judgment is motivating. In order to explain the connection between moral judgment and motivation, it has been thought, one must devise a sentimentalist account of moral judgment. But this problem of motivation and moral judgment arises already for moral judgment in young children. Young children judge harmful actions to violate normative prohibitions and they are also motivated not to violate those norms.[2] Thus, the problem of motivation and moral judgment needs to be addressed for three-year-olds, and the dissociation problem suggests that the neosentimentalist solution is unavailable for three-year-olds. It is plausible that whatever the solution is for three-year-olds, that solution will also apply to adults, with no radical changes along neosentimentalist lines.

6.2. Children *Do* Make Judgments about the Normative Appropriateness of Guilt

OBJECTION. Perhaps young children and people with autism do make genuine moral judgments, but the evidence on the understanding of emotion does not show that young children and people with autism lack an understanding of guilt. On the contrary, young children and individuals

---

2. The situation with motivation and moral judgment is rather complicated, as evidenced by the debate over internalism. I will discuss motivation and internalism more fully in chapter 5. For present purposes, though, it is important to note that there are presumably two different ways in which moral judgment is connected with motivation. First, moral violations fall into the class of rule violations and people are generally motivated not to violate rules. Secondly, moral rules often prohibit actions that are inherently upsetting, and hence to be avoided. Most saliently in the present context, harm in others generates considerable negative affect and so people are motivated not to do those things. This complication does not affect the present point though, because both of these strands of motivation—rule-based and emotion-based—seem to be present in young children (see chapter 5, section 4).

with autism probably *do* make normative judgments about the appropriateness of guilt.

REPLY. Of course, as is always the case with empirical results, future studies could overturn the claim that young children and people with autism do not understand guilt. But the available evidence certainly suggests that the understanding of guilt emerges relatively late and that young children cannot assess when guilt is normatively appropriate to a situation. In the face of this, one cannot make a persuasive case simply by adopting a skeptical stance. One needs to marshal evidence to overturn the claim.[3] Absent countervailing evidence, the data suggest that core moral judgment is indeed dissociable from the capacity to judge normatively in favor of a moral emotion.

6.3. Neosentimentalist Alternatives

OBJECTION. The studies only show a dissociation between moral judgment and the normative assessment of guilt. But the emotion that is implicated in neosentimentalism need not be guilt. It might be some other emotion about which children *do* make normative judgments. For instance, some neosentimentalists seem to suggest that the operative emotion is a sentiment of moral disapprobation (Wiggins 1991, 228). And it might well be that young children make normative assessments about when moral disapprobation is appropriate.

REPLY. Perhaps there is some other emotion that will serve the neosentimentalist better than guilt. But the challenge here is considerable. Neosentimentalists would need to show that there is some emotion or suite of emotions that fits into the neosentimentalist schema and which is sufficient to exclude nonmoral cases.[4] Maybe there is such a sentiment, but in order to meet the challenge one would need to provide a detailed account of the profile of the sentiment and provide evidence that children have an early understanding of this emotion and of when the emotion is

---

3. In looking for evidence, the neosentimentalist might reasonably be encouraged by the fact that the research on the moral/conventional distinction and the research on understanding guilt have important methodological differences. A worthwhile line of experimentation would be to look at the understanding of morality and the understanding of guilt in the same (young) subjects using similar measures.

4. The difficulty of this part of the neosentimentalist project is nicely illustrated in D'Arms and Jacobson's critique of Gibbard (D'Arms and Jacobson 1994). They argue that even guilt is inadequate in neosentimentalist accounts of moral judgment because one can think it appropriate to feel guilty about doing something without thinking that the action is immoral. At any rate, it is unlikely that the neosentimentalist can provide an adequate account with an emotional suite that is simpler than guilt.

normatively appropriate. Given children's problems with the moral emotions that have been studied, there is little reason to be optimistic that they have an early understanding of some moral sentiment that has not yet been characterized but that will serve the demands on a neosentimentalist account of moral judgment.

7. CONCLUSION

Thus the empirical evidence on moral judgment poses a serious problem for neosentimentalism. According to neosentimentalism, to judge an action morally wrong is to judge that it would be appropriate to feel a certain moral emotion in response to doing the act. The empirical research on moral judgment indicates that such accounts fail to capture the basic capacity for moral judgment. For apparently the capacity for moral judgment can be dissociated from the capacity to judge the normative appropriateness of moral emotions like guilt. By contrast, the Sentimental Rules account develop in chapter 1 is perfectly consistent with the evidence on young children. The affective mechanism that plausibly underwrites core moral judgment is present early in children. And the normative theory containing information about harm violations is also present in young children. So the fact that core moral judgment emerges when it does poses no problem. Unlike neosentimentalism, the Sentimental Rules account makes no commitments about the child's understanding of emotions. Hence, the dissociation between moral judgment and the understanding of moral emotions is fully consonant with the Sentimental Rules account.

5

Sentiment, Reason, and Motivation

Marky (aged 2 years, 2 months) dropped his lunch box on the stairs.

> Ross (aged 4 years, 1 month): "Marky don't drop it."
> Marky: "I didn't drop it."
> Ross: "The reason why I yelled at you was because you dropped your lunch box. A little boy's got to not drop his . . . The big boy doesn't drop his lunch box."
>
> —B. MacWhinney and C. Snow, "The Child Language Data Exchange System"

1. INTRODUCTION

I have argued that the empirical evidence on moral judgment poses a serious problem for neosentimentalism. However, neosentimentalism has been an extremely rich and productive theory, and one could hardly expect the dissociation problem by itself to uproot neosentimentalism, especially if there is no viable alternative in the offing. In the previous chapter, I set out the central constraints for developing an adequate sentimentalist account of moral judgment. I will argue in this chapter that the account sketched in chapter 1 provides a framework to develop a theory that meets the constraints. Moreover, this alternative is obviously sentimentalist in an important sense. Again, the basic idea is that core moral judgment depends on two mechanisms, a body of information prohibiting harmful actions and an affective mechanism that is activated by suffering in others. In the next two sections, I will consider whether this account can deliver the explanatory goods promised by neosentimentalism. In section 4, I will describe how the Sentimental Rules account maps to various distinctions in the internalism/externalism debate. In the fifth section, I will consider an important shortcoming in the Sentimental

Rules account—in contrast to traditional sentimentalist accounts, the Sentimental Rules account makes the relationship between emotions and norms seem suspiciously contingent.

2. SENTIMENTS IN MORAL JUDGMENT

Chapter 4 began by considering the constraints on an adequate sentimentalist metaethics. An adequate sentimentalist account must explain (1) how emotion plays a role in linking moral judgment to motivation; (2) how moral judgments can be made in the absence of emotional response; and (3) how reason can play an important role in moral judgment. Neosentimentalism offers a sophisticated and subtle account that explains these features of moral judgment, but the very sophistication of the account leads neosentimentalism into the dissociation problem. The Sentimental Rules account does not suffer from the dissociation problem. But can the Sentimental Rules account address the problems that neosentimentalism handles so impressively? I will suggest the Sentimental Rules account does indeed provide the beginnings of an account that can meet the central constraints on an adequate sentimentalist account.

On the Sentimental Rules account, an affective mechanism plays a crucial role in moral judgment. This mechanism is defective in psychopathy, and as a result, the capacity for core moral judgment is seriously compromised in psychopaths. Psychopaths also, notoriously, seem to lack the normal motivation that follows moral judgment. On the account I have sketched, it is plausible that the core affective deficit is responsible both for the deficit in moral judgment and for the deficit in moral motivation. Thus, the account of core moral judgment falls comfortably in line with the sentimentalist claim that emotions play a crucial role in moral judgment and moral motivation.[1] An important caveat is, however, re-

---

1. In the twentieth century, philosophical sentimentalists often used the open question argument to support sentimentalism (e.g., Hare 1952; Gibbard 1990; Darwall, Gibbard, and Railton 1992; D'Arms and Jacobson 2000). One way to cast the open question argument for sentimentalism is as follows. For any proposed definition of "wrong," it seems that one can judge that an action meets that definition without judging that one should not do that action. It will always "make sense" to ask whether one should refrain from acting in the way described in the analysis. However, this is not the case for the notion of wrong itself. To judge that an action is wrong is to judge that one should not do that action. If one agrees that an action is wrong, it doesn't make sense, the argument goes, to ask whether one should not refrain from so acting. Hence, the one feature that is essential about the notion of wrong is that it is "action-guiding."

Because the Sentimental Rules account is not an account of the semantics of moral terms, it does not address the open question argument. Neither, however, does it rely on the open question argument. And given the controversial nature of the open question argument (e.g., Lycan 1988), one might consider that a virtue.

quired. The Sentimental Rules account does not purport to give a conceptual analysis of moral terms, and so the proposed connection between moral judgment and emotions is not an analytic connection. Consequently, unlike philosophical sentimentalist views, the Sentimental Rules account is not committed to a conceptual connection between moral judgment and motivation. Hence there is an important difference between how the Sentimental Rules account and how philosophical sentimentalism handle the role of emotion and moral judgment. Some of these differences will be discussed further in sections 4 and 5 below. But for now, it suffices to note that the Sentimental Rules account accommodates the central sentimentalist idea that moral judgment is typically attended by emotion.

The second constraint on an adequate sentimentalism is that the account must be able to accommodate the fact that a person can judge that something is wrong even if she lacks an emotional response to the transgression. This is easily accommodated on the Sentimental Rules account, because one can have knowledge of the harm norms, and voice one's disapproval of harming others, even if one has lost the affective response. Thus, it is clearly possible for a person to judge an action wrong even if she lacks the relevant emotional responses.

Although the account allows for the possibility that one can judge something to be wrong even in the absence of affective response, the evidence on moral judgment signals an intriguing complication. The claim that we can judge something to be wrong after losing all disposition to feel is not obviously true if we focus on core moral judgment. For there remains an issue, broached in chapter 1, about how affect produces core moral judgment. The extreme on-line version would entail that in fact, core moral judgment cannot proceed in the absence of all dispositions to feel. That is, on the extreme online processing model, if a person were suddenly sapped of all disposition to feel negative affect at another's suffering, then that person would no longer treat harm norms as distinctive along the classic dimensions. On the other hand, the extreme developmental position would allow for the full complement of core moral judgment in the absence of any disposition to affective response at another's suffering. As noted in chapter 1, I suspect that both of these stories are too simplistic. Rather, it is likely that core moral judgment can persevere for at least some time after the emotions are eradicated. But it is also likely that over time, the tendency to treat harm norms as distinctive would wane. At any rate, this is really an empirical issue that poses no problem for the overall structure of a Sentimental Rules account. For that account allows that the set of normative rules is at least partly dissociable from the affective system. One might recognize that a certain action violates an internally represented body of rules without having any concomitant affect about the action. Hence, the Sentimental Rules account can meet the second constraint on an adequate sentimentalism, that a sentimentalist account must be able to accommodate the fact that a person can judge something wrong after losing all disposition to feel.

3. REASONING IN MORAL JUDGMENT

The final constraint on an adequate sentimentalism, that it accommodate the role of reasoning in moral judgment, has really been the central focus of much recent work in sentimentalist metaethics, so I want to devote more time to this issue here. As sketched in chapter 4, a number of philosophers invoked the role of reasoning in moral judgment as a problem for various sentimentalist accounts. So, Toulmin noted that if one is pressed for why one feels obligated to return a borrowed book, one is charged with producing "reasons," for example, "I ought to, because I promised to let him have it back" and "Because anyone ought to do whatever he promises anyone else that he will do." (Toulmin 1950, 146). Baier appealed to a different kind of reasoning, in which we assess the relative weight of various moral considerations (Baier 1958, 170). And Geach promoted simple cases of reasoning with modus ponens (Geach 1965, 463). An adequate sentimentalism must be able to accommodate the evident roles of reasoning in these examples.

Of course, in the Sentimental Rules account, there is a pretty obvious explanation of this kind of reasoning. For on that account, moral judgment depends on two dissociable mechanisms: an affective system and a normative theory. Much of everyday moral reasoning might be explained as disputes about the content of the normative theory. Moreover, this kind of reasoning over a normative theory can, at least in principle, be carried out dispassionately. In the case of arguments about a normative theory consisting of etiquette rules, this kind of reasoning often *is* carried out dispassionately, as when we debate whether one should leave one's napkin on the chair when one leaves the table.

The capacity to reason about a normative theory seems, like core moral judgment, to be present in three-year-olds. It is worth dwelling a bit on some of the details about children's abilities to reason about moral issues, and about their reasoning abilities more broadly. For children's surprisingly good reasoning abilities will, I suggest, impose a tighter constraint on an adequate sentimentalist account of moral judgment.

NORMATIVE REASONING IN YOUNG CHILDREN. The enormous literature on human reasoning provides ample evidence that humans are bad at what seem to be elementary reasoning problems. Some of the best known results involve standard indicative conditionals. Normal adults fumble the evaluation of simple indicative conditionals. For instance, people are bad at determining the truth of conditionals like "If a book was published in 1997, it has a recycling stamp on it" (Cummins 1998, 40). But it turns out that adults are good at other kinds of reasoning. Much of the discussion over reasoning abilities has been pursued recently in debates over the status of evolutionary psychology. One side in the debate (e.g., Cosmides 1989) maintains that evolutionary considerations explain why humans are good in some reasoning tasks but not others; the other side (e.g., Fodor 2000), rejects this story. For our purposes, this lively debate can be ignored. What is especially important for us are issues of ontogeny, not phylogeny. And, as it happens, the kinds of reasoning at which adults excel tend to be available early ontogenetically.

To begin, although adults remain flummoxed by indicative reasoning, even young children are good at counterfactual reasoning. For instance, in one recent experiment, children were shown drawings in which a woman, Mrs. Rosy, calls her husband to show him the flower she just planted. When the husband opens the door, the dog runs through the door and tramples on the flower, making the woman sad. The children were then asked, "What if the dog hadn't squashed the flower, would Mrs. Rosy be happy or sad?" Even three-year-old children are good on this task and related tasks (German and Nichols 2003; see also Harris, German, and Mills 1996; German 1999).[2] This ability is really rather striking when one considers the relative status of indicative and counterfactual conditionals in formal logic. For the simple indicative conditional has had a definitive logic for over a century. By contrast, counterfactual conditionals remain logically mysterious. The prevailing account, Lewis's (1973) possible worlds account, is widely used, but not, I dare say, widely believed. What is striking, then, is that although most people are bad at the kinds of conditionals that are easily accommodated by formal logic, even young children are adept with counterfactual conditionals, which continue to puzzle logicians.

The experimental literature further indicates that young children have a considerable capacity to reason about normative violations. By the age of four, children are adept at detecting transgressions of familiar precautionary rules. For instance, in an experiment by Paul Harris and Maria

---

2. There are findings that suggest that young children have difficulties with counterfactuals (e.g., Riggs et al. 1998). However, children's difficulties in these experiments seem to be a product of the complexity of the inference in the tasks, rather than any intrinsic difficulty with counterfactuals (German and Nichols 2003).

Núñez, children were told that Sally's mom said that if Sally plays outside, she must put her coat on. Children were then shown four pictures: one picture showed Sally inside with no coat, another showed her inside with her coat on, a third showed her outside with no coat, and a fourth showed her outside with her coat on. Children were then asked, "Show me the picture where Sally is being naughty and not doing what her Mum told her" (Harris and Núñez 1996, 1577). Three- and four-year-old children perform well on these and related tasks.

The above rule is familiar and sensible, so one might maintain that it just shows the child's overall familiarity with those kinds of situations. Harris and Núñez (1996) went on to explore young children's understanding of novel rules. They gave young children rules that were clearly arbitrary. For instance, in one task, they said "One day Carol wants to do some painting. Her Mum says if she does some painting she should put her helmet on" (1581). Again, children were shown four pictures: two pictures depicted Carol painting, one with and one without a helmet; in the other two pictures, Carol is not painting, but in one of these pictures she has a helmet on. Children were asked, "Show me the picture where Carol is being naughty and not doing what her Mum told her?" Even on these tasks with unfamiliar and arbitrary rules, three- and four-year-old children tend to get the right answer.

In addition to children's success in identifying transgressions, children are also able to give some justification for their choice. For instance, in the task described above, after they answer the question about which picture depicts a transgression, the children are asked "What is Carol doing in that picture which is naughty?" (Harris and Núñez 1996, 1581). The children in these experiments tended to give the right answer even here—they invoked the feature of the situation that was not present, for example, they noted that Carol isn't wearing her helmet. Harris (2000) maintains that this suggests that children's capacity for deontic reasoning implicates their capacity for counterfactual reasoning. The child knows what the target actually did, and then reconstructs what feature of the situation would have had to be different in order to avoid the transgression. Whether children's justificatory practices actually involve counterfactual reasoning remains to be seen, but it is clear that children have an early emerging capacity for both counterfactual and deontic reasoning.

This facility with prescriptive rules has been compared directly with young children's ability to evaluate indicative conditionals (Cummins 1996; Harris and Núñez 1996). In light of the fact that adults do poorly with indicative conditionals and children do well with deontic conditionals, it will come as no surprise that young children have more difficulty evaluating whether a conditional is true than whether a rule has been broken. In yet another experiment reported by Harris and Núñez, they gave subjects either a set of deontic conditional cases analogous to those above or a set of parallel indicative conditional cases. For instance, one of the deontic cases was identical to the case above in which the child is told that Carol wants to paint and "Her Mum says if she does some painting she should put her helmet on" (1585). In the parallel indicative case, the experimenter says, "One day Carol wants to do some painting. Carol says that if she does some painting she always puts her helmet on" (1585). Subjects were shown the usual complement of pictures and in the indicative case were asked, "Show me the picture where Carol is doing something different and not doing what she said" (1585). Both three- and four-year-olds did much worse with these kinds of questions than with the parallel deontic questions (see also Cummins 1996). Despite the close similarity between deontic and indicative conditionals, young children were much better at evaluating whether deontic conditionals were met than whether indicative conditionals were true.

Núñez and Harris (1998) extend these finding by showing that children also consult the actor's intentions when evaluating transgressions. For instance, in one task, children are told that Carol's mother has said that if Carol does some painting, she must keep her apron on. As in their earlier experiments, Núñez and Harris showed children four pictures. As they set down each picture, they described it. For instance, for one picture, they said, "Here's Carol doing some painting. Look! She's taken her apron off"; for another picture, they said, "Here's Carol doing some painting. Look! Her apron is torn and has fallen off" (Núñez and Harris 1998, 170). After being shown all the pictures, children were asked, "Show me the picture where Carol is being naughty and not doing what her Mum told her." Both three- and four-year-olds performed much better than chance on these tasks, selecting the picture that depicts the child intentionally flouting the rule.

The above evidence shows a strikingly early competence with normative reasoning. In particular, it shows that young children are capable of assimilating information about which sorts of actions are prohibited and then using this information appropriately to judge whether a given action is prohibited. There is more specific developmental evidence on their reasoning about harm-based transgressions. As we have seen, young children will maintain that the reason it is wrong to pull hair is because it hurts the other person (e.g., Smetana 1993). Further evidence indicates that the child's reasoning about moral transgressions does not depend merely on a simple rule that says that an action is wrong if it causes harm. First, young children's judgments about moral violations are sensitive to consequences of the action. For instance, they regard actions that cause greater harms as worse than actions that cause lesser harms (e.g., Rotenberg 1980). Also, in an early study that partly anticipates Núñez and Harris (1998), Nelson-Le Gall (1985) found that in making moral judgments, children attend to whether the action is intentional or unintentional. In one study, children were given stories in which a person either intentionally or unintentionally hurts another person. Here are two such stories:

1. Nick is playing with his ball, throwing it against the fence. Nick is angry with Pat. Nick sees Pat coming and so he hides behind the fence where Pat can't see him. Nick throws the ball again, trying to hit Pat. The ball hits Pat and Nick runs away laughing.
2. Nick is playing with his ball, throwing it against the fence. Nick is angry with Pat. Nick is busy thinking of something mean to do to Pat. Pat is walking along quietly on the other side of the fence. Nick doesn't know Pat is there. Nick throws the ball again, and just then Pat steps out from behind the fence and the ball hits him. Nick is surprised because he didn't know Pat was around to get hit by the ball. (Nelson-Le Gall 1985, 334)

Even though the consequences are the same and a negative motive is present in both cases, young children (mean age three years, ten months) rated the intentional harm as significantly worse than the unintentional harm (Nelson-Le Gall 1985).

These experimental findings indicate, then, that even young children engage in elementary moral reasoning. This is corroborated by observational studies on children in natural environments. In studies done on children at home, Smetana found that already at the age of three, children appeal to rights in the context of moral transgressions (but not conventional transgressions) (Smetana 1989, 504). Further, Dunn and Munn (1987) found that three-year-olds provided justifications for their actions in disputes with their mothers and siblings. Not surprisingly, most of these justifications appealed to the child's own feelings, but even at this young age children were beginning to appeal to social rules and others' feelings in justifying their actions (794–95; see also Dunn 1988, 51).

Before wrapping up this presentation of young children's moral reasoning, I'd like to review an ingenious bit of work done by Judith Smetana. Smetana presented preschool children (mean age four-and-a-half years) with transgression scenarios in which the actual transgression is not specified. Rather, in lieu of transgression terms, she used nonsense words such as "frammel," "wuffle," and "piggle." Some transgressions were modeled on the criteria associated with conventional transgressions (context specific, appeal to rules), other transgressions were modeled on criteria associated with moral transgressions (generalizable; child cries). Here is an unspecified conventional transgression, reprinted in full:

Mary is a little girl about your age. In her house, her mommy and daddy always let her _____, but in her nursery school, there is a rule that children are not allowed to _____. One day during story time at school, she felt like _____, and so she did. The teacher got mad and said to her, "Mary, you know you're not allowed to _____ here. It's against the rules. If you _____ again, you'll have to stay inside during recess."

Mary went home. Later that day, when she was having dinner with her mommy and daddy, she _____. Her parents didn't say anything, because she was allowed to _____ at home. So she told her mommy what had happened to her that day in school. Her daddy said to her. "Mary, it's OK if you _____ here. But you have to follow the rules at school, so it's okay to _____ here, but you shouldn't _____ at school. (Smetana 1985, 21)

And here is an unspecified transgression modeled on moral transgressions:

Sally is a little girl about your age. She goes to a nursery school just like this one. One day, Sally's best friend Jessica was playing with a bright shiny new toy. That made Sally mad because she wanted to play with the toy too. So she _____. Jessica began to cry. Just then, Mrs. Green, the teacher, walked by and said, "We're not supposed to _____ here."

Sally went home that night. She has a mommy and daddy and a baby brother named Michael. Sally and Michael were playing after dinner before bedtime. Sally went to find her favorite doll, but couldn't find it. So she got mad and _____. Michael began to cry. Their daddy came in the room and said, "Sally, did you _____? You know you shouldn't _____." (Smetana 1985, 21)

After each transgression was described, the children were asked questions that included the following: "What if there were no rule, would it be OK to frammel (piggle)?," "Would it be OK if the teacher decided to let kids frammel (piggle)?," and "What about in another country, would it be OK to frammel (piggle) there?" Smetana found significant differences on all three of these dimensions between these kinds of cases. Children were more likely to think that the unspecified moral transgression would be wrong even if there was no rule and even if the teacher allowed the behavior; they also were more likely to say that the unspecified moral transgression would be wrong in another country. In these cases, children are able to reason about transgressions based on minimal features associated with an action. Children reason in systematically different ways about actions associated with context-specific, rule-driven transgressions and actions associated with generalizable, distress-causing transgressions.

REASONING IN CHILDREN AND METAETHICS. I have spent a good bit of time here describing the kinds of normative reasoning that seem to be available to young children. If we now look back to the classic philosophical examples of moral reasoning lodged as problems for sentimentalism, many of these examples parallel the reasoning of young children. So, for instance, classic examples of moral reasoning include reasoning from moral principles, as in Toulmin's example of returning a book because one promised to return it. Young children do something that seems analogous when they judge that it is wrong to pull hair because it hurts the other person. Presumably the child reasons that it is wrong to pull hair because pulling hair hurts the person and hurting people is prohibited. Indeed, in the study just reported by Smetana, she found that when children were asked to explain why the unspecified moral transgression was wrong, children appeal to welfare considerations. In this case, they do not even know what the transgression is, but they maintain that it is wrong because it causes harm (Smetana 1985, 25).

Another classic philosophical example of moral reasoning involves judging which of one's reasons is weightiest (e.g., Baier 1958). We have seen that in a rudimentary fashion, young children do something like this as well. They judge that intentional harms are worse than unintentional harms and that actions that produce greater harm are worse than actions that produce lesser harms.

Finally, consider the example that is supposed to be especially threatening for certain sentimentalists, Geach's example of reasoning.

> If doing a thing is bad, getting your little brother to do it is bad.
>
> Tormenting the cat is bad.
>
> *Ergo*, getting your little brother to torment the cat is bad. (Geach 1965, 463)

Smetana's (1985) work suggests that young children are able to navigate this kind of reasoning as well. The point is perhaps easiest to see by considering the conventional transgressions. Children are told that Mary shouldn't piggle at school, but it is okay for her to piggle at home. From this, they tend to infer that in another country, it is okay to piggle. Now, in order to move from the information to the conclusion, the child presumably relies on some inductive premise of the sort, "If an action is okay at home but not at school, it is likely that the action is okay in another country." That is, children seem to do something very like the reasoning in Geach's example:

> If an action is okay at home but not at school, then it is probably okay in another country.

Piggling is okay at home but not at school.

Ergo, piggling is okay in another country.

Indeed, what is especially striking about Smetana's finding is that children negotiate this reasoning without knowing what piggling is!

Children seem able, then, to engage in the kind of elementary moral reasoning that sentimentalists seek to explain. Now we can see how the findings on children's moral reasoning suggest a tighter constraint on an adequate account of moral judgment. The young child apparently enjoys and exploits the capacity for basic moral reasoning. As a result, an adequate account of moral judgment needs to be able to explain not simply the fact that moral reasoning is central to moral judgment, but that moral reasoning is central to moral judgment in young children. That is, we need an account of the capacity for moral reasoning that can extend to cover moral reasoning in young children.

In the previous chapter, I noted that young children are motivated by moral judgments, so one needs an adequate account of core moral judgment in children that will address the problem of motivation. That account cannot, because of the dissociation problem, be a neosentimentalist account. Now it turns out that the other feature that drives neosentimentalism, reasoning, is also present in young children and we need an account for this capacity. Once again, neosentimentalism is not a good candidate. For young children apparently engage in moral reasoning before they are capable of the kind of reasoning to which neosentimentalism adverts to explain the rationality of ethical discourse. According to neosentimentalism, when we engage in moral reasoning, we are reasoning about whether it is appropriate to feel guilt (or some other moral emotion) on doing an action. As discussed in the previous chapter, young children apparently lack the capacity to judge the appropriateness of feeling guilt in response to performing a certain action. However, young children seem capable of engaging in elementary moral reasoning. This presents the neosentimentalist with another serious problem. Before children are capable of engaging in neosentimentalist reasoning, they can engage in the kind of basic moral reasoning that sentimentalists seek to explain.

Hence, the capacity for neosentimentalist reasoning seems not to be essential to the capacity for moral reasoning. We need an account of the young child's capacity for basic moral reasoning, but that account cannot be a neosentimentalist account. On the Sentimental Rules account, as noted above, the obvious way to explain moral reasoning is to appeal to the normative theory that plays a role in core moral judgment. Moral argument and moral discourse can largely be construed as reasoning over the content and implications of the internally represented normative theory. The developmental evidence on children's moral reasoning accordingly poses no problem for the Sentimental Rules approach. On that account, young children have some grasp of a normative theory prohibiting harmful actions. What the developmental evidence on reasoning indicates is that from a young age, children are able to reason in impressive ways over this normative theory.

Of course, the child's normative theory is quite limited early on. For instance, as noted in chapter 1, the three-year old child's normative theory might not include prohibitions against lying, since three-year-olds have an extremely limited understanding of lying. More interestingly, William Damon has charted children's developing understanding of distributive justice as it continues to change into adulthood. Damon gave children a variety of tasks that involved distributing resources. For example, in one set of experiments, children first made various objects then were given ten candy bars to divide among themselves (in groups of three plus an absent fourth child). In this experiment, Damon found that six-year-olds follow a pretty inflexible equality line. Everyone gets an equal amount, regardless of the quality or intensity of their work. Older children are sensitive to differences and are more likely to distribute resources partly on the basis of merit. To get a feel for the pattern, it is useful to have an anecdote or two in hand. In one of Damon's experiments, the experimenter has told the subject a story in which several children made bracelets at the request of their teacher. The subject is then asked a series of questions about how much money each of the children should get. The inflexible equality approach to distributive justice is expressed by a seven-year-old child in the following exchange:

> *Experimenter.* Clara said that she made more things than everybody else and she should get more money.
> *Child*: No. She shouldn't because it's not fair for her to get more money
> . . .
> *Experimenter.* Should she get a little more?
> *Child*: No. People should get the same amount because it's not fair. (Damon 1977, 81)

Older children are more likely to allow merit considerations to come into play. For instance, the following is an exchange with an eight-year-old child:

> *Experimenter.* So, would you give Rebecca, who made more things, more of the money?
> *Child*: Well, she would get a little more. (Damon 1977, 85)

Not surprisingly, there is a good deal of variation in the ages. So for instance, one of the clearest statements of a merit-based distributive justice comes from a six-year-old:

Experimenter: Rebecca thought that she should get the most because she made the most things. Do you think that's fair?
Child: Well, if she made more things, then she'd get more money. . . .
Experimenter: What about the lazy kid?
Child: Well, he shouldn't get as much if he didn't work as much, if he didn't do his work. (1977, 83)

But the overall trend is that children tend to move from a strict equality notion of distributive justice to a form that is sensitive to merit considerations as well.

On the present proposal, at least part of the process documented by Damon's work reflects the development of an increasingly sophisticated *normative theory*. There is a range of interesting questions about this reasoning.[3] But there is no reason to think that the child ever abandons the elementary reasoning depicted by the studies above (e.g., Harris and Núñez 1996; Núñez and Harris 1998; Smetana 1985). Indeed, much of this kind of reasoning has also been demonstrated in adults (e.g., Cosmides 1989; Cheng and Holyoak 1985; Turiel 1983).

Clearly the picture I have presented leaves open a vast array of questions about the nature of moral reasoning. But we do not need to await the answers to these questions to see that there is a stark contrast between the account of moral reasoning that I'm suggesting and that proffered by neosentimentalism. According to neosentimentalism, in moral discourse, we are arguing about the appropriateness of feeling some emotion. I do not want to deny that one can engage in normative evaluations of one's emotions. One can ask all sorts of such questions about when emotions are rational, appropriate, and fit. But much of the disagreement and argument we find in moral discourse can be accounted for more simply by adverting to the content of an internally represented normative theory. Of course, this would also allow us to explain why it is that when we talk about moral issues, it does not seem like we're talking about emotions at all. That's because typically we're not talking about emotions. We're talking about the content and implications of a largely shared normative theory.

4. INTERNALISM AND SENTIMENTAL RULES

At this point, I won't argue further for the Sentimental Rules account. Rather, I will locate the position with respect to a nest of distinctions in

---

3. One possibility is that the normative theory proscribing harmful violations is simply a subset of rules stored in a large and domain-diverse body of information about transgressions. A quite different alternative is that the normative theory proscribing harmful violations is stored in a domain specific

the internalism/externalism discourse. This is a delicate business. Teasing out different notions of internalism makes ideal fodder for the tools of philosophers, and the literature is deliriously sophisticated (e.g., Railton 1986; Brink 1989; Darwall 1995). But I would like to cut the pie in yet another slightly different way.

One prominent notion of internalism that I want to chart only to ignore, is internalism about reasons. The idea of reasons-internalism is that if one has a reason to do something, then one has some motivation to do that thing (e.g., Railton 1986). Because our focus is on narrowly moral judgments, it is not absolutely essential to consider reasons-internalism. I'm content to neglect it on those grounds.

The kind of internalism that is relevant for our purposes is *internalism about moral judgment*. We will need to draw our distinctions here. Let us begin with a deliberately vague characterization of the claim of internalism about moral judgment (IMJ):

> IMJ: Making a moral judgment that X is wrong carries with it a motivation not to do X.

As stated, IMJ does not distinguish between a conceptual claim and an empirical claim about the relationship between moral judgment and motivation. That is the first distinction we need. One might embrace a kind of *conceptual internalism about moral judgment*, according to which it is part of our concept of making a moral judgment that moral judgments carry motivation with them. It is, on this view, a conceptual truth that judging something to be wrong carries with it a motivation to refrain from doing that thing. One might draw a rather different claim from IMJ, though. One might say that it is an *empirical* fact that when one judges that X is morally wrong, one is motivated not to do X.[4]

The account of moral judgment presented in chapter 1 aims to provide an empirical account of what moral judgment is, rather than a semantic or conceptual analysis of what moral terms and concepts mean. As a result, the account itself remains silent about conceptual internalism.

---

information structure like a module. Indeed, it is possible that the normative theory is stored in several different modules. It is also possible that some normative information is stored in modules and other normative information is stored in domain general systems.

4. The distinction here is closely related to the distinction in chapter 3 between conceptual rationalism and empirical rationalism. But in that case, the distinction teased apart two different rationalist claims. So, although the conceptual rationalist claim is related to the conceptual internalism about moral judgment, it differs insofar as conceptual internalism about moral judgment (CIMJ) need not say that the connection between moral judgment and motivation is mediated through rationality. For a sentimentalist might be thoroughly opposed to rationalism and yet embrace CIMJ. Empirical internalism is, of course, a different claim from empirical rationalism.

However, as discussed in chapter 3, there is reason to doubt that it is part of the lay concept of moral judgment that moral judgments are always motivating. The amoralist challenge poses a serious problem for the claim that it is part of the commonsense concept of morality that understanding a moral claim carries with it motivation (Brink 1989). For it seems conceptually possible that a person might know that some action is morally wrong but lack any motivation to refrain from performing that action. There is little actual evidence on the issue, but what evidence there is indicates that people in our culture are quite willing to allow that a psychopath might make genuine moral judgments without being motivated by those judgments (see chapter 3). So there is reason to think that conceptual internalism about moral judgment runs afoul of lay intuitions about moral judgment. Because commonsense intuitions are the central recourse for conceptual internalism, this counts as a major obstacle for conceptual internalism as I have characterized it. Of course, even if conceptual internalism is false, this does not uproot empirical internalism about moral judgment.

Empirical internalism about moral judgment presents a more interesting case, because here the empirical work suggests a new distinction between different internalisms. The distinction emerges because there is evidently a difference between the capacity for core moral judgment and the capacity for judging that it is wrong to harm others. So we need to distinguish between *empirical internalism about core moral judgment* and *empirical internalism about harm-norm judgment*. Empirical internalism about core moral judgment is the claim that judging that something is distinctively morally wrong (as reflected by the moral/conventional task) carries with it a motivation not to do that thing. That is, core moral judgment is nomologically connected with motivation. Empirical internalism about harm-norm judgment is the simpler claim that judging that it is wrong (i.e., counternormative) to harm other people carries with it the motivation not to harm other people. Let us consider the latter kind of internalism first.

Just as the conceptual possibility of the rational amoralist poses a problem for conceptual internalism, the real empirical findings on psychopaths pose a problem for empirical internalism about harm norms.[5] The problem is that psychopaths seem to be well aware of the harm norms, but at the same time, they seem to lack the appropriate motivation to refrain from harming others. This requires some elaboration. Psychopaths know that one is not supposed to harm others. On the moral/con-

5. See Roskies 2003 for a similar argument based on evidence from acquired sociopathy.

ventional task, they consistently maintain that the moral violations are indeed wrong. The awareness of norms is also reflected in the comment of Ted Bundy's: "It is wrong for me to jaywalk. It is wrong to rob a bank. It is wrong to break into other people's houses. It is wrong for me to drive without a driver's license. It is wrong not to pay your parking tickets. It is wrong not to vote in elections. It is wrong to intentionally embarrass people" (Michaud and Aynesworth 1989, 116). Bundy here shows a knowledge of a wide range of norms, and he apparently recognizes that the norms apply to him. But psychopaths also, notoriously, lack the normal emotional and motivational response to harm violations, as reflected in this snippet of an interview with a psychopathic prisoner: "When asked if he experienced remorse over a murder he'd committed, one young [psychopathic] inmate told us, 'Yeah, sure, I feel remorse.' Pressed further, he said he didn't 'feel bad inside about it'" (Hare 1991, 41). Despite the fact that psychopaths know the harm-norms and know that the norms apply to them, knowing that it is wrong to hurt others does not motivate them the way it motivates the rest of us. Rather, their motivation for following harm norms seems to be largely external. For instance, they are aware of criminal laws, and they try to evade detection when they violate those laws. They follow the harm norms opportunistically, rather than as any nomological consequence of making the judgment that it is wrong to harm others.

The psychopath's relation to harm norms might be compared to the relation some (nonpsychopathic) people have towards a range of etiquette norms. For some people, knowing that an action is proscribed by etiquette carries no intrinsic motivational force not to perform that action. Einstein, for instance, is said to have thought Emily Post's etiquette book terribly funny. The important feature of the etiquette analogy is that I can know that a rule of propriety applies to me without being motivated to act in accordance with that rule. This is nicely illustrated by Philippa Foot's famous observation that etiquette norms are "non-hypothetical," but one might nonetheless fail to be motivated by them. Foot makes the point by noting first that on Kant's characterization, hypothetical imperatives are "those telling a man what he ought to do because . . . he wants something and those telling him what he ought to do on grounds of self-interest" (Foot 1972, 306). At least some pronouncements of etiquette norms are not hypothetical in this self-interested sense. Foot's etiquette example is the norm that invitations addressed in the third person should be answered in the third person, and she claims that "the rule does not *fail to apply* to someone who has his own good reasons for ignoring this piece of nonsense, or who simply does not care about what, from the point of view of etiquette, he should do" (Foot 1972, 308; emphasis in original).

Foot's example suggests that, at least intuitively, there is no nomologically necessary connection between recognizing that an etiquette norm applies and being motivated to follow it. Consider Foot's other example: "The club secretary who has told a member that he should not bring ladies into the smoking-room does not say, 'Sorry, I was mistaken' when informed that this member is resigning tomorrow and cares nothing about his reputation in the club" (Foot 1972, 308–9). For our purposes, we can assume that the club member is fully aware that what he is doing is against the rules. But he does not care about the rules. Under these assumptions, the case nicely illustrates that some people know the rules without caring about following them. We do not need to run any experiments to know that it is an empirical fact that people can know the rules that apply to them without caring to follow the rules.

Foot's etiquette examples are useful because they provide clean anti-internalist exemplars. The club rules apply to the member, and he knows it, but this does not motivate him to follow the rules. Similarly, the harm norms apply to psychopaths and they apparently know it, but this alone does not motivate them to follow the rules. Hence, psychopaths cast doubt on the empirical internalist hypothesis that knowing that it is wrong to harm other people is nomologically tied to being motivated not to harm people. It would seem that, if one is a psychopath, one can judge that it is wrong to harm others without being thereby motivated not to harm others.

When we turn to the final form of internalism, empirical internalism about core moral judgment, things look rather brighter for the internalist. For, as suggested in chapter 1, core moral judgment plausibly implicates an affective mechanism that is sensitive to suffering in others. Despite their fluency with harm norms, psychopaths are less likely to accord those norms the distinctive status that harm norms receive from the nonpsychopathic population. Psychopaths also exhibit a deficit in their affective response to suffering in others. Thus, it seems that an emotional response is nomologically connected with core moral judgment, and because emotional responses are paradigmatically motivational, this suggests that core moral judgment is nomologically connected to motivation. That is, there is some plausibility to the claim that people who judge that harming others is distinctively morally wrong (in the sense tapped by the moral/conventional task) also tend to be motivated not to harm others.

The foregoing suggests the (tentative) internalist tree depicted in Figure 5.1. However, there are important questions about core moral judgment that would need to be resolved before one could be confident about the extent to which core moral judgment always carries motivational force with it. The central problem is that it is not yet clear whether core moral judgment can be preserved if the affective response to suffering in others

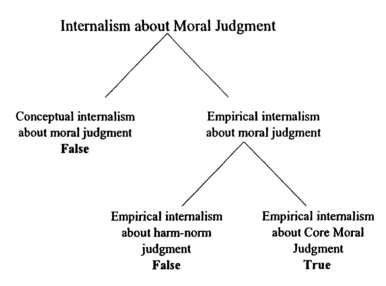

FIGURE 5.1 Internalism under the Sentimental Rules account

is damaged in later life. As noted in chapter 1, one possibility is that the affective response is essential during a critical developmental period, but then plays no further role in sustaining core moral judgment. In that case, if the affective mechanism were destroyed in adulthood, it is possible that the capacity for core moral judgment might persevere while the attendant motivation does not. The available data provide no reason to believe that such an extremist critical period view is right, though. And it would be rather surprising if the emotions played no role in sustaining the capacity for core moral judgment.

So much for the range of distinctions. What about moral motivation in those of us who have intact affective mechanisms? Well, it is likely that our motivation to behave in accordance with harm norms is multifaceted. We presumably share with the psychopaths an externalist motivation to obey the rules prohibiting harm norms. People are, after all, often motivated to obey even the conventional rules under which they fall. This is evident from childhood. Children want, for instance, to stay in their parents' good favor, and obeying the conventional rules is required for this. And, although conventional rules vary significantly across cultures, there is cross-cultural evidence that children the world over have some motivation to follow the local conventional rules (see Dunn 1988, 74–75).

This kind of externalist motivation to follow the rules presumably contributes to the motivational package of moral norms. Work in the Piaget-Kohlberg tradition is instructive here. For in Kohlberg's first stage and perhaps in later stages as well, the motivation to follow the moral rules is patently externalist. In Kohlberg's first stage, one follows the rules because one wants to avoid punishment. In the second stage, the motivation for following the moral rules is instrumental—to benefit from reciprocity. Children explicitly invoke these sorts of externalist justifications for their decisions to follow certain moral rules, as confirmed by a massive amount of data in the Kohlbergian tradition (see Lapsley 1996 for review).

In addition to this externalist motivation to follow the rules, we obviously have an additional nonexternalist fount of motivation as well. Our emotional systems are tuned to find suffering in others upsetting. So we are by nature disinclined to engage in actions that will produce those cues. There are multiple affective systems that respond to suffering in others and, as we have seen, these systems are present early in life (see chapter 2). So again, this source of motivation to refrain from harming others is present in the young child.

Thus there are two obvious ways that we are motivated to refrain from harming others, one rooted in the desire to obey the rules, the other rooted in the emotional response generated by suffering in others. It is possible that core moral judgment brings with it yet another distinctive kind of motivation, a motivation that cannot be attributed merely to the accumulated motivational contributions of rule-based and emotion-based motivations. The recognition of the distinctiveness of harm norms—that they are especially serious, generalizable, and not authority-contingent—might also carry with it greater motivation. This issue is largely unexplored, but there is a smattering of evidence showing a correlation in preschool children between moral reasoning and moral motivation (e.g., Eisenberg-Berg and Hand 1979).

5. THE COORDINATION PROBLEM

This chapter has largely paraded the virtues of the Sentimental Rules account and how that account addresses the constraints on an adequate sentimentalism, without falling into the dissociation problem. However, it is time to confess a significant shortcoming to the theory. On the Sentimental Rules account, the relation between emotions and normative judgment seems awkwardly contingent. By contrast, neosentimentalism locates the connection between emotions and normative judgment deep in the nature of normative judgment itself. Before bringing this chapter to a close, I want to reflect briefly on this important difference between neosentimentalism and the Sentimental Rules account.

On the Sentimental Rules account, core moral judgment is, of course, tied to the emotions in an important way. There is a nomological connection between having certain emotions and treating certain norms distinctively. What the Sentimental Rules account does not explain, however, is why we happen to have a large cluster of norms that are closely connected with our emotions. We have norms prohibiting harming others, and these norms are closely connected to our responses to suffering; we have norms against the gratuitous display of bodily fluids, and these norms are closely connected to our disgust responses. But why is it that we have so many norms that fit so well with our emotional repertoire? We might think of this as the *coordination problem*. The Sentimental Rules account has no principled explanation for the coordination between the norms we have and the emotions we have. Of course, on the Sentimental Rules account, one would expect that ontogenetically, norms and emotions can come to be coordinated in complex and interpenetrating ways. What is not explained, however, is why our natural emotional repertoire should be so closely connected to our characteristic normative commitments.

This shortcoming is hardly debilitating. It is unlikely that all norms are coordinated with emotions. For instance, some norms of etiquette (e.g., the fork is supposed to be on the left) are not grounded by emotion. However, it is not just table etiquette. There are norms about games (e.g., do not look at your cards until all hands have been dealt); norms about office behavior (e.g., do not tie up the phone line with personal calls; do not leave the coffee pot empty); norms about school behavior (e.g., do not chew gum in class; do not stand up during story time); religious norms (e.g., go to church on Sunday); and even some putatively moral norms (e.g., pay your income tax; vote in local elections) that are probably not neatly coordinated with emotions.[6] So the situation is not as bad for the Sentimental Rules account as it might seem. For many norms are not closely connected to our basic emotions. Nonetheless, there is a serious issue here on which the account is at least incomplete. The issue is: why does so much of our normative life fit so closely our natural emotional endowment? In the case of central interest, the moral norms, we might ask why the moral norms we have are connected to affective responses. The Sentimental Rules account provides one level of explanation for this—because our moral norms prohibit harming others and we have an affective system that is built to respond to harm in others. However, this might seem not to answer the deeper question about why these norms that are so tightly connected to affect exist at all. As a result, on the Senti-

---

6. Perhaps there is some general emotion of disapprobation that attends all normative violations. I am rather skeptical of this, but in any case, it is not relevant to the present issue. The point here is just that there are many norms (like table setting-norms) that do not seem to be coordinated in obvious ways with our emotional repertoire.

mental Rules account, the connection between norms and emotions seems rather accidental—we have some norms that happen to be backed by affect for a large portion of the population.

On this point, there is no doubt that neosentimentalists can appeal to a tighter connection. Philosophical sentimentalists in the last century have sought to find the connection between morality and emotion in the very semantics of moral terms. The philosophical accounts maintain that emotion concepts are infused into the meaning of moral concepts. As a result, on philosophical sentimentalist accounts, it obviously follows that moral norms will be coordinated with our emotions. This feature is shared by sentimentalist accounts throughout the twentieth century, from Ayer to Gibbard.[7] This does provide philosophical sentimentalists with a noncontingent connection between moral judgment and emotion. I have gone to some lengths to argue that the philosophical sentimentalist accounts are empirically problematic. Yet surely it is no accident that our norms are connected to our emotions in important ways. That is, it is no accident that normal people's views about the moral wrongness of harm turn out to correlate with their emotional responsiveness. If we abandon philosophical sentimentalism, we need some other explanation for why our norms are coordinated with our emotions.

6. CONCLUSION

Thus far, I have argued that the psychological work on moral judgment poses serious problems for philosophical sentimentalist accounts of moral judgment. Further, the psychological work points to a positive account of moral judgment that might explain the central features of moral judgment. If this approach is right, the psychological work contributes significantly to our understanding of moral judgment. But this approach leaves us with a major lacuna. How do we get norms like this, connected with affect as they are? Not, I have argued, because emotions form part of the definition of wrongness. I think a more promising approach is to consider the genealogy of these norms. That is, rather than attempt to give a semantics of moral concepts or try to determine how individuals arrived at the affectively charged moral norms ontogenetically, we ask how these norms were arrived at historically.

7. Blair's VIM-account (see chapter 1) also has a principled explanation for the coordination between emotion and moral judgment. For Blair maintains that the actions that are judged immoral are precisely those that trigger VIM-based affect.

6

A Fragment of the Genealogy of Norms

It is unseemly to blow your nose into the tablecloth.

—From *Ein spruch der ze tische kêrt*, quoted in N. Elias, *The Civilizing Process*

1. INTRODUCTION

Where do our moral norms come from? Why do we have the norms we do? How did they become fixed in our moral outlook? These are large and deep questions to which one would like to have comparably deep answers. Unfortunately, the project of discerning the genealogy of morals has not produced any kind of received view about how to answer these questions. The Sentimental Rules account developed in the earlier chapters might provide answers to some of our metaethical questions, but it is entirely silent on why we have these norms that happen to be coordinated with our emotions. In this chapter, I will make a rather indirect argument that emotions played a crucial role in the historical process that led to our contemporary norms. Although the issues here are grand, my treatment will lack any claim to grandeur. Indeed, we will be reduced to discussing spitting and nose blowing in our attempt to glimpse the genealogy of morals.

The attempt to uncover the genealogy of morals has a rich history in philosophy. Hobbes, Rousseau, and Nietzsche all tried to develop stories about the origins of the moral norms that hold forth in our culture. In the twentieth century origin stories continued to proliferate, but there is nothing even approaching a consensus about the origin of moral norms. Recent developments in cognitive anthropology, however, offer a promising new approach to exploring the genealogy of norms. On the "epidemiological" approach to cultural evolution, rather than searching for the origin of cultural items, one attempts to determine which cultural items are likely to survive; in order to assess such cultural viability, epidemiologists maintain that one must attend closely to the details of human psychology (e.g., Sperber 1996; Boyer 2000). In this chapter, I will extend the epidemiological account by arguing that epidemiologists should allow that basic affective systems play a crucial role in cultural evolution in general, and in particular, affective systems plausibly influence the cultural viability of norms. After sketching the epidemiological approach, I will proceed first by arguing that existing work on affect suggests that epidemiological approaches should recognize affective systems as important factors in determining which cultural items get preserved. I maintain that emotional responses will affect the cultural viability of norms as well as other cultural items. In particular, norms prohibiting actions that elicit negative affect will, I argue, be more likely to survive than affectively neutral norms. I will then consider some historical evidence on the development of manners in our culture, and I will argue that the historical evidence confirms the hypothesis that norms prohibiting emotionally upsetting actions are more likely to survive. In addition, as I will discuss in the final section, the theoretical and historical considerations brought to bear in the case of norms suggest that current scientific approaches to cultural evolution need to accord greater attention to the role of emotion. Indeed, although the chapter will focus largely on etiquette norms, this case suggests more broadly that emotion is a powerful force in affecting which mental representations get preserved in a culture.

2. ORIGIN STORIES

Most genealogical accounts of norms focus on moral norms, and the most familiar attempts to explain the genealogy of morals strive to give an account of the origin of moral norms in our cultural past. According to one prominent naturalistic proposal, "evolutionary ethics," moral norms are evolutionary adaptations (e.g., Ruse and Wilson 1986). Although there has been a great deal of interest in evolutionary ethics among philosophers of science, there is widespread skepticism about such evolutionary explanations of why we have the moral norms we do. Indeed, even those who are attracted to an evolutionary explanation of basic mental capacities often remain dubious of evolutionary explanations of specific norms (e.g., Ayala 1987, 1995; Kitcher 1990, 1994). Darwin himself expresses skepticism about the view that moral norms are adaptations (Darwin 1871, chapter 4).[1]

In this chapter, I will develop an alternative naturalistic approach to explaining the genealogy of norms that does not assume that the moral norms are themselves adaptations. Critics of evolutionary ethics have suggested that culture might be a better place to look than biology for determining the genealogy of morals (e.g., Ayala 1995; Kitcher 1994; Rottschaefer and Martinson 1990; Sober 1994). That is precisely where I want to look as well. But a major obstacle remains even if we restrict ourselves to nonadaptionist explanations for the origin of moral norms in the culture. The problem with such origin explanations is not that we don't have any good explanations, but rather that we have too many good explanations, and not enough historical evidence to decide between them. Here is a quick and incomplete catalog of some candidate explanations of the cultural origins of moral norms prohibiting harming others.

1. Nietzsche's "slave morality." The weak invented the norms as a self-serving strategy to protect themselves against harm from the powerful (Nietzsche 1887; see Boehm 1999 for a related view).
2. Reciprocal altruism. Individuals agree not to harm each other because (at least if resources are not scarce) this agreement is beneficial to both parties (cf. Trivers 1971).
3. Indirect reciprocity. Adopting the norm of not harming others might make one more attractive for alliances (cf. Alexander 1987; Frank 1988).
4. Kin selection. Adopting the norm not to hurt kin might confer a selective advantage, and the norm prohibiting harm might then be generalized to the group (cf. Sober and Wilson 1998).
5. Emotional sensitivity. The emotions might play a key role in the origination of the norms against harming others. Witnessing the suffering of others is emotionally upsetting, and it is possible that the norms against harm arose as a concession to this emotional sensitivity. For instance, the !Kung care deeply about how they are received by others (e.g., Marshall 1976), so it could be that members of the community developed norms against harming others (even the weak) so as not to provoke the distress of other members of their community.
6. Random mutation. The origin of harm norms might have been an arbitrary fluke that was promoted by a dominant individual who happened to wield unusually strong influence. One way that this might be implemented is if the dominant individual punishes transgressors and punishes those who do not punish transgressors (Axelrod 1986; Boyd and Richerson 1992).

---

1. This view is discussed further in chapter 7, footnote 3. I discuss recent arguments for the innateness of moral principles in Nichols (in press).

I think that we must frankly acknowledge that all of these stories are possible accounts of the origin of norms against harming others. No doubt further possible origin stories could be cooked up. However, while origin stories have proliferated over the last several decades, the crucial historical details that could decide between the stories remain elusive. To confirm such an origin story, one would want to have a detailed record of a culture that lacked harm norms and then developed them. We have no such detailed records, which is not surprising since harm norms are culturally ubiquitous and historically ancient.

A further problem with the origin stories is that we cannot assume that a single origin account applies to all cultures. It might be that harm norms originated for one reason in one culture and for another reason in another culture. So even if we were presented with the crucial historical details for how the harm norms arose for some tribe in the Pleistocene, we could not casually generalize this origin story to other groups.

Given this problem with the proliferation of origin stories in the absence of the relevant historical evidence, one might become abjectly discouraged about the possibility of getting any insight into the actual genealogy of these norms. I think that a rather different genealogical goal offers greater promise for success. Instead of seeking an account of the origin of moral norms, we might try to determine which features make certain norms more likely to prevail than other norms. This might then help us explain why harm norms prevailed. To pursue this project, we need to turn to cognitive anthropology.

3. CULTURAL TRANSMISSION

Rather than ask for the origin of cultural items like norms, one might try to determine which cultural items are more likely to survive in a culture. Such "cultural transmission" stories have been widely discussed and explored for decades (e.g., Dawkins 1976; Dennett 1995). I will not take the time to review this literature. Rather, I will simply begin by adopting one of the most promising and interesting recent approaches to cultural transmission—the epidemiological account introduced by Dan Sperber (1996) and taken up by a few colleagues (e.g., Atran 1998; Boyer 1994, 1999, 2000).[2]

2. For a critique of rival transmission accounts, see Sperber 1996, chapter 5. It should be noted that some of these rival transmission accounts have generated an impressive body of work on cultural evolution. In particular, Boyd and Richerson (1985) have a sophisticated account that is gaining empirical confirmation (e.g., Henrich and Boyd 1998, Henrich and Gil-White 2001). However, Boyd and Richerson's account is not really directed at predicting the kinds of cultural *content* that are likely to be pre-

The epidemiological approach focuses on a crucial class of cultural items—mental representations. Because norms are widely regarded as mental representations, this focus will suit us well. According to Sperber, in trying to evaluate which cultural items (in the form of mental representations) are likely to prevail, one needs to look not only at ecological factors, but also at the details of human psychology. In this section and the next, I want to present and try to extend the general epidemiological approach to cultural transmission. I will eventually bring these points to bear on the transmission of norms.

One crucial idea behind the epidemiological approach is that if you want to understand cultural transmission, it is not enough to look at the cultural items themselves. You need to look at human psychology, because you need to see which cultural items are likely to be attractive to creatures who have the kind of psychology that we do. Sperber illustrates this by noting that some variants of "Little Red Riding Hood" are more likely to survive than others, because different versions differ in their "attractiveness": "In the logical space of possible versions of a tale, some versions have a better form: that is, a form seen as being without either missing or superfluous parts, easier to remember, and more attractive. The factors that make for a good form may be rooted in part in universal human psychology and in part in a local cultural context" (Sperber 1996, 108).

What do we need to know about human psychology to know which cultural items will enjoy greater cultural fitness? Sperber is somewhat less systematic here than one might like in the progenitor of a new methodology. But there are a couple of points on which Sperber is quite clear. First, one wants to know which features of human psychology are universal. Sperber adopts the view, now prominent in evolutionary psychology, that the mind is composed of a set of modules that are adaptations to the environment. So, there is a module for reasoning about physics, a module for reasoning about psychology, and so forth. Moreover, these modules are species general—every normal member of the species has the modules (or will have them if they are allowed to mature). Sperber embraces modules as vital forces in cultural transmission: "Mental modules . . . are crucial factors in cultural attraction. They tend to fix a lot of cultural content in and around the cognitive domain the processing of which they specialize in" (Sperber 1996, 113). Similarly, Pascal Boyer's (1994, 1999, 2000) deployment of the epidemiological model appeals to species universal, but domain specific, cognitive mechanisms. Boyer focuses on a

---

served. The epidemiological approach, on the other hand, has this as a primary goal—to explain which kinds of contents will likely get preserved in the culture.

particular cluster of domain specific bodies of information—intuitive physics, intuitive biology, and intuitive psychology. Boyer maintains that all of these should be considered part of basic "intuitive ontology."

To understand which cultural items are likely to survive, then, we need to know as much as possible about universal human psychology. The species-general mechanisms are likely to affect attraction and shape the kind of information that we retain. But this still does not give us much guidance about how to measure whether one item is more culturally fit than another. How can we test, experimentally, whether a given cultural item is more likely to survive? Sperber and Boyer offer few hints here. But one experimental approach rises to the top of the list for both: cultural items are more likely to survive if they are easier to remember. For instance, Sperber writes, "Potentially pertinent psychological factors include the ease with which a particular representation can be memorized" (Sperber 1996, 84; see also Sperber 1996, 62, 73, 74–75). Similarly, Boyer focuses on differences in whether a representation is likely to be recalled as "one aspect that is crucial to differences of cultural survival" (Boyer 2000, 105). Indeed, in their work on religious ideas, Boyer and Justin Barrett have been investigating whether "counterintuitive" representations (i.e., representations that violate some aspect of intuitive ontology) are more likely to be remembered than representations that are distinctive but not counterintuitive. They find that counterintuitive representations *are* more likely to be remembered; more importantly for present purposes, this evidence on retention is the central experimental evidence offered to support the claim that counterintuitive representations enjoy greater cultural fitness (see Boyer 2000, 105).

I have set out two central features of the epidemiological approach, and both of these features will be important in what follows. First, on the epidemiological approach, we need to attend closely to the universal features of human psychology. Second, we can expect that cultural items that are more easily remembered will have greater cultural fitness.

A further feature of the epidemiological approach worth emphasizing is that it is well equipped to deal with the apparently enormous variation we find in norms across cultures. As we will see in somewhat more detail in chapter 7, anthropologists have uncovered what seem to be vast differences in what different cultures regard as acceptable harm. For instance, in some cultures, wife beating is regarded as permissible (at least by the men), whereas in our culture, wife beating is not typically regarded as permissible (even by the men). Prima facie, the best explanation of this is that not all cultures embrace the same harm norms. There are, of course, subtle moves one might make to maintain that the culture really agree about the normative claims and only disagree about the facts. But the epidemiologist need not resort to subtle moves, because the epidemiological approach is entirely consistent with rich normative diversity. The epidemiological approach merely tries to explain which norms, once they emerge in a culture, will survive better.

One of the virtues of adopting a cultural transmission approach is that the transmission of cultural items (unlike the origin of culture items) can capitalize on cumulative effects. As work in evolutionary biology has richly illustrated, even traits that confer small advantages often become pervasive after many generations. This point plausibly extends to cultural evolution as well. Cultural items that enjoy relatively small advantages can become widespread after many generations as a result of the cumulative effects of the small advantages. So explanations that are naïve as origin stories can become fairly plausible forces in transmission stories. For instance, it is regarded as jejune to maintain that religious beliefs have their origin in the desire to salve one's fears of death (e.g., Boyer 2001, 19ff). It is implausible that people concocted the idea of life after death as a religious bromide to ease their fear of death. But it is much easier to make a case that a religious doctrine that promises life after death will be more likely to succeed than other religious doctrines that carry no motivational benefits (Nichols [in press a]).

4. AFFECT AND EPIDEMIOLOGY

As Sperber and Boyer develop the epidemiological approach, they recommend that to understand cultural transmission, we attend to species-general information-based cognitive mechanisms like intuitive physics and intuitive psychology. However, there is a different class of basic mental mechanisms that are almost certainly crucial on an epidemiological approach: emotion systems. Sperber and Boyer devote little attention to the role of affective mechanisms as forces of cultural attraction. Yet a number of affective mechanisms are regarded as universal denizens of human psychology. And the idea that affective mechanisms partly determine which cultural items succeed is certainly consistent with the epidemiological approach. I will try to put some detail on this suggestion over the next couple of pages.

There is, of course, a simple commonsense reason why we might expect emotion to be a powerful force in cultural transmission. Emotional items are typically accorded extra importance. Put crudely, we care more about information that is emotionally gripping for us. And it seems likely that information that we care more about will be more culturally viable.

But this commonsense idea needs to be sharpened in the context of the epidemiological approach.

In contemporary psychology, emotions provided the battleground for one of the most important early debates over human universals. Paul Ekman and his colleagues generated a varied and impressive array of data indicating that there is a set of universal basic emotions that have a cluster of features including the following: automatic appraisal, quick onset, involuntary occurrence, distinctive physiology, and distinctive facial expression. Further, across cultures, there are common elements in the contexts that elicit a basic emotion. Among the emotions that fit all the criteria of basic emotions are sadness, anger, fear, and disgust (Ekman 1994). These emotions are taken to be evolutionary adaptations that are universally instantiated in the species, although there might be important cultural variations in some of the eliciting conditions and some of the ways the emotions are displayed (e.g., Mallon and Stich 2000). Knowing the character of universal affective systems will presumably help us to determine which cultural items will succeed. But we still have not considered *how* emotions might facilitate cultural transmission. As we saw above, one crucial experimental assay for cultural fitness is the retention test. Items that are better remembered will have an edge in cultural fitness. As it happens, we already have in the coffers of science a heap of evidence that affect confers this advantage.

Over the last forty years, there has been an impressive experimental tradition tracking the effects of affect on memory. The broad pattern of findings indicates that increased emotion at encoding facilitates retention (for reviews, see Heuer and Reisberg 1992 and Revelle and Loftus 1992). This pattern is what matters particularly for us, because we want to see whether affect will facilitate cultural survival. However, some of the details of this research are worth examining a bit more closely.

One interesting fact is that emotion facilitates long-term retention much better than it does short-term retrieval. In one famous series of studies on word recall, subjects were shown affectively neutral and affectively charged words (e.g., "rape"). Subjects exhibited worse recall for the emotion words when asked two minutes after being given the word lists. However, when the same subjects were tested for recall a week later, they recalled the emotion words better than the neutral words (Kleinsmith and Kaplan 1963). This finding has been widely replicated, and the broad interpretation of these and related findings is that emotional arousal improves memory, so long as memory is not tested shortly after encoding (e.g., Heuer and Reisberg 1992, 161).

There are two important points about cultural transmission to draw from these findings. First, the crucial mnemonic dimension for cultural fitness is long-term retention, and that is exactly the dimension that affect most clearly facilitates. Second, the retention benefits cannot be attributed to a self-serving bias to remember things that are affectively pleasing. For the evidence indicates that retention benefits are generated when the stimuli elicit negative affect. Indeed, virtually all of the experiments showing that affect facilitates retention have been done using negative affect. For example, in the word recall experiments, the affectively charged words were words that generate considerable unease (e.g., "rape" and "vomit"). So, stimuli that are emotionally valenced contribute to greater retention even though the valence is negative.

Another interesting feature of the work on memory and emotion is that, although emotion facilitates memory for the central events in an emotional stimulus, emotion also seems to undermine memory for peripheral information. In one study, subjects were shown a film in which a teacher and a student get into an argument. One group saw a film in which the argument escalates into an emotional confrontation; the other group saw a film in which the argument remained civil. Subjects in both groups remembered the central elements of the story well, but subjects in the emotion-condition had poorer memory for peripheral features of the film (Kebeck and Lohaus 1986). Subjects also apparently show impaired memory performance for stimuli presented shortly before or shortly after an emotional stimulus (e.g., Bower 1994). One explanation of this phenomenon is that emotional stimuli attract and command attentional resources, which are then unavailable for processing peripheral stimuli (Christianson 1997). Thus, it seems that affect not only facilitates long-term retention, affect seems to determine which information gets reliably encoded.

There are several possible mechanisms that might be responsible for the effects of emotion on memory. Emotional events are often more distinctive than other events, and distinctiveness in general enhances retention. So one mechanism that plausibly facilitates the retention of emotional stimuli is distinctiveness. However, Christiansen and Loftus (1991) pitted distinctiveness against emotion and found that a fairly common emotional stimulus (a picture of a woman in an accident) produced better retention for central features (e.g., the color of the woman's coat) than a neutral stimulus (a woman riding a bike) and an affectively neutral but distinctive stimulus (a woman carrying a bicycle upside-down on her shoulder).[3] Heuer and Reisberg (1992) suggest that there is also a kind

---

3. As noted in section 3, Boyer and Barrett find that "counterintuitive" stimuli also boast better retention effects than distinctive but noncounterintuitive stimuli. It would be interesting to see how emotional stimuli compete with counterintuitive stimuli on retention. Would emotional stimuli show

of physiological explanation for the beneficial effects of emotion on memory (169). Emotional stimuli induce arousal, which might increase glucose production, and higher levels of glucose have been shown to enhance memory (e.g., Manning et al. 1990). A third possible explanation for the retention effects is that because emotional items have greater salience, they are more frequently recalled and rehearsed (Heuer and Reisberg 1992). A related explanation is that emotional events get encoded in more elaborate ways because they typically have "greater implications for the individual's sense of self and integrity" (Christianson and Engelberg 1999, 222).

Although it is not yet clear which mechanisms underlie the contribution that affect makes to retention, we do not need to know this to see that the work on the emotions and memory already provides an important tool for epidemiological approaches. For instance, the work suggests that the emotional elements of stories will have greater cultural fitness than the nonemotional parts of stories. So, if we could trace transmission of stories in an oral tradition (cf. Sperber 1996, 74–75), we should find that the emotional elements of the stories are better preserved across the ages than the nonemotional elements. Further, because the psychological evidence indicates that emotional stimuli actually impede retention for peripheral information, the greater cultural fitness of emotional elements might come at the expense of lower cultural fitness for surrounding elements.

So far, I have tried to elaborate the epidemiological approach to include affective systems as crucial forces in cultural transmission. Affective systems provide a rich source of likely human universals, and there is considerable evidence that affective systems contribute to greater retention. We can combine these two facts to generate a fairly interesting prediction: cultural items that are likely to elicit a basic emotion will be more culturally fit than cultural items that are affectively neutral. This is significant because insofar as there are eliciting conditions for basic emotions that are broadly consistent across cultures, we can expect cultural items that have those features to be better remembered and hence have greater cultural fitness.

5. AFFECT AND THE EPIDEMIOLOGY OF NORMS

Epidemiological theorists note that we need to know features of human psychology to explain cultural transmission. This is as true for norms as it is for religious beliefs or scientific beliefs. That is, if you want to under-

---

greater or lesser retention facilitation than counterintuitive stimuli? The answer to this will have to await further study, but something perhaps even more important does not need to await further study—it stand the cultural transmission of norms, the epidemiological approach suggests that you need to know some general features of human psychology. In the preceding section, I tried to make the case that affect is an important factor in the transmission of cultural items, and this will certainly apply to the transmission of norms. Indeed, affect might be especially important to the transmission of norms. I will argue that norms that are connected to affect in a certain way enjoy an edge in cultural fitness in virtue of their Affective Resonance.

The first thing to note is that the retention benefit afforded by affect will apply to norms as it does to other cultural items. Normative claims that are "affect-backed," that prohibit an action that is emotionally upsetting, will be better remembered than non-affect-backed normative claims.[4] Thus, if more memorable representations have greater cultural fitness, then affectively salient norms will plausibly accrue this advantage just as much as affectively salient stories.

There is reason to think that the viability of norms would be especially strongly influenced by affective systems, because a norm would plausibly gain cultural sway if, for instance, it prohibited an action that elicits negative affect. That is, a norm prohibiting an action that is likely to elicit negative affect would presumably have enhanced cultural fitness because the proscribed action is already regarded as unpleasant. In fact, the evidence on disgust norms recounted in chapter 1 lends credence to the claim that norms prohibiting actions that elicit negative affect are regarded as especially important. To recap that evidence, affectively neutral normative violations (e.g., a dinner guest drinks tomato soup out of a bowl) were pitted against affectively charged normative violations (e.g., a dinner guest spits into a water glass before drinking from it) (Nichols 2002b). Subjects rated the affectively charged, "disgust-backed," violations as much worse than the neutral violations. Subjects also were more likely to say that the disgust-backed violations would be wrong even if the host had said that it was okay. Furthermore, subjects with low disgust sensitivity judged a disgusting violation as less serious than subjects with high disgust sensitivity. Low disgust subjects were also more likely to say that the disgusting violation would not be wrong if the host had said it was okay. The evidence thus suggests that affect makes a significant

---

seems likely that counterintuitive items that are emotionally valenced will be more successful than counterintuitive items that are affectively flat. And this might be important to evaluating the transmission of, inter alia, religious ideas.

4. The norms I will focus on here are norms associated with negative emotion, and the affect-memory research has also focused on negative affect. So, a more careful way to frame this would be to say that negative-affect-backed norms will have an edge in cultural fitness. But the terminology is already so awkward that I have opted for the less precise locution.

contribution to the salience of norms. Disgust-backed violations are treated as more serious and authority independent. And this seems to be partly a function of the level of disgust sensitivity.

So affect-backed norms are regarded as more serious and important than affectively neutral norms. And the evidence on affect and memory suggests that affect-backed norms will be easier to recall than non-affect-backed norms. This provides ample reason to expect that affect facilitates transmission of norms, and that, in particular, norms prohibiting actions likely to elicit negative affect will have enhanced fitness. We might now frame this as an "Affective Resonance" hypothesis:

> A. Normative prohibitions against action X will be more likely to survive if action X elicits (or is easily led to elicit) negative affect.

It is important to be clear that the hypothesis is not that *only* affect-backed norms are culturally fit. No doubt societal factors play an enormous role in determining which norms survive, and it is possible that biological factors play an important role as well (e.g., Durham 1991). My claim is only that by virtue of the connection to affect, affect-backed norms have a survival advantage over non-affect-backed norms.

6. NORMS: A HISTORICAL APPROACH

Although I have argued that affect-backed norms should have a survival advantage over affectively neutral norms, I have not actually provided any evidence that helps to confirm that affect-backed norms in fact do survive better than affectively neutral norms. One might worry that there are lots of other features of normative transmission, like the processes that send norms to fixation in an individual, and these other features might subvert any alleged survival advantage for affect-backed norms. So it is important to have some kind of confirmation that affect-backed norms have fared better than affectively neutral norms. I aim to provide a bit of evidence along these lines in what follows. Although the norms that are of particular philosophical interest are the moral norms, I will not focus on moral norms. Jerry Fodor once remarked that if one is interested in sorting out whether nonbasic sciences can be reduced to physics, one should not use psychology as the focal nonbasic science, because there are lots of other problems facing psychology. Rather, Fodor proposes that one should approach reductionism by considering nonbasic sciences that do not suffer the extra problems of psychology, for example, geology. A similar lesson applies in the present context. Moral norms are contentious on multiple fronts. So if we want to understand how norms are transmitted in a culture, it will be best to explore first the transmission of less controversial norms. I will focus on norms governing manners in our culture.

The hypothesis that I will promote is that affect-backed manners norms enjoy greater cultural fitness than affectively neutral manners norms. To evaluate this hypothesis, we need first to know what the manners norms were—that is, we need a list of norms from our culture's past. As these things go, we happen to be in a surprisingly good evidentiary situation. The closest thing we have to primary sources on past norms are etiquette manuals, and the history of etiquette manuals in the West is rich and long. The genre really began to flourish in the fifteenth and sixteenth centuries, shortly after the introduction of the printing press. Indeed, one of the first books to be published in English was an etiquette manual, Caxton's fifteenth-century *The Boke of Curtesye*. These documents reveal the culture's norms from the perspectives of people within the culture itself, rather than through the distorting telescope of historical hindsight. There are, of course, lots of problems with using etiquette manuals. To list a few of these worries: Are the books really representative of the prevailing norms? To what extent are they written to instill new norms rather than reflect prevailing norms? What audience are the books written for? Did the authors have other agendas in mind that corrupt their presentation? It would be much better to bring sixteenth-century Europeans into the lab. Nonetheless, by the standards that apply to historical evidence, the etiquette manuals constitute a fantastically rich vein of information. We are extremely fortunate to have such a detailed historical record in our own cultural heritage, and they provide us with the best window on past manners we could reasonably hope to have.

The twentieth-century tour guide for European etiquette manuals is Norbert Elias, whose work, *The Civilizing Process* provides the best known treatment of the materials (Elias [1939] 2000). Perhaps the most celebrated feature of Elias's account is his claim that people's sense of disgust actually becomes more refined as the culture develops a more refined sense of manners. He maintains that with the rise of the modern state, societal pressures shaped our emotions, and he uses excerpts from the manners books to argue for this thesis. He explains his use of these excerpts as follows: "Images must be placed together in a series to give an overall view . . . of the process: the gradual transformation of behaviour and the emotions, the *expanding threshold of repugnance*" (Elias [1939] 2000, 71, emphasis added; see also 98).

Elias builds his case by tracing the prohibitions in manners books from the Middle Ages to the present. He considers several different areas, including bodily functions, nose blowing, and spitting. The pattern he sets out can be elucidated by focusing on any of these domains. I have opted for spitting. To illustrate the changes in the norms surrounding spitting, Elias digs out gems like the following from medieval etiquette verse: "Do not spit across the table in the manner of hunters" (130); "Do not spit into the basin when you wash your hands, but beside it" (129). With Erasmus's etiquette book, *On Good Manners for Boys* (1530), we get a slightly more refined set of admonitions: "Turn away when spitting, lest your saliva fall on someone. If anything purulent falls on the ground, it should be trodden upon, lest it nauseate someone" (Elias [1939] 2000, 130). Elias reports the following elaboration on this norm from a 1714 manual on civility: "Do not spit so far that you have to look for the saliva to put your foot on it" (131). But, according to Elias, already in the seventeenth century, the norms against spitting are showing signs of much greater restrictions. He writes that the next step in the development of spitting norms is exhibited by Courtin in 1672, who wrote: "Formerly . . . it was permitted to spit on the ground before people of rank, and was sufficient to put one's foot on the sputum. Today that is an indecency" (130). The emerging norm was to spit into a handkerchief, as expressed in a 1729 manual: "When you are with well-born people, and when you are in places that are kept clean, it is polite to spit into your handkerchief while turning slightly aside" (131). Within another 150 years, spitting is more roundly rejected. Elias quotes from a nineteenth century English etiquette manual that briefly advises, "Spitting is at all times a disgusting habit. I need say nothing more than—never indulge in it" (132).

Elias's agenda, as noted, is to argue that societal pressures force us to have a lower threshold of repugnance. It is possible that this is so. However, for present purposes, I am interested in drawing a less theoretically burdened lesson from Elias's review. His review suggests the following descriptive claims. First, many activities that are likely to elicit disgust and that are now regarded as counternormative in our culture (e.g., spitting beside the basin, spitting into a handkerchief, blowing the nose with two fingers) were once regarded as permissible in the culture. This, of course, fits with broader anthropological findings of cultural differences in etiquette norms. More interestingly, Elias's review suggests that when disgust-backed norms became part of the culture's manners, those norms were, by and large, preserved. That is, at least in our culture, normative prohibitions against disgusting actions typically did not go away. Elias reports no cases in which disgusting prohibitions are repealed. Rather, new prohibitions against disgusting actions were introduced, and those prohibitions were then preserved in the culture.

This trend depicted by Elias fits the hypothesis I'm urging, namely, that disgust-norms will fare well because affect facilitates transmission. But one might worry that my attempt to exploit Elias's review for my hypothesis is thwarted by Elias's own interpretation of the pattern. For when Elias claims that social pressures expand the threshold of disgust, what he is saying, effectively, is that the norms come first and the emotions are then shaped by the norms. What I want to claim is that the norms succeed in part because of the emotions that are already in place.[5]

If emotional responses were entirely malleable, then Elias's review probably cannot support the hypothesis I am pushing. But there is no reason to think that emotions are that malleable. Even if Elias is right that the social pressures expand the threshold of disgust, it is likely that a crucial feature here is that the disgust mechanism is at least predisposed to find saliva and mucous objectionable. That is, we come prepared to be disgusted by certain things and not others (cf. Seligman 1971; Garcia 1990). As noted earlier, disgust is a basic emotion (Ekman 1994; Izard 1991; Rozin, Haidt, and McCauley 2000, 638–69), and by common consensus, body products are at the core of the eliciting conditions for disgust (Rozin, Haidt, and McCauley 2000, 647). Indeed, Haidt and colleagues maintain that it is useful to distinguish "core disgust," which is elicited by body products, food, and animals (especially animals associated with body products or spoiled food) (Haidt, McCauley, and Rozin 1994). Similarly, Rozin and colleagues write that "Body products are usually a focus of disgust . . . There is widespread historical and cultural evidence for aversion to virtually all body products, including feces, vomit, urine, and blood" (Rozin, Haidt, McCauley 2000, 640). For present purposes, then, it will be safest to focus on core disgust, and even somewhat more conservatively, on body products as the important elicitor category for core disgust. Given this more conservative notion of disgust, we can now formulate a sharper instance of the Affective Resonance hypothesis to suit our purpose:

> B. Norms prohibiting "core-disgusting" actions (i.e., actions that are likely to elicit core disgust) will enjoy greater cultural fitness than norms prohibiting actions that are unlikely to elicit core disgust (or other emotions).

Once the hypothesis is thus sharpened, it largely sidesteps the concern over the ductile nature of human emotion. For core disgust is plausibly a basic emotion that has been in the human repertoire for millennia. On this more restricted hypothesis, Elias's review still fits the hypothesis be-

---

5. It is important to note that it is possible to feel disgust for a behavior without regarding the behavior as violating norms. For instance, dissecting pig fetuses in high school biology classes is not counternormative, but many find it quite disgusting.

cause activities like spitting and nose-blowing fit squarely in the elicitor category for core disgust.[6]

7. TESTING THE HYPOTHESIS

In the previous section I suggested that Elias's review of manners fits with our hypothesis. But there is a crucial body of information that Elias's review entirely neglects. What Elias's review fails to do is to compare the norms that survive with the norms that fall into desuetude. In effect, Elias only gives us one dimension, the dimension that traces the manners that survive. At a minimum, to evaluate hypothesis B, one needs to consider another dimension: the norms that do not survive. And hypothesis B generates a clear prediction: if we look to the manners books from our cultural past, we should find that the norms prohibiting core-disgusting actions are more likely than the non-affect-backed norms to be part of contemporary manners in our culture.

To join this task in a systematic fashion, one needs to examine closely the manners at some particular juncture in our culture's past, and because our primary data are etiquette manuals, this means focusing on some particular manners book. Thus, the first question to answer is which manners book to use. I used a simple method—I chose what is likely the most important manners book in history: Erasmus's *On Good Manners for Boys*. This text was enormously popular and influential. There were 130 editions of the book. It was first published in Latin (1530), but was quickly translated into English (1532), and shortly thereafter into French, German, and Czech. Erasmus's treatise also exerted a huge influence over later etiquette manuals, many of which simply lifted large portions of Erasmus's text. In addition to its enormous influence, this book was one of the first manners books in this tradition to be aimed at the general population rather than the members of the court. Finally, this text occupies the central place in Elias's review. Elias treats Erasmus's treatise as the pivotal work in beginning the "civilizing process" (Elias [1939] 2000, 47ff.). So Erasmus provides an excellent place to join the project.

In fact, Erasmus's book looks to me to be a remarkable miscellany that includes prohibitions that seem completely arbitrary and prohibitions

---

6. Another prediction that flows from this hypothesis is that norms that restrict behavior likely to elicit core disgust, like natural functions, should be cross-culturally common. And, indeed, these kinds of norms are apparently quite common. In his famous "partial list" of human universals, Murdoch includes "modesty concerning natural functions" (Murdock 1945, 124).

of things too obviously repulsive to need mentioning. But I do not expect that my intuitions about this are sufficient to support the theoretical conclusions. After all, I had a clear agenda in mind when I read over Erasmus's text—I hoped to find that the text confirmed my hypothesis. As a result, I tried to develop this into something a little more methodologically reputable. Independent coders who were blind to the hypothesis evaluated large portions of Erasmus text, and the results of the coding were analyzed. It is important to be clear about the methods here, so I want to supply some of the details in what follows (see also Nichols 2002c).

On Good Manners for Boys includes hundreds of normative proclamations, but to explore the issue of interest, it suffices to look at a representative sample. The goal is to explore whether prohibitions against core disgusting actions are more likely to survive than other manners-norms. So I sought out items that were plausibly connected to core disgust and included those items and the surrounding items as well. Prohibitions against core-disgusting actions appear in several places in *On Good Manners*. To help ensure representative samples, where possible complete entries for given areas were used.

There remains the difficult issue of how to individuate the norms. Relying on etiquette books provides us with a means of individuating norms that is at least relatively unbiased. For Erasmus basically presents the norms as a list, and we can simply adopt his listing procedure. This is exactly what was done, using the items verbatim from the English translation, as far as possible.

There were two coding processes. One coder determined which items forbid something likely to elicit "core disgust," which items permitted something likely to elicit core disgust, and which items did not involve anything likely to elicit core disgust. The coder was instructed that core disgust was elicited by body products including especially bodily fluids. Two other coders independently judged whether the normative claim fit or did not fit with contemporary manners.[7] For items that did not fit with contemporary manners, the coders had to note whether contemporary manners is neutral about the action or forbids the action.

For a handful of the items coded as likely to elicit core disgust, Erasmus maintains that the action is permissible. The following are the items that fit this category:

> It is permissible to clear your nose with two fingers, so long as you immediately ground under foot any matter that falls on the ground.

---

7. Interrater agreement on whether the items were part of contemporary manners was high.

TABLE 6.1

	Not part of contemporary manners	Part of contemporary manners
Action likely to elicit core disgust	1	12
Action not likely to elicit core disgust	32	12

It is permissible to spit disgusting material onto the ground, so long as it is ground under foot.

If it is impermissible to ground spit under foot, catch up the spittle with a cloth.

There are some who lay down the rule that a boy should refrain from breaking wind by constricting his buttocks. But this is no part of good manners. If you may withdraw, do so in private. But if not, then in the words of the old adage, let him cover the sound with a cough.

The manners-coders maintained that all four of these items are prohibited by contemporary manners. But what we really need to consult are the prohibitions in Erasmus's list.

To see the relation of most interest for evaluating our hypothesis, it will be helpful to consult a table of the raw numbers (table 6.1). What we want to know is whether the sixteenth-century norms prohibiting core-disgusting actions are more likely to be part of contemporary manners than the sixteenth-century norms prohibiting actions unlikely to elicit core disgust. Prohibitions against core-disgusting actions were indeed more likely to survive than prohibitions against actions that are not core-disgusting.[8] (See figure 6.1.)

The findings thus confirm the hypothesis. Sixteenth-century norms prohibiting core-disgusting actions are significantly more likely to be part of contemporary manners than sixteenth-century norms that prohibit ac-

8. When I present this material, I am often asked which of Erasmus's prohibitions against a disgusting transgression was regarded as acceptable now. The item is the following: "Some have the distressing habit of coughing slightly while speaking, not through need but through habit." The disgust-coder rated this as connected to core disgust, but the manners-coders regarded this as not prohibited by contemporary manners. I think that one might dispute whether the item really involves core disgust, but it's bad form to argue with your independent coders.

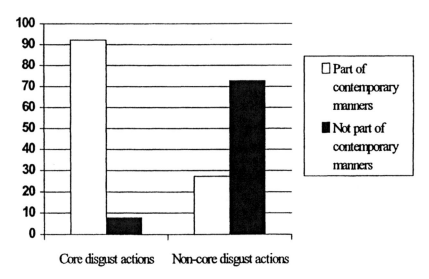

FIGURE 6.1

tions unlikely to elicit core disgust. To underscore the nature of the findings, let me add some more anecdotal remarks on Erasmus's treatise. As the coders bore out, several of the items from Erasmus now seem simply arbitrary or even run against contemporary etiquette:

> The person who opens his mouth wide in a rictus, with wrinkled cheeks and exposed teeth, is . . . impolite. (276)

> When sitting down [at a banquet] have both hands on the table, not clasped together, nor on the plate. (281)

> If given a napkin, put it over either the left shoulder or the left forearm. (281)

On the other hand, many of the claims that prohibit core disgust actions are now so deeply entrenched that they seem too obvious to mention. Consider, for example, the following:

> It is boorish to wipe one's nose on one's cap or clothing, and it is not much better to wipe it with one's hand, if you then smear the discharge on your clothing. (274)

> Withdraw when you are going to vomit. (276)

Reswallowing spittle is uncouth as is the practice we observe in some people of spitting after every third word. (276)

To repress the need to urinate is injurious to health; but propriety requires it to be done in private. (277)

While the norms prohibiting core-disgusting actions have sustained their normative strength, the non-core-disgust norms have often simply disappeared from the culture. Of course, it is also the case that some of the etiquette rules that have prevailed have nothing to do with core disgust or with any other emotion. For instance, Erasmus tells us that: "The cup and small eating knife, duly cleaned, should be on the right-hand side" (281). This remains part of our tradition of etiquette today. But this in no way threatens our hypothesis, which is probabilistic, not categorical: norms prohibiting actions that elicit negative emotions are more likely to survive than affectively neutral norms.[9] The evidence from Erasmus looks to provide impressive confirmation for this hypothesis.

Although I have focused on Erasmus's text for systematic evaluation, similar trends are apparent in etiquette books that were not influenced by Erasmus. For instance, in John Russell's *The Boke of Nurture* (1460), the table settings (which are typically clear cases of manners norms that do not connect with core disgust) differ significantly from contemporary settings (e.g., lines 200–212). The text also offers the following variegated set of prohibitions in quick succession: "wrye not youre nek a doyle as hit were a dawe; put not youre handes in youre hosen youre codware for to clawe.... with youre eris pike not/ ner be ye slow of herynge/ reche / ne spitt to ferre / ne haue lowd laughynge" (lines 285–86, 289–90). That is: do not twist your neck, do not claw at your crotch, do not pick your ears, do not be slow to hear, do not retch, do not spit too far, do not laugh loudly. Contemporary manners is rather tolerant of twisting one's neck, being slow to hear, and laughing loudly. But contemporary manners continues to frown upon groping at one's crotch, ear picking, retching, and projectile spitting.[10]

---

9. The probabilistic nature of the hypothesis can also accommodate the fact that sometimes we develop norms that run against our emotions. Perhaps it is worth noting as well that we need not deny that Elias's civilizing process plays a role in the relationship between the norms and the emotions. In the case of manners, it is possible that there are rich feedback loops between disgust and etiquette judgments. That is, I have argued that manners norms that easily recruit disgust responses are more likely to survive; but it may also be the case that the culture's norms partially tune the actual disgust responses of the individual.

10. See also the medieval Italian and German etiquette verse collected in Furnivall (1869), especially da Riva, Barbarino, and the summary of rules from Thomasin's *The Italian Guest* (Furnivall 1869, II, 113–7).

8. IMPLICATIONS

I have argued that a central chunk of our manners norms seems to be preserved partly because the norms are connected to core disgust. This argument was intended to help confirm the hypothesis that norms gain greater cultural fitness when they prohibit actions that are likely to elicit negative affect. The line of argument I have been pushing has primarily been an attempt to contribute to our understanding of the genealogy of norms. However, the apparent role of emotion in the genealogy of norms also signals some broad implications for work in cultural evolution. In sections 4 and 5, I argued that mental representations that are affectively salient would enjoy enhanced cultural fitness. This claim is reinforced by the historical evidence on etiquette norms. Emotion systems seem to play a powerful role in securing which mental representations survive in a culture. As a result, epidemiological theorists would do well to pay greater attention to the role of emotion in cultural transmission. For instance, some of the most interesting work in the epidemiological tradition has focused on the cultural transmission of religious representations (Boyer 1994, 2000). But given the potential significance of affect for cultural transmission, a deeper understanding of the transmission of religious representations requires charting the role of affect in preserving religious representations. For, like etiquette norms, religious norms and beliefs plausibly gain in cultural fitness as a function of being connected to affective systems.

The role of emotion in cultural transmission also has a rather different implication for epidemiological theorists. In keeping with the orientation of earlier work in the epidemiological tradition, I have focused on apparently universal features of human affective systems. However, some theorists maintain that there is considerable cross-cultural variation in emotion systems. For example, in some cultures anger seems to be elicited and displayed in different ways than in other cultures (see Mallon and Stich 2000 for a useful discussion). If there are such systematic cross-cultural differences, they might help epidemiologists explain why some norms and ideas are more likely to survive in some cultures than in others. In any case, epidemiological approaches to cultural evolution will need to be sensitive to such potential systematic differences in the affective repertoire of people in different cultures.

Of course, these implications for the epidemiological approach are only crudely sketched. The actual deployment of epidemiological accounts requires careful attention to both the empirical details of emotion systems and the historical patterns of cultural representations. But the available historical and empirical evidence certainly indicates that the emotions played a significant historical role in determining which norms survived into the present, and this evidence also suggests that an adequate naturalistic account of cultural evolution must begin to accommodate the role of affect in cultural transmission.

Closer to our present interests, the Affective Resonance account developed in this chapter begins to address the coordination problem that was broached at the end of chapter 5. As moral philosophers in the Humean tradition are fond of pointing out, it is a striking fact that our norms are often closely coordinated with our emotions. Why is it that the norms we happen to have are so closely tied to the emotions we have? On the Sentimental Rules account of moral judgment, there is an important sense in which the norms are only contingently connected to the emotions. Although emotions affect the processing of norms, the Sentimental Rules account does not explain why the norms we happen to have are connected to the emotions we happen to have. This leaves the Sentimental Rules account without an adequate answer to the coordination problem. Philosophical sentimentalists, on the other hand, explain the connection between norms and emotions by maintaining that emotions are implicated in the very semantics of normative terms. As a result, philosophical sentimentalists have a direct and thoroughgoing explanation for the fact that our moral norms are so closely coordinated with our emotions. The coordination is an obvious consequence of the semantics of moral terms.

The naturalistic genealogical approach I have taken in this chapter offers a radically different explanation of the striking fact that so many of our norms are closely coordinated with our emotions. At least part of the reason our norms are connected with our emotions is that affect-backed norms have greater cultural fitness and hence are more likely to persevere. Norms with Affective Resonance are more likely to survive than norms that fail to engage our affective responses. Thus, our norms are plausibly connected to our emotions not through semantics, but through history. Our emotions played a historical role in determining which norms survived into the present.

9. CONCLUSION

The goal of this chapter was to get some purchase on the genealogy of norms. One promising way to investigate the genealogy of norms is by considering not the origin of norms, but rather, what makes certain norms more likely to prevail. Emotional responses, I argued, constitute one important set of mechanisms that affects the cultural viability of norms. Norms are more likely to be preserved in the culture if the norms resonate with our affective systems by prohibiting actions that are likely to elicit negative affect. The claim that norms with such Affective Resonance will enjoy cultural success gains support, I have argued, from the history of etiquette norms in the West. Norms prohibiting disgusting actions seem to have thrived in our culture, whereas affect-neutral norms have proved much more feeble.

7

Moral Evolution

> The object is to explore the huge, distant and thoroughly hidden country of morality, morality as it has actually existed and actually been lived, with new questions in mind and with fresh eyes.
>
> —Friedrich Nietzsche, Preface to *The Genealogy of Morals*

1. INTRODUCTION

The evolution of norms prohibiting disgusting actions carries at least a vulgar sort of interest. But our primary interest here is in the moral norms, and in this chapter, I will turn to harm norms, that is, norms against causing pain and suffering in others. First, I will set out a range of facts that need to be captured by a genealogy of harm norms. This will require a review of some basic claims in anthropology and social history. What needs to be explained are the broad similarities and differences in harm norms across cultures, and the characteristic evolution of harm norms. I will consider the most prominent explanation of these patterns—the appeal to moral progress. Then I will propose an alternative account of the genealogy of norms that draws on the Affective Resonance approach developed in the preceding chapter. Finally, I will compare this account more explicitly with the moral progress view.

2. HARM NORMS: VARIATIONS ON A THEME

Before we try to determine the best explanation of the basic historical and cultural patterns in harm norms, it will be important to get a richer description of these basic patterns. As in the first chapter, by "harm norms," I mean norms prohibiting actions that cause pain and suffering. An adequate account of the genealogy of harm norms needs to accommodate the ubiquity of harm norms, the cross-cultural variation of such norms, and the characteristic development of harm norms. So I will give a brief description here of each of these explananda.

2.1. Ubiquity of Harm Norms

In one sense, harm norms show robust cross-cultural consistency. Nearly all cultures that have been studied by anthropologists have been found to have norms prohibiting a range of harmful actions (e.g., Westermarck 1906–8; Murdock 1945; Kluckhorn 1953). More recent work in cross-cultural psychology has confirmed this (e.g., Haidt, Koller, and Dias 1993; Miller [in press]). Some anthropologists suggest that there are cultures in which harm norms are absent, for example, the Dobu (Benedict 1934) and the Ik (Turnbull 1972). These claims are often regarded with suspicion (e.g., Heine 1985), but even if it is true that the Ik and the Dobu lack harm norms, these count as striking exceptions to a rather profoundly confirmed trend that virtually all the cultures that have been studied clearly have harm norms. The alleged exceptions should not be taken to undermine the manifest truth that harm norms are effectively ubiquitous.

2.2. Variation in Harm Norms

Despite the ubiquity of harm norms, it is a mistake to assimilate all basic harm norms into a homogeneous paste. Anthropologists like to regale us with stories of the astonishingly alien norms and practices found in other cultures. Indeed, claims of cross-cultural variation in harm norms have been rife in anthropology since the nineteenth century. One of the best known examples in philosophy comes from Richard Brandt. Brandt found that the Hopi thought it was morally permissible for children to capture birds, tie them up, play with them roughly, and let them starve to death. According to Brandt (1954), the Hopi believed that the bird felt pain, but still did not regard the treatment as seriously wrong (213–15). The history of the Aztecs provides an even more disturbing picture. According to de Sahagun's sixteenth-century account, the Aztecs ritually killed and cannibalized huge numbers of slaves and prisoners taken in battle, including children. De Sahagun [1578–79] (1981) reports that the victims were often tortured in unspeakably gruesome ways before they were killed, and this was done as part of a public celebration. Perhaps the most compelling illustration of differences in harm norms comes from the treatment of women in other cultures. Chagnon (1992) maintains that the Yanomamö routinely beat their wives, often to display their fierceness to other men in the group (17). The Yanomamö also try to abduct women when raiding enemy villages. According to Chagnon, "A captured woman is raped by all the men in the raiding party and, later, by the men in the village who wish to do so but did not participate in the raid. She is then given to one of the men as a wife" (190). Of course, in our own culture, we regard it as impermissible to torture birds, prisoners, and every other sentient being. We also regard rape and abduction as impermissible regardless of whether the woman is part of an enemy group.

Many of the cross-cultural differences in harm norms can be attributed to differences in who is regarded as part of the moral community. Allegedly, in many tribal cultures, only people in the tribe count as part of the moral community (e.g., Benedict 1934; Edel and Edel 1968). However, there is another dimension on which harm norms vary. Some harms to members of the moral community are regarded as acceptable in some cultures and unacceptable in others. This is nicely illustrated by looking, not to anthropology, but to social history. In eighteenth-century England, flogging school children (and even college students) was regarded as acceptable (e.g., Scott 1959). In late twentieth-century England, however, such punishment was roundly rejected. It was outlawed in 1986, though it was little practiced for many years before that. The culture of eighteenth-century England knew, of course, that flogging hurt the child, but they viewed these harms as acceptable. The English culture of today regards these kinds of harms as intolerable.

2.3. Characteristic Evolution of Harm Norms

It has become a commonplace in discussions of moral evolution that, in the long run, moral norms exhibit a characteristic pattern of development. The familiar account is that harm norms tend to evolve from being restricted to a small group of individuals to encompassing an increasingly larger group. That is, the moral community expands. The trend is bumpy and irregular, but this kind of characteristic normative evolution is affirmed by a fairly wide range of contemporary moral philosophers, including Peter Singer (1981), Peter Railton (1986), Thomas Nagel (1986, 148), David Brink (1989, 208–9), and Michael Smith (1994, 188). As far as I know, there has not been a systematic cross-cultural study of normative evolution that confirms this. But I suspect that the pattern is real. It is manifestly the case in our own culture that the moral community has shown this kind of development. Perhaps the most extensive record comes from Western European culture since the Middle Ages. In this case, we have a dramatic picture of the development of increasingly inclusive moral norms. Indeed, this is regarded as one of the hallmarks of the Enlightenment. Over the last several hundred years, Western culture has shown increasing prohibitions of violence in general (e.g., McLynn 1991, 297). The particular character of this evolution is richly illuminated by work in social history (e.g., Thomas 1983; Spierenburg 1991; Dulman 1990; Weisser 1979). It is worth recounting part of this social history in some detail to give a richer idea of the actual changes. I want to focus on two points. First, in European culture the prohibition against harming others seems to have been expanded to prohibit cruelty to animals. Second, harsh corporal punishment has declined sharply since the Middle Ages. I choose these cases for a couple of reasons. First, the examples are at a greater historical remove than issues about, say, civil rights, and this makes the issues somewhat easier to discuss dispassionately. The second reason I choose these cases is more opportunistic—these topics have received excellent scholarship in social history.

CRUELTY TO ANIMALS. General disapproval of cruelty to animals has become increasingly entrenched in Western society since the seventeenth-century. In Keith Thomas's (1983) magnificent *Man and the Natural World,* he describes the growing opposition in England to needless killing and cruelty to animals. In the seventeenth-century, blood sports like cock-fighting were popular, as was the practice of bear baiting, in which dogs were set on a bear that was tied to a post. Thomas maintains that "In the case of animals what was normally displayed in the early modern period was the cruelty of indifference. For most persons, the beasts were outside the terms of moral reference" (Thomas 1983, 148). Gradually, English society, and Western culture more broadly, expanded the moral community to include animals as moral patients.

Perhaps the simplest way to trace this change is by looking to legislative records. No European country had any laws protecting animals before the nineteenth century (Maehle 1994, 95). But the first half of the nineteenth century saw several prominent developments:

> In the 1820s and 1830s the first important animal protection societies were founded. In 1824 the Society for the Prevention of Cruelty to Animals was established in London. . . . The successes of the humane movement in Britain are well known: after the Act of 1822 to "Prevent cruel and improper treatment of cattle," in 1835 a Cruelty to Animals Act established the illegality of blood sports involving the baiting of animals, the keeping of cock-pits and of places for dog-fights. Cock-fighting as such was prohibited by an Act of 1849 'for the more effectual Prevention of Cruelty to Animals.' . . . In 1876 Britain enacted the world's first law regulating experiments on living animals. (Maehle 1994, 100)

The nineteenth century also saw the emergence of animal protection laws in Europe more widely (Maehle 1994, 100).

One of the striking features of this history is that it makes clear that it is naïve and simplistic to assume that there is a single origin story for norms prohibiting cruelty to animals. In some cases, the norm against cruelty to animals seems to have emerged out of a concern about how such cruelty might also foment cruelty towards people (Thomas 1983, 150–51). This view has a precedent in Biblical sources. Opposition to cruelty to animals was also based on a rather different appeal to theological considerations. Cruelty was regarded as "an insult to God, a kind of blasphemy against his creation" (Thomas 1983, 156, 162). Among Puritans, cruel animal sports were opposed partly because of their connection with gambling and disorder (Thomas 1983, 158). In his *History of England,* Thomas Macaulay quipped that Puritans denounced bear baiting not because of the suffering it caused the animal, but because of the pleasure it gave to the observers (Thomas 1983, 158). Of course, another basis for opposition to animal cruelty came from people's own emotional reactions to the suffering of animals (Thomas 1983, 177). In some of these cases, the anticruelty norm was promoted by pet owners, who seem to have developed heightened sensitivity to the plight of animals (Thomas 1983, 119–20; see also Serpell and Paul 1994). This serves to reinforce worries about trying to find *the* origin of harm norms. For in the case of norms against harming animals, there is no single origin. We might then, be leery of undertaking to find *the* origin of norms against harming people.

CORPORAL PUNISHMENT. The other example that I'd like to give in some detail focuses on the growing rejection of graphically violent forms of punishment. The first thing to note is that in the Middle Ages, there simply *was* more violence in everyday life and people were more tolerant of violence. In Europe before the sixteenth century, people brooked physical aggression and the infliction of pain to a much greater extent than we do in contemporary society. There were also fewer legal measures restricting violence, and even minor insults would often provoke a violent response (Spierenburg 1991, 195; see also Halsall 1998). In light of this tolerance for violence, it is less difficult to comprehend the tolerance for severe corporal punishments.

In the late Middle Ages, a range of what now seem appalling punishments were available, including maiming, blinding, and branding. This is reflected in the German Empire's *Constitutio Criminalis Carolina* of 1532. This statute describes the punishments to be meted out for various offenses. Among other things, the statute gives guidelines for sentencing. Here is one example: "When . . . it is decided that the condemned person should be torn with glowing tongs before the execution, the following words shall in addition stand in the judgment, viz.: 'And he shall in addition before the final execution be publicly driven around upon a wagon up to the place of execution, and the body torn with glowing tongs, specifically with N. strokes'" (Langbein 1974, 303).

Severe corporal punishments, like maiming, began to recede in the early modern period. By the sixteenth century in Germany, blinding was rare. Cutting off of hands was more frequent, but it too was on the wane in the sixteenth century (Dulman 1990, 47–48). Spierenburg summarizes the trend: "An unambiguous development consisted in the disappearance of visible mutilation. Some corporal penalties which have become horrible to us, such as blinding and cutting off hands or ears, were no longer practiced. This development took place throughout Western Europe, although at different points in time. In Amsterdam such punishments were applied in the first half of the seventeenth century at the latest" (Spierenburg 1991, 211; see also Emsley 1987, 202; Langbein 1977, 27–28). Flogging continued to be a prominent punishment throughout the eighteenth century (e.g., Dulman 1990, 49; McLynn 1991), but of course, flogging has now largely disappeared from the European catalog of punishments.

Just as severe corporal punishments were on the wane, there were successful movements to abolish judicial torture in several European countries in the eighteenth and early nineteenth centuries (e.g., Peters 1985).[1] Executions were also becoming increasingly less common in the Netherlands (Spierenburg 1991, 212) and England (Emsley 1987, 201). More generally, there has been a decline in capital punishment in European countries since the 1500s. Where capital punishment survives, it retains none of the corporal abuse that formerly attended it (Foucault 1977, 11–12). This too can be traced through the early modern era. At the close of the Middle Ages, horrifically painful methods of execution, such as breaking on the wheel and burning alive, were in use. Further, executions would sometimes be preceded by additional corporal punishments (e.g., Dulman 1990, 77–79). Gradually the additional punishments and pains were largely eliminated from executions. In the United States, for instance, considerable effort has been expended to make the ultimate penalty relatively painless.

Thus, there are important broad cross-cultural similarities in harm norms. Within our own culture at least, there are also important historical trends

1. In the aftermath of recent terrorist attacks, there has actually been renewed support for torture in the United States (e.g., Dershowitz 2002). Of course, this does not undermine the central claim of interest. We are considering broad historical trends, and those trends will obviously be affected by a number of factors, including religion and perceived threats to the well being of one's community.

in harm norms.[2] We want a genealogical account that can explain such similarities and historical trends as well as the cross-cultural differences in harm norms across cultures. That is, of course, a preposterously ambitious project. My goal here will be to try to provide a partial explanation of the similarities and changes in a way that is fully compatible with the differences. Before I move on to the business of pursuing these goals, I need to make a brief detour to address a worry that the anthropology of ethics provokes almost reflexively for philosophers, the worry over "ultimate ethical disagreement."

3. A BRIEF INTERLUDE ON CROSS-CULTURAL NORMATIVE DISAGREEMENT

Early in the twentieth century, William Sumner (1906) and Edward Westermarck (1906–8) provided lengthy potpourris of anthropological exotica, recording, among other things, the unusual normative lives found in other cultures. Sumner and Westermarck thought that their anthropological reviews constituted evidence for some form of ethical relativism. However, in the wake of these works, scholars expressed skepticism about whether the alleged cultural differences were really differences in the basic norms embraced by the culture. For instance, Sumner relays that the indigenous peoples of Australia are reported to cannibalize their own infants: "Sickly and imperfect children were killed because they would require very great care. The first one was also killed because they thought it immature and not worth preserving. Very generally it was eaten that

---

2. One would like to have cross-cultural evidence of the trends in moral evolution. As far as I can tell, the moral evolution enthusiasts mentioned above (Singer, Railton, Brink, Nagel, and Smith) do not have any evidence to adduce, and neither do I. It is thus a substantive assumption for all of us that, ceteris paribus, other cultures will show similar historical trends in moral evolution.

To be sure, the kind of cross-cultural evidence that would be most useful is not easy to obtain. Ideally, we would like to have evidence on moral evolution in other cultures in the absence of Western influences, or at least in the absence of Western Enlightenment influences. For we want to see whether there is something like convergent moral evolution. For this, we need to look to non-Western civilizations that have an historical record dating back well before Western Enlightenment influences on the culture. China, in fact, provides a promising case. For China had a thriving civilization for many centuries before the Western Enlightenment. In China, blood sports never achieved any prominence as they did in Europe. Neither did the Chinese ever have a tradition of chattel slavery. Hence we cannot look for changes on these dimensions. The Chinese do, of course, have a history of penal practices (as does every civilization), and the record here parallels the kind of evolution we find in the Western penal system. Mutilation, including branding on the forehead, cutting off the feet and cutting off the nose, was a common form of punishment before the Han dynasty (206 BCE—220 CE). But beginning with the Han, mutilation punishments gradually fell into disuse, and they were not reinstated (McKnight 1992, 331). Of course, that is a rather breezy gesture to throw at a vast topic. To explore systematically the cross-cultural similarities and differences in moral evolution would be extremely difficult and extremely valuable.

the mother might recover the strength which she had given to it. If there was an older child, he ate of it, in the belief that he might gain strength" (Sumner 1906, 316). This is indeed a startling accusation to make of another culture—that they eat their young! Even if one accepts that the foreign culture engages in the behavior, what one wants to know is whether such cases reveal genuine normative disagreement between our culture and the culture under anecdote, or whether the exotic customs merely reveal disagreement over some nonmoral facts. The question is whether there is "ultimate" or "fundamental" disagreement about morality, or whether all disagreement can be attributed to disagreement over facts.

This worry over how to interpret the anthropological evidence was pressed in a particularly influential way by Gestalt psychologists like Karl Duncker. Duncker maintained that simply because we find people disagreeing about what the right thing to do is does not mean that the people really disagree about the norms. It might well be that they are interpreting the situation differently. Duncker takes the celebrated example of killing elderly parents as a case in point. "'Killing an aged parent' may, according to circumstances, mean sparing him the miseries of a lingering death or an existence which, as a born warrior, he must feel to be exceedingly dull and unworthy; or it may mean protecting him against injuries from enemies or beasts, or causing him to enter the happy land which is not open save to those who die by violence" (Duncker 1939, 42). Westermarck himself had worried about this issue in the concluding pages of his mammoth *The Origin and Development of the Moral Ideas* (1906–8, II, 745–46). Later in the century, the philosopher Richard Brandt took this problem very seriously. Indeed, these kinds of worries drove Brandt, in one of the more admirable acts of twentieth-century naturalistic philosophy, to embark on his own sustained anthropological project. He studied the Hopi Indians over the course of several years. Brandt wanted, among other things, to see whether there were normative disagreements that were not disagreements about the facts. So, when he discovered that the Hopi thought it was acceptable for children to catch birds and let them starve to death, Brandt proceeded to explore whether perhaps they thought that the birds did not feel pain or that the birds would get some reward in the afterlife. Brandt could find no factual disagreement surrounding this issue, and so he tentatively suggested that this was a case of fundamental ethical disagreement (Brandt 1954, 213–15; 1959, 102–3).

This issue continues to inspire debate. For instance, Richard Boyd maintains that it is "useful to remember the plausibility with which it can be argued that, if there were agreement on all the nonmoral issues (including theological ones), then there would be no moral disagreement"

(Boyd 1988, 213). More recently, Michele Moody-Adams (1997) offers a sustained critique of Brandt and John Doris and Stephen Stich (in press) offer a state-of-the-art defense. My own sympathies lie with Brandt, Doris, and Stich, but fortunately, I do not need to defend fully those sympathies for present purposes. For it is crucial to distinguish between two claims about moral disagreement:

1. All moral disagreements are really disagreements about the nonmoral facts.
2. All moral disagreements are rationally resolvable under ideal conditions (of impartiality, etc.) once the parties agree on the nonmoral facts.

Note that the above quote from Boyd is ambiguous between these two claims. However, virtually all of the recent critical literature on moral disagreement (including Boyd) focuses on the latter claim. The latter claim is the claim that invites difficult and intractable debate. For on the latter claim, one needs to provide reason to affirm or deny that fully informed, fully rational, and fully attentive subjects will converge on their moral views. That claim is, to say the least, hard to test. Even if the ethics review board agreed, the requisite training study is prohibitive. However, for the purposes at hand, what is especially important is to reject (1). For the project here is merely to explain the normative phenomena as we find them, not as they would be under idealized conditions. Because few if any prominent figures in the contemporary debates actually defend (1), the rejection of (1) is not terribly controversial. Again, this is not to say that there wouldn't be convergence were all the participants supremely smart, rational, and knowledgeable. The claim is simply that it is plausible that the work in anthropology and social history reveals some cases of moral disagreement that can't be attributed to disagreement about the nonmoral facts.

4. MORAL EVOLUTION AND MORAL REALISM

Let us now return to the central question of this chapter—how are we to explain the similarities, differences, and characteristic evolution of harm norms? Perhaps the most important answer to this question begins with the last phenomenon—the characteristic evolution of moral norms. As recounted in section 2, the historical trend in our own culture has been towards increasingly inclusive and antiviolent norms. The idea that this pattern counts as a kind of moral progress, is familiar from Enlightenment thinkers (e.g., Condorcet, Voltaire) as well as the chroniclers of the

Enlightenment (e.g., Macauley 1913; Trevelyan 1942). Over the last two decades, a number of prominent moral philosophers have resuscitated this interpretation of the characteristic pattern of moral evolution as a pattern of moral progress (Singer 1981; Nagel 1986, 148; Brink 1989, 208–9; Smith 1994, 188; Sturgeon 1985). What has happened, according to these theorists, is that people have been getting closer and closer to the truth about right and wrong. This view provides an important and powerful explanation of the pattern of moral evolution. Not only does this view promise to explain moral evolution, it also, as we shall see, offers a basic explanation for the ubiquity of harm norms.[3]

In recent years, Nicholas Sturgeon, David Brink, and other self-described "moral realists" have provided the most visible and developed appeal to moral progress (e.g., Brink 1989, Sturgeon 1985).[4] The invocation of moral progress serves, according to these theorists, to support the claim that there are moral facts. Briefly, the idea is that the best explanation of the historical trends is that there are moral facts which people gradually come to recognize. Before we continue, we need to get a clearer picture of this view. First, there is an important terminological issue. The label "moral realism" is used for markedly different positions. In some cases, "moral realism" maintains only that some moral claims are true (e.g., Sayre-McCord 1986, 3). On this construal, moral realism is perfectly consistent with a thoroughgoing relativism, according to which moral claims

3. As noted in chapter 6, evolutionary ethics provides a different approach to explaining why we have harm norms. In the critical literature that has arisen around evolutionary ethics, most of the attention has focused on whether evolutionary ethics can tell us what norms we ought to embrace. There has been considerably less critical attention to the issue of interest here—why we have the norms we do. However, even this part of the evolutionary ethics view has not attracted many followers, and there is at least one prominent opponent. In a widely cited paper, Francisco Ayala explicitly rejects the idea that the specific moral norms we have are evolutionary adaptations. In setting out his objections, he appeals to both the diversity of moral norms and the evolution of moral norms: "[M]oral norms differ from one culture to another and even 'evolve' from one time to another. Many people see nowadays that the Biblical injunction: 'Be fruitful and multiply' has been replaced by a moral imperative to limit the number of one's children. No genetic change in human population accounts for this inversion of moral value" (Ayala 1987, 250). Ayala thus maintains, sensibly, that it is implausible to explain the diversity and evolution of moral norms in terms of genetic changes. By itself, this does not tell us why we should reject the idea that no specific moral norms are adaptations. An advocate of evolutionary ethics might maintain that he only seeks to maintain that ubiquitous moral norms are adaptations. However, one obvious way to fill out Ayala's argument is to note that we need some explanation of the diversity and evolution of moral norms. That explanation will, according to Ayala, appeal to cultural forces (1987, 1995). And we might expect that the cultural explanation of diversity and change will also extend to explain such ubiquity as there is. Hence, at this point, there is no reason to think that the best explanation of the ubiquity of harm norms is that the ubiquitous norms are adaptations.

4. Peter Railton (1986) also draws on moral evolution to defend a kind of moral realism. However, Railton's approach is somewhat different from the approaches offered by Brink and Sturgeon, so I put Railton's account to the side for present purposes. I will address his account in section 6.

are true, but relativized to an individual or a culture (e.g., Benedict 1934). In other places, "moral realism" is used to pick out the view that moral claims are not just true, but that they are true apart from any particular perspective and independent of people's beliefs about right and wrong (e.g., Brink 1989, 20). The appeal to moral progress is typically used in defense of this stronger form of moral realism.[5]

The appeal to moral progress is supposed to support the claim that there are moral facts. Here is how Sturgeon makes the point:

> Do moral features of the action or institution being judged ever play an explanatory role? Here is an example in which they appear to. An interesting historical question is why vigorous and reasonably widespread moral opposition to slavery arose for the first time in the eighteenth and nineteenth centuries, even though slavery was a very old institution; and why this opposition arose primarily in Britain, France, and in French- and English-speaking North America, even though slavery existed throughout the New World. There is a standard answer to this question. It is that chattel slavery in British and French America, and then in the United States, was much *worse* than previous forms of slavery, and much worse than slavery in Latin America. (Sturgeon 1985, 64)

According to Sturgeon, chattel slavery prompted opposition because it was morally worse than previous forms of slavery. In order to explain the historical changes, on his view, we need to appeal to the greater immorality of the new form of slavery. A similar line is pushed by Brink:

> Most people no longer think that slavery, racial discrimination, rape, or child abuse is acceptable. Even those who still engage in these activities typically pay lip service to the wrongness of these activities . . . Cultures or individuals who do not even pay lip service to these moral claims are rare, and we will typically be able to explain their moral beliefs as the product of various religious, ideological, or psychological distorting mechanisms. This will seem especially appropriate here, since the relevant changes in moral consciousness have all been changes in the same direction. That is, with each of these practices, in almost all cases where people's moral attitudes toward the practice have undergone informed and reflective change, they have changed in the same way (with these practices, from approval to disapproval and not the other way

---

5. This description of moral realism is broad enough to include very different forms of moral realism. For instance, a moral realist might maintain that the moral facts are grounded in human capacities and so the facts are species specific. A moral realist might alternatively make the stronger claim that moral facts, like "it is wrong to torture puppies," are entirely independent of human capacities.

around). When changes in moral consciousness exhibit this sort of pattern, this is further reason to view the changes as progress.
(Brink 1989, 208–9)

Brink goes on to say that this kind of moral convergence counts as "(de-feasible) evidence of moral progress" and hence support for moral realism.

Both Brink and Sturgeon acknowledge Slote (1971) as an early exponent of this kind of argument from historical trends to realism about value judgments (Brink 1989, 209; Sturgeon 1985, 255). Slote's argument is actually focused on aesthetic value judgments, but it is instructive to consider his line of argument, because it remains one of the clearest presentations of this argumentative strategy. Slote maintains that there is an intriguing pattern of "unidirectionality" in aesthetic preferences and opinions (Slote 1971, 822, 834n5). For instance, most serious listeners of classical music prefer Mozart to Bruckner. Slote maintains that the best explanation of this pattern is that "the more people study and are exposed to music, the more they like what is good in the field of music and the less they like what is mediocre or bad in the field of music, and that Mozart is, in fact, a greater, a finer, a better composer than Bruckner" (824).

One of the nice features of Slote's presentation is that he makes the argument form wonderfully clear. The argument is a form of inference to the best explanation, and Slote is explicit that the realist explanation of unidirectionality should be accepted if but *only if* it is the best explanation: "When scientists attempt to explain a given fact or phenomenon, they generally consider various possible alternative explanations of the fact or phenomenon, and accept one of these explanations as correct only if it is clearly more reasonable, in terms of certain standards of scientific methodology and according to the available evidence, than any of the alternative explanations that they have been able to think up" (Slote 1971, 823–24). Slote adopts an analogous approach to defending the realist explanation of unidirectionality. He proceeds to consider all the alternative explanations he can think up and he argues that all of the alternatives are inferior to the realist explanation. He thus concludes that aesthetic value judgments are indeed rational judgments about objective qualities in the works.[6]

Now, if we exploit this form in trying to assemble the analogous argument for moral realism, the argument goes something like the following.

---

6. Slote maintains that his argument supports the view that we have the ability "to make rational, reasonable, objective aesthetic value judgment" (Slote 1971, 821). Elsewhere, Slote expresses cautious attraction to moral progress as well (Slote 1982).

One explanation for the evolution of moral norms is that it is *true* that, for example, slavery is morally wrong, and this is something that rationality leads us to recognize. What are the available competing explanations in the moral case? On this point, Brink (1989) and Sturgeon (1985) say little. However, Peter Singer pushes a similar line of argument, and he does offer one alternative to the realist explanation:

> the shift from a point of view that is disinterested between individuals within a group, but not between groups, to a point of view that is fully universal, is a tremendous change—so tremendous, in fact, that it is only just beginning to be accepted on the level of ethical reasoning and is still a long way from acceptance on the level of practice. Nevertheless, it is the direction in which moral thought has been going since ancient times. *Is it an accident of history that this should be so*, or is it the direction in which our capacity to reason leads us? (Singer 1981, 112–13, emphasis added)

Thus, Singer suggests that the pattern of moral evolution is either explained by rational processes or the pattern is an "accident of history." Obviously if those are the choices, the realist story is attractive because it is rather less plausible that the trajectory is purely an historical accident.

The historical accident account of moral evolution scarcely counts as an explanation at all. By contrast, the appeal to moral facts has considerable explanatory power. It can accommodate all three features that we started with. Certain core harm norms are virtually ubiquitous because everyone has figured out this much about morality. The norms evolve in a characteristic way because people tend to get closer to the truth. And there is considerable variation because the process is a difficult one, distorted by self-interest and cultural idiosyncrasies.

Despite its manifest virtues, the appeal to moral progress has been attacked on a number of fronts. In philosophy, one familiar complaint is that it is not clear that the changes in moral attitudes can be attributed to any kind of rational process. Rorty makes this point in a characteristically inflammatory way:

> To get whites to be nicer to blacks, males to females, Serbs to Muslims, or straights to gays . . . it is of no use whatever to say, with Kant: notice what you have in common, your humanity, is more important than these trivial differences. For the people we are trying to convince will rejoin that they notice nothing of the sort. Such people are *morally* offended by the suggestion that they should treat someone who is not kin as if he were a brother, or a nigger as if he were white, or a queer as if he were normal, or an infidel as if she were a believer. (Rorty 1998, 178; emphasis in original)

A rather different critique comes from revisionist historians, who often ridicule appeals to moral progress as Pollyanna and Whiggish. For instance, Foucault (1977) maintains that the decline of harsh corporal punishment had nothing to do with increasing humaneness but only with new and more effective means of state-sponsored oppression (see also Ignatieff 1978). This is not the place to engage the details of such debates. But there is an important sense in which the complaint of Whiggishness is not really fair to the moral progress view. For the moral progress claim appeals to a broad set of changes in norms, over hundreds of years and in many different arenas. It is this broad trend that needs to be explained. It would indeed by striking if the entire truth were to be told by a series of individual revisionist stories. Then the trend would be chalked up to historical accident after all, and that, as noted above, seems highly unlikely. No, if we are to successfully challenge the moral progress account, we need an alternative explanation for the broad trend. Merely finding fault with the moral progress proposal will not suffice. One really needs to develop an alternative. Now, finally, I will turn to that task.

5. AFFECTIVE RESONANCE AND HARM NORMS

In the previous chapter, I argued that a central cluster of our etiquette norms seems to be preserved partly because the norms are connected to core disgust. This argument was intended to help confirm the Affective Resonance account, according to which norms gain greater cultural fitness when they prohibit actions that are likely to elicit negative affect. It will come as no surprise, then, that I will maintain that some of our moral norms, the harm norms, gained an edge in cultural fitness by prohibiting actions that are likely to elicit negative affect.

As we saw in chapter 2, witnessing or learning of suffering in others often excites considerable affective response in humans. This emotional responsiveness to others' suffering emerges early in human development. Indeed, emotional responses to suffering in others seem to be present in infancy, such responses are almost certainly cross-culturally universal, and they exhibit quick onset. Suffering in conspecifics seems to provoke negative affect even in some nonhuman animals (see chapter 2, section 11). Evidently, we come pre-tuned to be upset by the distress signals of others. There are, as discussed in chapter 2, importantly different kinds of affective response to suffering in others. Reactive distress can be triggered by low-level cues of harm (e.g., pained facial expression, audible crying), whereas concern is triggered by (inter alia) knowledge that the target is in pain. Some forms of reactive distress are found in infancy and even concern seems to be present well before the second birthday. By eighteen months or so, children seem to be emotionally sensitive not just to distress cues, but to the knowledge that someone else is in pain.

Although none of the forms of reactive distress or concern appears on standard lists of basic emotions (e.g., Ekman 1992), some of these responses do plausibly have the features that matter for building an epidemiological account—they are universal and have characteristic sets of eliciting conditions. Indeed, some of the eliciting conditions for reactive distress, for example, crying, seem to be hardwired. In addition, like basic emotions, the response to suffering in others seems to be at least largely insensitive to background knowledge. Knowing that inoculations are for the best does not eliminate the discomfort one feels on witnessing a child get inoculated.

In the previous chapter, I argued that norms prohibiting actions that are likely to elicit negative affect, "affect-backed norms," will have an advantage in cultural evolution. In keeping with this, I suggest that our emotional sensitivity to suffering in others helped to secure for harm-norms the central role they occupy in our moral outlook. Suffering in others leads to serious negative affect, so harm norms would prohibit actions that are likely to elicit negative affect. Thus, if affect-backed norms are more culturally fit, the norms against harming others should have increased cultural fitness over norms that are not backed by affective response. That is, harm norms, like norms against disgusting behavior, enjoy Affective Resonance, which enhances their cultural fitness.

The thrust of the preceding is simply that harm norms will have an edge in cultural fitness. Now we need to see whether this can provide insight into the genealogy of morals. The cultural advantage enjoyed by affect-backed norms provides at least part of an explanation for the ubiquity of harm norms. In chapter 6, I reviewed several stories about how harm-norms originated. I maintained that we lack the evidence to determine which of these stories is right, and, moreover, that it is possible that no single origin story is right. The work in social history makes vivid the possibility that norms prohibiting harms actually had multiple different origins. For in the case of the norms prohibiting animal cruelty, it seems that these norms did have multiple different origins (see section 2). Nonetheless, whatever story or stories one prefers about how the harm-norms were generated, the fact that we are emotionally sensitive to others' suffering helps to explain why the harm norms ended up being so successful. For as harm norms entered the culture, their emotional resonance would have contributed to their cultural cachet.

It is worth noting that the above explanation of the ubiquity of harm norms is fully consistent with rich diversity in harm norms. For the claim is simply that harm norms will have enhanced cultural fitness. This allows for considerable normative diversity, because it concedes that cultural processes play a vital role in the development of norms. Because cultural processes implicate a complex and variegated set of forces, it is hardly surprising, on this view, that there is so much diversity in the norms found in different cultures. Indeed, the Affective Resonance approach is even consistent with the radical claims that the Dobu and the Ik lack harm norms altogether. For the account only claims that normative prohibitions that resonate with our emotions will be more likely to survive. The account does not necessitate that the norms will be present.

The appeal to Affective Resonance also provides an explanation for much of the evolution of harm norms. Two central characteristics of the evolution of harm norms might be teased apart. First, as we've seen, harm norms seem to become more inclusive, that is, cultures seem to develop a more inclusive view of the set of individuals whose suffering matters. Second, harm norms come to apply to a wider range of harms among those who are already part of the moral community—that is, there is less tolerance of pain and suffering of others (e.g., Macklin 1999, 251; Railton 1986). Both of these patterns can be explained by the Affective Resonance of harm norms. Because we respond affectively to a wide range of distress cues and even to the knowledge that someone is in pain, the Affective Resonance account obviously explains why new norms prohibiting old harms would have a fitness advantage. In addition, because low-level cues of distress are affectively powerful, we know that the underpinnings of the affective-response to suffering in others is promiscuous. We apparently come pretuned to be emotionally upset by distress cues that are exhibited by all humans, regardless of ethnicity or gender. So harm norms that include more of this group will gain an advantage in cultural evolution.

Indeed, our responses to suffering in others are more promiscuous still. Although there is not much experimental evidence available, it is plausible that we respond to the sufferings of some animals with reactive distress or concern. Some of the cues of suffering in animals are similar to the cues of suffering in humans (e.g., bleeding, convulsing, shrieking), and knowledge that an individual is in pain can provoke concern. As a result, humans are likely predisposed to respond affectively to much animal suffering. There is actually a bit of evidence, from an unlikely source, on (adult) human responses to animal distress. In Milgram's famous obedience studies (Milgram 1963), subjects were told to deliver increasingly severe shocks to a "learner" person, culminating in a switch labeled "450-volt, XXX." Notoriously, in several versions of the experiment, subjects tended to give shocks all the way to the end of the scale (see Milgram 1974). In Milgram's study, the "learner" was actually a confederate, and there was no genuine victim. Critics complained that the absence of a real victim might have contributed to subjects' behavior in the study. In light of this criticism, Sheridan and King (1972), in an experiment which would probably be disallowed by most university ethics boards, replaced the confederate with a real victim—a "cute, fluffy puppy" (1972, 165).[7] Paralleling the Milgram study, the subjects were told to shock the puppy when the puppy failed on a discrimination task. Sheridan and King found that subjects behaved much as they did in several of Milgram's experiments—the majority of subjects gave shocks all the way to the end of the scale. Now, what's of greater interest for us is the incidental responses subjects exhibit. First, in the original Milgram experiments, it is important to note that, although subjects would go to the end of the shock scale, they were *not* happy about this. Subjects who went to the end of the scale were typically an emotional wreck. Something similar was true in the puppy study. Sheridan and King report that the subjects "typically gave many indications of distress while giving shocks to the puppy. These included such things as gesturally coaxing the puppy to escape the shock, pacing from foot to foot, puffing, and even weeping" (1972, 166). This provides some reason to think that we are predisposed to feel serious negative affect in reaction to the distress of nonhuman animals.

Consequently, so long as one remains within the confines of species that are likely to inspire reactive distress or concern (this will probably exclude lots of insects), harm norms that are more inclusive will have a survival advantage over other norms. Thus, the Affective Resonance account seems well suited to explain the evolution of norms against cruelty to animals. These norms plausibly resonated with a preexisting tendency to respond emotionally to the suffering of animals.

The promiscuousness of reactive distress and concern also explains why norms against corporal punishment would have a fitness advantage. Witnessing or hearing about harsh corporal punishments is likely to trigger reactive distress or concern. Indeed, because our immediate responses to another's suffering is largely insulated from background knowledge (see chapter 2), even if one is convinced of a convict's guilt, witnessing severe punishments on that individual is likely to elicit reactive distress or concern. As a result, norms prohibiting those kinds of punishments will gain some fitness advantage.

The preceding remarks indicate that some of the core facts about the genealogy of harm norms fit with the Affective Resonance account. However, as with the case of etiquette norms, it is not really enough just

---

7. Thanks to John Doris for drawing my attention to this study.

to point out that the pattern of evolution fits with the hypothesis. Perhaps moral norms tend to be preserved in all cases. So we need to see whether the moral norms that fall into desuetude tend not to be connected to strong core emotions. Our evidentiary situation here is not nearly so good as in the case of etiquette. Nonetheless, as with etiquette norms, it is plausible that there are lots of "moral" norms that have largely lost their cultural grip.[8] For instance, a few hundred years ago, pride, greed, lust, envy, gluttony, anger, and sloth were all regarded as seriously immoral—the Seven Deadly Sins. Many of these dispositions or tendencies are now regarded largely as peccadilloes and, in some cases (e.g., pride, envy, anger), as barely counternormative. This is supported by a glance at the moral equivalent of etiquette manuals. The tradition of moral manuals was not nearly so rich as that of etiquette manuals. Nor has it received the kind of insightful attention that Elias brought to the etiquette manuals. Nonetheless, we can get some idea of prevailing seventeenth- and eighteenth-century moral norms by looking to these manuals. One manual emerges as particularly widely known and influential: Allestree's *On the Whole Duty of Man* (1684). As a youth, apparently Hume paid close attention to the precepts set out in the manual, though he later would eschew this catalogue of virtues (see MacIntyre 1998, 171; 1984, 231). We find in the *Whole Duty* admonitions against "Being injurious to our neighbor," "Murder, open or secret," "Maiming or hurting the body of our neighbor" (166). These kinds of normative prohibitions are obviously retained in contemporary morality. But the *Whole Duty* also warns against immoral behaviors like "Greedily seeking the praise of other men," "Uncontentedness in our estates," "Eating too much," "Making pleasure, not health, the end of eating," "Being too curious or costly in meats," "Immoderate sleeping" (165–66). Some of these admonitions now strike Western Europeans as at best prudential advice, other items, for example, the puritanical restrictions on cuisine, seem positively quaint. These norms that have fallen away, of course, also have the feature that they prohibit actions that are unlikely to elicit reactive distress or concern (or any other core emotion). Hence, as the Affective Resonance account would suggest, the norms that are connected to reactive distress and concern seem to survive well, whereas many norms that are not so connected have disappeared.

It bears emphasizing that the Affective Resonance explanation is not

---

8. There is a delicate issue, of course, about when a norm counts as moral. I have assiduously avoided trying to define the moral domain, and I do not intend to change course now. In the present case, we want to look at norms that the culture treated as moral, at least in some salient respects, but that are not connected to core emotions. Perhaps some would maintain that such norms only count as moral in an inverted-commas sense; but we still might consider the extent to which such 'moral' norms survive.

that individuals typically recognize that certain norms fit well with their emotions and accordingly decide to adopt those norms. The idea that people deliberately try to achieve some kind of equilibrium by bending their norms to fit their affect seems rather implausible. Rather, the Affective Resonance proposal approaches the phenomena from the broad vantage of cultural evolution. The central idea is simply that on balance, affect-backed rules will be more attractive and this advantage will accumulate down the ages.

Before closing this section, it is worth recalling the significant forces at work to help secure affect-backed norms in the culture. We can look back to the psychological research on normative judgment to see some of the ways in which affect-backed norms are more psychologically salient. First, affect-backed normative rules will be more memorable. More significantly, in the domains of both morals and manners, norms that prohibit intrinsically upsetting actions are treated as especially impermissible, more seriously wrong, and less contingent on authority than actions prohibited by affect-neutral norms. Indeed, people who lack the relevant emotion tend to regard these violations as less serious and less authority independent. In the etiquette case, subjects with low disgust response were more likely to regard disgust-backed violations as less serious and less authority independent (Nichols 2002b). In the moral case, the population of subjects with low response to suffering are also more likely to regard harmful violations as less authority independent (Blair 1997). As a result, the affective response seems to play a major role in determining the strength of one's normative commitments. In addition, the affect-backed norms are treated as having justifications that go beyond the conventional. Subjects are less likely to appeal to societal norms in explaining why these actions are wrong. These psychological facts about affect-backed norms make for a compelling case that affect-backed norms will enjoy a considerable advantage in the struggle for cultural success. People are more impassioned about the affect-backed norms and that will make them more outspoken and impassioned advocates for the norm. Perhaps more important, it will be easier to convince someone that an action is wrong if that action is easily regarded as affectively offensive. Against this background, it would be surprising if affect-backed norms failed to show cultural resilience.

6. COMPARISON WITH ALTERNATIVES

In the previous section, I set out the explanation of moral evolution provided by the Affective Resonance hypothesis. This explanation provides an alternative to the moral realist proposal. Now it is time to consider in a bit more detail whether Affective Resonance provides a better explanation than moral realism. After all, the form of argument under investigation is inference to the best explanation.

First, however, a word is in order about a more general worry: why did the more inclusive and antiviolent norms emerge so recently in Western history? This is an interesting question, and again the work in social history is revealing. In the case of cruelty to animals, Thomas maintains that one crucial enabling condition was that animals were no longer threatening (Thomas 1983, 273–74). Humans had effectively eliminated the animals that competed for resources or posed a more violent threat to human well-being. By the sixteenth century, for instance, wolves had been eradicated from England. This, according to Thomas, made it possible for attitudes about animals to shift towards the more inclusive norms we know today. In the case of corporal punishment, the situation is rather complicated, but some maintain that the new forms of punishment, and in particular, the penitentiary, provided a viable alternative to corporal punishment (e.g., Ignatieff 1978; see also Emsley 1987). So it was only because an alternative emerged that people were able to shed themselves of corporal punishment. The details here are rich and fascinating, but for present purposes, the important point is just that it is likely that there were important historical factors that enabled the moral evolution we've charted. Both the Affective Resonance account and the realist account can comfortably acknowledge the importance of an enabling background for the evolution of norms.

6.1. Moral Realism Version 1

The simple appeal to moral facts is an interesting explanation of moral evolution, especially if the only alternative is the historical accident explanation. If one has to choose between moral realism and historical accident, then realism certainly seems like a better explanation of the patterns. One can simply say, as moral realists do, that the best explanation for the evolution is that people are getting a clearer picture of the moral facts. Of course, there is an important sense in which this is still a thin explanation. For without an independently established story about moral facts, the simple realist story does not generate specific predictions about the direction of moral evolution. What one needs to know antecedently is, what are the moral facts? The trouble is, of course, that there is no generally accepted story about moral facts. That's part of the reason, after all, that realists appeal to moral progress—to shore up their claim that there *are* moral facts. As a result, the simple realist story provides only the barest sketch of an explanation—if there were moral facts, then that would explain why there are robust trends. By contrast, the Affective Resonance story above offers a much thicker explanation of the pattern. It makes a broad range of predictions about what sorts of norms will likely succeed—norms that prohibit actions that are likely to elicit negative affect are more likely to succeed. This kind of explanatory thickness carries a danger, for it is much easier to disconfirm a theory that makes more specific predictions. If the specific predictions are flouted, then the Affective Resonance account is in trouble. However, the predictions of the Affective Resonance account are apparently not flouted. The historical trend seems rather to confirm the predictions made by the Affective Resonance account, and this suggests that the account has a major explanatory advantage over the simple realist explanation. It is a commonplace in philosophy of science that, all else being equal, a theory with greater predictive success and explanatory depth is to be preferred. On these grounds, the Affective Resonance is to be preferred to the realist account. For the realist account only explains why we find moral evolution, whereas the Affective Resonance account explains both why we find moral evolution, and why it takes the course it does.

None of the foregoing, of course, shows that morality is not objective or that the simple realist theory is wrong. Rather, the point is just that the Affective Resonance account provides a better explanation for moral evolution without invoking a role for moral facts. The simple appeal to moral facts does not seem to be the best explanation for the kind of moral evolution that has been our focus.[9] To make a case against moral realism would obviously require further argument. In the final chapter, I will exploit features of the Affective Resonance account to sketch a Humean argument against one kind of moral realism. First, however, we need to turn to a rather different approach to explaining moral evolution through moral realism.

6.2. Moral Realism Version 2

In the philosophical literature, one prominent realist explanation of moral evolution manifestly does not suffer from a lack of predictive specificity.

---

9. As Ron Mallon has pointed out to me, moral realists might adopt the following compatibilist line:

Affective Resonance is a mechanism by which we progress to the moral facts.

For present purposes, I want to remain neutral on this compatibilist position. I only want to maintain that, at least prima facie, the compatibilist's appeal to moral facts is an ancillary hypothesis that does not obviously contribute to the explanation of moral evolution. The Affective Resonance account itself makes no appeal to moral facts. If Affective Resonance does explain the moral evolution charted above, then, unless there is an independent argument for moral facts, the explanation of moral evolution need not

That explanation comes from Peter Railton. Railton argues that the characteristic evolution of norms is explained by "social rationality," and Railton makes the explicit prediction that norms will evolve in ways that minimize the risk of social unrest. This proposal has a number of virtues, and what I hope to show in the following is that, although it may tell part of the story, it also fails to tell an important part of the story about the evolution of harm norms.

Railton writes, "Moral norms reflect a certain kind of rationality, rationality not from the point of view of any particular individual, but from what might be called a social point of view" (1986, 190). In particular, the norms of a culture move in the direction that will alleviate risks of social unrest: "A social arrangement . . . that departs from social rationality by significantly discounting the interests of a particular group [will] have a potential for dissatisfaction and unrest" (191). Railton elaborates on this notion of the potential for unrest: "The potential for unrest that exists when the interests of a group are discounted is potential for pressure from that group—and its allies—to accord fuller recognition to their interests in social decision-making and in the socially instilled norms that govern individual decision making. It therefore is pressure to push the resolution of conflicts further in the direction required by social rationality, because it is pressure to give fuller weight to the interests of more of those affected" (193). As Railton notes, this generates the following, rough, prediction: "one could expect an uneven secular trend toward the inclusion of the interests of (or interests represented by) social groups that are capable of some degree of mobilization" (194–95). Railton goes on to note that this prediction is borne out by "patterns in the evolution of moral norms" (197). For instance, this account predicts that moral norms will increase in generality (197), which is, of course, one of the central patterns that we hope to explain.

Railton's proposal is intriguing. First, it does not suffer from the lack of predictive specificity that other realist accounts do. And there can be no doubt that social unrest has played a vital role in shaping the norms that we have. This is probably true for both moral and nonmoral norms. The proposal also helps to reinforce that, just as there are plausibly multiple different origins for moral norms, there are plausibly multiple factors influencing the evolution of moral norms. However, I think that there are strict limitations on the extent to which the social unrest model can explain the phenomena at hand.

---

invoke such facts. Of course, if there is an independently persuasive argument for moral facts, then the kind of compatibilism Mallon suggests might be welcome.

Before setting out its limitations, I want to address Railton's formulation of the prediction. Railton's prediction is that there will be a trend toward "the inclusion of the interests of (or interests represented by) social groups that are capable of some degree of mobilization." The parenthetical comment here dilutes the hypothesis to such an extent that it no longer makes any distinctive predictions. For basically any interests can be represented by social groups capable of mobilization. The substantive prediction follows when we focus on the interests of the social group itself. And that, indeed, is what Railton appeals to when he adduces the support for his proposal.

Although the social unrest theory surely explains some moral evolution, it is limited in several ways. First, I want to advert to a point raised by Railton himself. He notes that the work in the social history of unrest, "a common theme . . . is that much social unrest is re-vindicative rather than revolutionary, since the discontent of long-suffering groups often is galvanized into action only when customary entitlements are threatened or denied. The overt ideologies of such groups thus frequently are particularistic and conservative, even as their unrest contributes to the emergence of new social forms that concede greater weight to previously discounted interests" (193n33). If this is right, then it leaves an important gap in the social unrest story. If the risk of social unrest could be alleviated by merely restoring recently lost rights, why does it end up having such pervasive effects? If the long-suffering groups would be satisfied by mere restoration, why do the social reforms typically go beyond this? The social unrest story does not immediately provide an answer for this question.

A related limitation of Railton's account is that some moral evolution leads to norms that apply to groups that pose no serious threat from social unrest. As Railton notes, the moral evolution seems to result in extending the harm norms to include the entire species (197). But in most cases, we are at no serious risk of unrest from, say, the !Kung or the Yanomamö. So why do we extend our norms to include so many individuals who pose no threat to our society? The social unrest story lapses here. By contrast, the Affective Resonance account provides a plausible explanation. Our promiscuous responsiveness to cues of harm in others (and even thoughts about harm in others) explains why harm norms would become more inclusive than is required by social rationality.

In addition, as we saw above, the norms prohibiting harm have expanded to include norms prohibiting cruelty to animals. These norms have, like norms prohibiting harming outgroupers, grown in prominence and acceptance over the last several hundred years. The social unrest model clearly provides no explanation of this phenomenon, since nonhuman animals are no longer in any position to threaten us. Indeed, as noted above, Thomas maintains that it is partly *because* animals were in no position to threaten us that the norms prohibiting cruelty took hold. Of course, while the social unrest proposal stumbles on norms prohibiting cruelty to animals, the Affective Resonance account provides a natural explanation. Suffering in animals excites negative affect in humans, and as a result, norms prohibiting actions that cause suffering in animals will have an edge in cultural fitness.

Neither is the other historical pattern that we considered in detail, the decline of corporal punishment, easily explained by the social unrest account. For in many cases, the individuals who were subjected to the punishment were presumably in no position to foment unrest. For instance, the gradual elimination of corporal punishment from executions is not easily explained by the relevant party's likelihood to incite social unrest. By contrast again, the Affective Resonance account does explain this trend. Corporal punishment will prompt serious negative affect, and norms that prohibit this kind of thing will be more likely to survive than other sorts of norms. Thus, there is a range of cases central to the pattern of the evolution of harm norms that cannot be easily accommodated by Railton's model, but that are explained by the Affective Resonance account.

Finally, consider again the striking fact, discussed in the previous chapter, that the norms we happen to have are often tightly coordinated with the emotions we happen to have. The Affective Resonance account provides a broad-based explanation for this tight fit between emotions and norms. The reason so many of our norms fit so well with our emotions is, in part, that our emotions play a crucial historical role in securing the norms. The social unrest story, of course, provides no explanation for the evident connection between emotions and norms. As such, it is at best a quite incomplete story about the evolution of norms.

7. CONCLUSION

In this chapter, I have tried to extend the Affective Resonance account of the cultural evolution of norms to the particular case of harm norms. There are two striking facts about harm norms that need to be explained by a genealogical account. Harm norms are culturally ubiquitous and they seem to exhibit a characteristic pattern of evolution. The ubiquity and evolution of harm norms is often explained by appeal to moral facts— through reason we come to recognize the fact that it is wrong to harm others. I have argued that the Affective Resonance account provides a better explanation of the phenomena than the appeal to moral facts. For

Affective Resonance provides a richer explanation of the distinctive character of the evolution of harm norms.

The realist approach to moral evolution, it should be noted, is typically supposed to provide both an explanation and a justification for why we have the norms we do. We have the norms we do because reason leads us to the right norms. This both explains why we have the norms we do and implies that we are justified in embracing the norms. By contrast, the Affective Resonance account is intended only as an explanation for why we have the harm norms we do. The account harbors no pretensions about providing a justification for our embracing the norms. Rather, the Affective Resonance approach is essentially descriptive and historical, rather than prescriptive and justificatory. Indeed, in the next chapter, I will argue that the Affective Resonance account might play a part in an argument that moral judgments lack the kind of justification sought by some moral realists.

8

Commonsense Objectivism and the Persistence of Moral Judgment

> If we can depend upon any principle, which we learn from philosophy, this, I think, may be considered as certain and undoubted, that there is nothing, in itself, valuable or despicable, desirable or hateful, beautiful or deformed; but that these attributes arise from the particular constitution and fabric of human sentiment and affection.
>
> —Hume, "The Sceptic"

1. INTRODUCTION

Like most great philosophical questions, the issue of moral objectivity has its roots in commonsense. As a result, it is important to begin with as clear an account of the commonsense view as possible. In this chapter, I argue that commonsense is committed to a kind of moral objectivism that is undermined by the account of moral judgment developed in this volume. As a rough guide to the philosophical geography, we might impose a tree structure on the core questions about moral objectivism (see figure 8.1). The structure of this chapter follows the tree down. In section 2 I consider the claim that commonsense is committed to moral objectivity. This claim is advanced both by philosophers and developmental psychologists. I will argue that this claim is more problematic than commonly thought, but that there is an important nugget of truth in it. In section 3, I will pursue a tangent. I will argue that the origins of the commonsense commitment to moral objectivity might again be tied to affective response. In the subsequent section, I will consider the familiar Humean argument that morality is not objective because it depends on the emotions we happen to have. I argue that the account of moral judgment

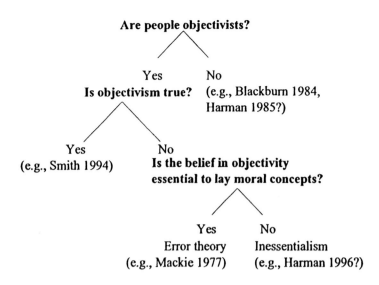

FIGURE 8.1 Commonsense moral objectivism tree

developed in this volume suggests that moral judgment does indeed depend on the emotions and that this provides a way of filling out the Humean argument against objectivism. However, abandoning objectivism would not settle whether or not we should adopt an "error theory," according to which all commonsense moral judgments are false because they all presuppose objectivity. In the fifth section, I will broach the last question on the tree—is the belief in objectivity essential to our moral concepts. Here I will not try to pronounce judgment. But I will provide some reason to think that moral judgment remains largely intact even after the rejection of moral objectivity. For many of the central characteristics of moral judgment can be preserved in the absence of a commitment to objectivity.

2. ARE PEOPLE MORAL OBJECTIVISTS?

2.1. Analysis and Moral Objectivity

Among analytic philosophers, it is widely assumed that people are moral objectivists in some sense. Unfortunately, the term "moral objectivity" has accumulated multiple definitions, and we will need to do some tidying before long. But first, let us consider some characteristic statements among analytic philosophers to the effect that lay people are moral objectivists. In *The Moral Problem*, Michael Smith claims that one of the central features of commonsense morality is the "objectivity of moral judgement": "we seem to think moral questions have correct answers; that the correct answers are made correct by objective moral facts; that moral facts are wholly determined by circumstances and that, by engaging in moral conversation and argument, we can discover what these objective moral facts determined by the circumstances are" (1994, 6). Similarly, Stephen Darwall writes, "Ethical thought and feeling have 'objective purport.' From the inside, they apparently aspire to truth or correctness and presuppose that there is something of which they can be true or false" (1998a, 25). Darwall defines "objective purport" as: "Seeming to be of something objective and independent of the perceiver (e.g., some objective fact or an objective property of some substance)" (1998a, 239).

Many of the philosophers who maintain that commonsense is committed to moral objectivity are themselves sympathetic to moral objectivity. And, at least in some cases, the alleged commonsense commitment to moral objectivity is taken as support for the truth of moral objectivity. Relatedly, one might maintain that if it is part of commonsense that morality is objective, then a metaethics that entails objectivism is better than a metaethics that does not entail objectivism. Rationalism and Intuitionism are thus thought to accrue plausibility because they entail objectivism (e.g., Smith 1994; Darwall 1998a, 56).

Although philosophers who embrace moral objectivity are often the most vocal proponents of the view that commonsense is committed to moral objectivity, even philosophers who are not so sympathetic maintain that lay people are moral objectivists. Indeed, perhaps the best known opponent of moral objectivism in recent years, J. L. Mackie, goes to some lengths to establish that ordinary people are committed to the "claim to objectivity":

> The ordinary user of moral language means to say something
> about whatever it is that he characterizes morally, for example a
> possible action, as it is in itself, or would be if it were realized, and
> not about, or even simply expressive of, his, or anyone else's rela-
> tion to it. But the something he wants to say is not purely descrip-
> tive, certainly not inert, but something that involves a call for action
> or for the refraining from action, and one that is absolute, not con-
> tingent upon any desire or preference or policy or choice, his own
> or anyone else's. (Mackie 1977, 33)

Thus, among analytic philosophers of different minds about the status of moral objectivity, we find an important island of agreement about the commonsense view—both objectivists and their opponents can agree that commonsense is committed to moral objectivity.

At this point, we can no longer forestall the task of stipulating a sense of "moral objectivism" that will sustain us throughout the remainder of the chapter. The first part of Mackie's above analysis will work nicely for a start. To claim that an action is objectively immoral is to claim that the action is wrong "as it is in itself" and not in relation to subjects. Cashing out "as it is in itself" is no pleasant undertaking, but we might focus on the negative claim, which Mackie seems to regard as an entailment. If morality is objective, then being morally wrong is *not* determined by a relation subjects bear to the action. Thus, to claim that an action is objectively immoral is to claim that the action is wrong "as it is in itself" and not in relation to other subjects. There are various quibbles that might be made over this characterization, but the underlying idea is familiar. According to the objectivist, if a particular action is morally wrong, then it is wrong simpliciter. So morally wrong actions are not merely wrong relative to certain populations. This point is easiest to appreciate by focusing on a particular example. Let's say that a teenage boy, Tom, intentionally kicks a small dog. It cannot turn out, according to the objectivist, that Tom's kicking the dog was morally wrong for some populations but not for other populations. If the action is morally wrong, it is wrong full stop. Thus, moral objectivism is committed to the view that (i) true moral judgments are nonrelativistically true and (ii) some moral judgments are true. Now, if we look back over the philosophical characterizations of moral objectivity, it is plausible that Smith, Darwall, and Mackie all regard commonsense as committed to something like this notion of moral objectivism.[1]

Although analytic philosophers routinely speak on behalf of commonsense's commitment to moral objectivity, empirically minded philosophers have expressed skepticism about whether adequate attention is accorded to how morality is actually viewed by lay people (e.g., Harman 1985; Stich and Weinberg 2001). Many people seem explicitly to disavow moral objectivism at least for some standard moral violations. Furthermore, the most vocal population of individuals who disavow objectivism are college students, and one might have expected academic philosophers to be familiar with this group. Stich and Weinberg press this point in response to Frank Jackson's (1998) claim that the folk are moral objectivists: "we find it simply astounding that Jackson attributes these 'ob-

---

1. This notion of moral objectivism is stronger than the inclusive notion of moral realism used in the previous chapter. For some moral realists, for example, Railton (1986), allow that the moral facts might be relative to the species. The notion of objectivity under consideration in this chapter makes no such concession. And, importantly, we will see that this stronger notion of moral objectivity probably tracks commonsense.

jectivist' views to the 'folk.' Indeed, we can't help wondering whether Jackson ever talks to undergraduates, since a significant number of *our* undergraduates claim to be moral relativists" (Stich and Weinberg 2001, 641; emphasis in original).

Such nonobjectivism among undergraduates is commonly dismissed by drawing attention to the fact that some college students will proclaim a broad metaphysical nonobjectivism in which they maintain that there is no fact of the matter even about whether the earth is flat. It is likely, the dismissal continues, that this apparent endorsement of metaphysical nonobjectivism ensues from a naive confusion, and that this confusion lies behind the students' apparent endorsement of moral nonobjectivism. Hence, we can safely disregard the undergraduate nonobjectivist. Undergraduates who endorse metaphysical nonobjectivism should, perhaps, often be regarded as confused. But this parry does not adequately address the issue. For recent experiments indicate that when presented with anonymous questionnaires describing scenarios of cultural disagreement, many college students say that although there is a fact of the matter about whether the earth is flat, there is not a fact of the matter about whether canonical moral violations (e.g., hitting and shoving) are wrong (Nichols 2004).[2]

Alternatively, many philosophers maintain that students should not be taken at their nonobjectivist word because it is easy to talk them out of their nonobjectivist rhetoric about morality. It is no doubt true that professors often talk students out of their nonobjectivist rhetoric, but this is a seriously tainted set of anecdotes. An effective professor can talk students out of many of their genuine commitments. Indeed, it is likely that an effective professor could talk many objectivist students (at least among those who are not theists) out of their commitment to moral objectivism. As a result, to investigate these matters, we need to take precautions to minimize the sort of biases that are endemic to the professor/student

---

2. Different versions of the objectivity question were used in different experiments. In some of the experiments, the wording of the *no fact of the matter* option was as follows:

> There is no fact of the matter about unqualified claims like ["It's okay to hit people just because you feel like it"/ "The earth is flat"]. Different cultures believe different things, and it is not absolutely true or false that [it's okay to hit people just because you feel like it / the earth is flat].

In another experiment, the wording of the *no fact of the matter* option for the moral violation was as follows:

> There is no objective fact, independent of what different people think, about whether it was wrong for Frank to hit Bill or Lisa to shove Nancy. These actions were "wrong for Ted" and maybe "wrong for me," but they aren't *objectively wrong* independent of what people think about them.

relationship. Presumably anonymous experimental procedures are a step in the right direction.

The foregoing is certainly not the last word on whether there is a population of undergraduate nonobjectivists.[3] But at a minimum, the above considerations render the claim that moral objectivity is part of commonsense far less obvious than analytic philosophers typically allow. Nonetheless, I suspect that there is an important truth buried in the claim that commonsense is committed to objectivism. However, digging out that truth requires looking to children rather than college students.

2.2. Development and Moral Objectivity

Although college students present us with a patchy map of commonsense objectivity, there might be another way to shore up the claim that the commitment to objectivity is part of commonsense. For it might turn out that moral objectivity is a default presumption of commonsense. Developmental psychology offers the most obvious source of evidence for such a view. As it happens, developmental psychologists do maintain that, from a young age, children are moral objectivists. For instance, Larry Nucci writes: "Preschool-aged children . . . understand that it is objectively wrong to hurt others" (2001, 86; see also Flanagan 1991, 348 fn3).

The evidence entered on behalf of childhood objectivism comes from the research on the moral/conventional distinction. In particular, Nucci adduces two key findings as evidence that children are moral objectivists (Nucci 2001, 86–87):

1. Children regard moral violations as less authority contingent than conventional violations.
2. Children regard moral violations as more generalizably wrong than conventional violations.

So, for instance, children will say that even if the teacher says that it is okay to pull hair, it is not okay to do that. By contrast, children are much more likely to allow that it is okay to chew gum in class if the teacher

---

3. One issue is whether the "nonobjectivists" (or some subpopulation of them) would sustain their nonobjectivism for more outrageous moral violations, like racist murder. For present purposes, it suffices that many undergraduates seem to think that canonical moral violations are not objectively wrong. For that is enough to call into question the idea that people are thoroughgoing moral objectivists. However, even if virtually no undergraduates would sustain nonobjectivism for egregious moral violations, there would still be a question about how to interpret the responses of those who say that there is no fact of the matter about the wrongness of hitting and shoving but there is about racist murder. For instance, one would really like to know whether people who hold such views regard the views as in tension or as happily consistent. If they are in tension, we would want to know how these students would resolve tension under reflective equilibrium. These issues have not been explored systematically.

says it is okay. On the other dimension, children are likely to say that pulling hair is not okay in other places, at other times, in other countries, and so forth. They are more likely to allow that chewing gum is okay in other places.

This work on the moral/conventional task does suggest that children reject conventionalism, the anti-objectivist view that what counts as morally wrong varies with the prevailing conventions (e.g., Benedict 1934). For children do not assimilate morality to convention. However, in philosophical ethics, a more prominent anti-objectivist position maintains that moral properties are not objective because they are "response dependent" (e.g., Hume [1739] 1964; Stevenson 1944; Gibbard 1990). There are different notions of response dependence, but the basic idea is that a property is response dependent just in case that property is constituted by the responses it elicits in a population; so the same object or event might have different response-dependent properties for different populations (e.g., Cohen [forthcoming]; Johnston 1989; Smith and Stoljar 1998; Wedgwood 1998). As a result, a commonsense exemplar of a response-dependent property is "icky." The same object might be icky for one population and not icky for another population. No thing is icky "as it is in itself." Rather, whether something is icky depends on the responses of the focal subjects.

It is easy to see how this hooks up with the earlier discussion of objectivity. If morality is objective, then the moral status of an action cannot be relative to a set of subjects the way icky depends on the responses of a set of subjects. Hume is sometimes interpreted as maintaining that moral judgments are indeed akin to judgments about properties such as tasty and icky. Perhaps, then, in making moral judgments, children regard moral properties as response dependent in a similar way. If so, then children are not moral objectivists after all. A related concern runs in the other direction. If children never treat *any* properties as response dependent, then one might worry that children really do not grasp the objective/nonobjective distinction.[4] And in that case, it might be misleading to say that children are objectivists. Hence, to sustain the view

---

4. Abundant data show that children recognize from a young age that people can have different desires, beliefs, and emotions than they themselves have (e.g., Gopnik and Meltzoff 1997; Nichols and Stich 2003). Children can detect, for instance, that while they regard a cookie as yummy, another person does not regard the cookie as yummy (e.g., Flavell et al. 1990). However, the fact that children recognize that people differ on whether a cookie is yummy does not show that children regard "yummy" as a response-dependent property. After all, adults are well aware of the fact that people differ on whether the mind is immortal, but this does not show that adults think that immortality is a response-dependent property.

that children are moral objectivists, one would hope to find that children treat moral properties differently from properties that are paradigmatically response dependent.

The prevailing measure for moral judgment, the moral/conventional task, does a poor job of assessing whether children regard moral properties as dependent on our responses. For simple response-dependent properties might themselves be regarded as "nonconventional," both by children and adults. Consider the two key questions above, authority contingency and generalizability. We can easily devise an authority contingence question for response-dependent properties. For instance, one might ask the following: "If the teacher said that liver is yummy, would liver be yummy?" Adults, and presumably children as well, regard the teacher as in no position to make liver yummy. If this is right, then merely showing that moral transgressions are regarded as authority independent does not show that moral properties are regarded as response independent. For the generalizability dimension, the problem is that in the context of response-dependent properties, generalizability questions are notoriously ambiguous. If asked whether onions are icky in another country, an onion-hater might well assent. For she might interpret the question as asking whether onions in another country would be icky to her.

One might now look back on the developmental research and maintain that the moral/conventional task does not, after all, settle the question of childhood objectivism. For it does not exclude the possibility that moral judgments about, say, good and bad, are analogous to judgments about response-dependent properties like fun and icky. If children do regard moral properties as akin to such response-dependent properties, then the claim that children are moral objectivists is thoroughly compromised.

The foregoing merely suggests that the traditional moral/conventional task is inadequate to addressing whether children are moral objectivists. For it does not test the possibility that moral judgments are akin to judgments about response-dependent properties. In light of this lacuna in the evidence, Trisha Folds-Bennett and I have recently conducted a pair of experiments exploring children's judgments about moral and response-dependent properties (Nichols and Folds-Bennett 2003).

The first experiment, on children aged four to six years, looked at positive properties in three categories: moral (good), aesthetic (beautiful), and paradigmatically response dependent (fun, yummy). For each item, children were asked whether a property applied to something, for example, "Are grapes yummy?" Following a "yes" response the child was asked a generalizability question and a preference dependence question.

GENERALIZABILITY
Now, think about a long time ago, before there were any people. There were still grapes, just like the grapes now. Way back then, before there were people, were grapes yummy?

PREFERENCE DEPENDENCE
You know, I think grapes are yummy too. Some people don't like grapes. They don't think grapes are yummy. Would you say that grapes are yummy *for some people* or that they're yummy *for real*?

One of the moral items involved one monkey helping a hurt monkey, and we asked parallel generalizability and preference dependence questions:

GENERALIZABILITY
Now, think about a long time ago, before there were any people. There were monkeys back then too. Way back then, before there were people, when one monkey helped another monkey that got hurt, was that good?

PREFERENCE DEPENDENCE
You know, I think it was good for the monkey to help the other monkey. Some people don't like it when monkeys help each other when they're hurt. They don't think it's good when monkeys do that. Would you say that when one monkey helps a hurt monkey that is good *for some people* or that it's good *for real*?

For one of the aesthetics cases, we asked "Are roses beautiful?" Again, this was followed by generalizability and preference dependence questions:

GENERALIZABILITY
Now, think about a long time ago, before there were any people. There were roses back then too. Way back then, before there were people, were roses beautiful?

PREFERENCE DEPENDENCE
You know, I think roses are beautiful too. Some people don't like roses. They don't think roses are beautiful. Would you say that roses are beautiful *for some people* or that they're beautiful *for real*?

On the generalizability question, we found no significant differences in response between the three categories. The children tended to regard all of the properties as generalizable—before there were people, roses were beautiful and grapes were yummy. Matters were different for the preference dependence question. On this question, children tended to treat yummy and fun as preference dependent, and they were significantly less likely to treat good and beautiful in this way. Rather, they tended to say that the actions are good "for real" and that flowers are beautiful "for real" (Nichols and Folds-Bennett 2003).[5]

In a second experiment on five-year-olds, we focused on negative properties, including morally bad (e.g., pulling another child's hair), icky, and boring. Again, we asked children whether the property applied to some object or activity (e.g., "Is it boring to clean house?"), and we proceeded to ask questions about preference dependence and generalizability (e.g., "In another country or some place far away is it boring to clean house?"). As in the first experiment, we found that children tended to regard the paradigmatically response-dependent properties (icky, boring) as preference dependent, and they were significantly less likely to treat the moral property as preference dependent. In addition, unlike in the previous experiment, we found a significant difference between response-dependent properties and moral properties on the generalizability question. Children were more likely to treat the moral property as generalizable. That is, they were more likely to say that pulling hair and hitting are wrong in other countries than that onions are icky in other countries.[6]

The results of the above experiments indicate both that children appreciate that certain properties are response dependent and that children do not treat moral properties as preference dependent. Of course, these results do not exclude the possibility that children regard moral properties as response dependent in some other sense. The experiments probe only a simple kind of response dependence. There are more sophisticated kinds of response dependence, and it is possible that children regard moral properties as response dependent in some more sophisticated way. Thus there are many further empirical questions about whether children regard moral properties as entirely independent of responses. Nonetheless, the available data give no reason to think that children will depart from objectivism under other circumstances. Moreover, as we move to more sophisticated kinds of response dependence, it becomes less plausi-

5. Some have worried about whether young children really understand the locution "for real". As is often the case in doing experiments on young children, it is nontrivial to devise questions that both get at the issue and are plausibly comprehensible for the participants. In pilot studies leading up to this experiment, we tried several different formulations and settled on "for real" only after hearing my four-year-old daughter and her friends spontaneously using the expression. More importantly, though, the worry about whether the children understand the expression is mitigated by the fact that there was a clear effect. That is, children clearly drew a distinction between "yummy" and "good" on the "for some people/for real" criterion. So the question does somehow tap into an important difference in the way children regard the different properties.

6. Although there was a significant difference here, in this study as well as in the positive properties study, the majority of subjects treated the response-dependent properties as generalizable. The difference between moral and response-dependent properties emerged because all the subjects treated the moral properties as generalizable.

ble to maintain that young children even appreciate the operative sense of response dependence (cf. chapter 4). The above experiments show both that children understand preference-dependent properties and that they do not assimilate moral properties to preference-dependent properties.

With these results in hand, we can begin to refigure the received view that commonsense is committed to moral objectivity. Together with previous findings that moral violations are not merely conventionally bad, these results support the claim that children are indeed moral objectivists. They seem to regard moral properties as real and independent of both conventions and preferences. Thus, on the notion of objectivity adopted above, this provides evidence that children are objectivists about morality. They regard certain actions as bad, and they seem to resist the idea that whether a particular action is bad varies as a function of relations to subjects. The data on young children thus suggest, as a working hypothesis, that moral objectivism is the default setting on commonsense metaethics.

Of course, we lack the evidence to advance this hypothesis with beaming confidence. The lack of cross-cultural data is perhaps the most significant gap. A growing body of work in cross-cultural psychology reveals striking differences in cognitive processes and intuitions in different cultures (e.g., Machery et al. 2004; Miller [in press]; Nisbett et al. 2001; Weinberg et al. 2001). It is possible such differences exist in attitudes about moral objectivity as well and that in some cultures children never embrace moral objectivism. Nonetheless, given the available data, default objectivism is a plausible working hypothesis, and I will adopt it in this chapter.

We should now get a clearer picture of the contours of this default commonsense objectivism. The kind of objectivity sketched in section 2.1 says that some moral claims are true and that true moral claims are non-relativistically true. This bald claim entails an unqualified antirelativism according to which the truth of moral claims is not relative to the species or other groups of organisms. So as the claim to objectivity is characterized above, if a moral claim is true, then rational aliens who demur from it are making a mistake. For instance, if it is morally wrong to torture puppies, then if there are rational aliens who think that it is okay to torture puppies, those aliens are mistaken. This account fits with Mackie's description of the claim to objectivity (1977, 33), and the commonsense commitment to objectivity plausibly runs this far in both children and adults.[7] That is, default commonsense objectivism is likely committed to

---

7. Indeed, in one experiment on moral objectivism, students were actually presented with a case of moral disagreement (over puppy torture) involving aliens and humans. As with all of these experiments, there were a number of subjects who maintained that there is no fact of the matter about whether the earth is flat, but after screening off these subjects, a majority of participants maintained that it is

an unqualified antirelativism. If that's right, commonsense objectivism is not the nuanced objectivism of naturalistic moral realists like Peter Railton, who maintain that moral truths are grounded in the details of human nature and accordingly relativized to those details (e.g., Railton 1986). Rather, commonsense objectivism rejects relativizing morality to any group of subjects.

If moral objectivism is the default setting on commonsense metaethics, this setting is apparently defeasible in some measure. For although many undergraduates proclaim a thoroughgoing moral objectivism, many other undergraduates deny it. These repudiators apparently depart from the default setting. Which factors incline individuals to depart from moral objectivism? This question has not been explored in any systematic fashion, but a natural proposal is that education and other cultural forces play a crucial role in leading people to relinquish moral objectivism.[8]

This has all become increasingly speculative, taking fairly large leaps from fairly little evidence. But we have now arrived at a position where we can reformulate in a more empirically responsible way the received view that people are moral objectivists. The available evidence suggests that it is crude to say simply that commonsense thinks that morality is objective. For there are plenty of people who deny objectivism about central moral cases. Still, it is plausible that moral objectivism is a default position on lay metaethics and that this default position has been overturned in those who are nonobjectivists about canonical moral violations. Again, it is worth emphasizing that the available data scarcely secure this view. However, at this early stage in the empirical exploration of intuitions about moral objectivity, the view of moral objectivity as a default but defeasible setting on commonsense is sufficiently promising to merit provisional adoption.

3. THE ORIGINS OF OBJECTIVITY

3.1. Acquisition

Even if we go along with the provisional claim that objectivism is a default setting on commonsense metaethics, that leaves open important and in-

---

wrong to torture puppies, and aliens who think otherwise are mistaken (Nichols 2004). Although young children have not been tested on "alien" cases, presumably children's views on this are continuous with adults'. For there is little reason to expect that the commitment to objectivity is more carefully qualified in children than it is in college students.

8. This fits with Jonathan Haidt's work on moral judgment in groups of different socioeconomic status (SES). SES groups are typically distinguished by level of education, and Haidt found that high SES

teresting questions about how this postulated setting is achieved. How do people come to believe in moral objectivity? In philosophy, Mackie (1977) offers the most visible discussion of this issue. Mackie defends an error theory, according to which all commonsense moral judgments are false, because all such judgments carry the false presumption that morality is objective. It is incumbent on the error theorist, Mackie thinks, to explain the common belief in objectivity. The error theorist "must give some account of how other people have fallen into what he regards as an error, and this account will have to include some positive suggestions . . . about what has been mistaken for, or has led to false beliefs about, objective values" (17–18). Mackie sets this task for the error theorist, but a natural reading of the charge is to provide an account of the acquisition of the commonsense belief in objectivity. This charge extends to anyone interested in gleaning the origins of objectivity. As a result, I too want to consider the source of the belief in objectivity.

Mackie offers a multipronged explanation for the belief in objectivity. He does not try to maintain that there is a single factor that explains why people have the belief in objectivity. It will be worth considering the more prominent of Mackie's proposed explanations. First, Mackie suggests that the belief in objectivism partly results from our projecting our feelings onto the world: "If we admit what Hume calls the mind's 'propensity to spread itself on external objects,' we can understand the supposed objectivity of moral qualities as arising from what we can call the projection or objectification of moral attitudes. This would be analogous to what is called the 'pathetic fallacy,' the tendency to read our feelings into their objects. If a fungus, say, fills us with disgust, we may be inclined to ascribe to the fungus itself a non-natural quality of foulness" (42). Thus, Mackie seems to suggest, certain objects and actions give rise to bad feelings in us and we projectively attribute the badness to the objects or actions themselves. Although the suggestion that we drape our feelings over the world is seductive, it does not provide a very deep explanation of our commitment to moral objectivity. The easiest way to see this is by considering again the findings on young children's differential treatment of moral and response-dependent properties. Children are significantly less likely to say that onions are icky for real than they are to say that hitting is bad for real. That is, they are less likely to project their own views about the ickiness of onions onto the world. So even young children do not indiscriminately project their feelings onto the objects that provoke the

---

groups were more likely than low SES groups to be tolerant of offensive behavior in others (see Haidt et al. 1993).

feelings. As a result, we cannot rest content with the suggestion that such projection explains why children objectify moral properties.

Another of Mackie's explanations appeals to the role of religion in promoting the objectivity of values. Mackie advances the suggestion that "ethics is a system of law from which the legislator has been removed. . . . There can be no doubt that some features of modern European moral attitudes are traceable to the theological ethics of Christianity" (45). Although religion might contribute in some ways to beliefs about moral objectivity, the appeal to religion probably cannot explain the objectivist tendencies uncovered in children. Larry Nucci's research is particularly important in this context. As noted in chapter 1, Nucci found that Amish teenagers regarded the impermissibility of religious transgressions as contingent on God's authority, but they did not regard the impermissibility of moral transgressions as similarly contingent on God's authority. Even if God did not have a rule against hitting, it would still be wrong to hit; but if God did not have a rule against working on Sunday, it would be okay to work on Sunday (Nucci 1986). Hence, although Mackie is surely right that some features of our moral attitudes can be traced to Christian ethics, it is not at all clear that the belief in objectivity can be so traced. For Nucci's evidence suggests that children regard God's laws as conventional, and as we have seen, children regard moral properties as neither conventional nor response dependent.

A third explanation from Mackie for why people believe in moral objectivism appeals to motivational considerations: "There are motives that would support objectification. We need morality to regulate interpersonal relations, to control some of the ways in which people behave towards one another, often in opposition to contrary inclinations. We therefore want our moral judgments to be authoritative for other agents as well as for ourselves: objective validity would give them the authority required" (43). Mackie is rather vague on how he thinks motives engender the belief in objectivism. But direct motivational explanations for why we objectify morality are generally unsatisfactory. I seriously doubt that most children come to believe in moral objectivity because they want moral judgments to be authoritative so as to secure the regulation of interpersonal relations.

What are the other options? There is a wide range of possibilities. At one end of the spectrum, one might maintain that morality really is objective and that children discover this fact in a process of theory-building. Like Mackie, I am skeptical about moral objectivity (for reasons set out in section 4), so I am not inclined to explain acquisition as a discovery of the truth of objectivity. A more promising approach, I think, is to advert again to affect. The core idea is that affect somehow infuses harm norms with objective purport. Recall that the case for childhood objectivism comes from evidence that children regard moral violations as wrong in a way that is (i) authority independent, (ii) generalizable, and (iii) preference independent. So we need to uncover the factors that contribute to these aspects of moral judgment in children.

In the case of judgments about authority contingence, we have already seen (in chapter 1) two different reasons for thinking that affect plays an important role. First, the evidence on psychopathy suggests that children with psychopathic tendencies are more likely to treat moral violations as authority contingent, and psychopathy also involves a diminished emotional responsiveness to suffering in others. Second, disgusting violations, which involve a clear emotional component, are not treated as authority contingent. In addition, subjects with low disgust-sensitivity were more likely to treat a disgusting violation as authority contingent than subjects with high disgust-sensitivity. This all suggests that affect somehow mediates judgments of authority contingence.

Those data provide the beginnings of an affect-based case for the acquisition of the commitment to moral objectivity. But they do not address whether affect might contribute to the child's judgment that moral violations are generalizably bad. There is some evidence now, though, that encourages an affect-based account of judgments of generalizability as well. In the study on negative response-dependent properties discussed earlier, children were also presented with cases of disgusting violations (e.g., spitting in water before drinking it). Children treated these cases much like the moral cases. Like the moral violations, the disgusting violations were judged to be bad in a fully generalizable way. Every child said that each disgusting violation would be bad in another country or some place far away (Nichols and Folds-Bennett 2003). Hence, children apparently treat disgusting violations as wrong in a way that closely parallels their treatment of moral violations. An obvious explanation for this is that somehow the emotional response of disgust itself leads the child to treat the violations as generalizably bad. Similarly, then, the emotions of reactive distress and concern might be responsible for the child's judgment that harmful transgressions are generalizably bad.

When we turn to judgments about response dependence, the situation looks a bit different. Again, disgusting violations are treated like moral violations—they are judged to be bad in a way that is independent of preferences (as compared with icky and boring). However, in this case it is less clear whether affect plays the pivotal role. For even conventional violations tend to be treated as preference independent.[9] Hence, it is not

9. In the study relayed above (Nichols and Folds-Bennett [2003]) there were no significant differences between judgments about conventional violations and judgments about response-dependent prop-

clear that it is a distinctive feature of affect-backed norms that they are treated as preference independent. It might be a general feature of normative judgment that normative violations are judged as bad in a preference independent way. But in any case, being an affect-backed norm is obviously sufficient for being regarded as preference independent.

The core indicators of childhood objectivism—preference independence, authority independence, generalizability—are found with disgust norms. This conforms to the hypothesis that objective purport derives from affective response coupled with normative commitment. Simple noncognitive responses, like those underlying judgments that something is fun or icky, do not suffice for treating properties like fun or icky as objective. For children treat properties like fun and icky as dependent on preferences. One obvious difference between these kinds of cases and the moral cases is that there is no normative prohibition dictating that onions are icky or that cleaning house is boring. However, being normatively prohibited is not sufficient for being regarded as objectively bad. For transgressions of conventional normative prohibitions are less likely to be judged as bad independent of authority and in a generalizable way. Apparently both a body of information about normative violations and a noncognitive response play a role in generating the full suite of indicators of childhood moral objectivism.

The suggestion that judgments of normative objectivity implicate both norms and feelings leaves open a vast range of empirical possibilities for how this commitment to normative objectivity is secured. From an ontogenetic vantage, one might marshal a developmental contingency model, according to which the child will come to treat certain normative violations as objectively bad only if the child has, at some critical period, both a body of information delimiting a set of transgressions and an affective mechanism that is independently sensitive to actions of the forbidden type. An extreme version of this view would maintain that once the child comes to treat certain norms as having objective purport, the affective system is no longer relevant at all, and the individual will continue to treat those norms as having objective purport regardless of what happens to the emotion systems subsequently. Alternatively, one might eschew developmental considerations altogether in favor of on-line processing. An extreme version of this view would maintain that people treat normative violations as objectively bad whenever the described action triggers a

---

erties. However, there was a clear trend—conventional properties were typically treated as less preference dependent than properties like "icky" and "boring." As a result, we do not want to build our account of the acquisition of the notion of objectivity on the assumption that conventional properties are regarded as preference-dependent. That assumption is likely false.

(negatively valenced) affective response. But of course, one need not be an extremist of either variety. Perhaps judgments of objective purport depend both on critical developmental precursors and on on-line processing. The available research does not shine enough light to see many details.

For philosophical purposes, the details of implementation are rather less important than the rough claim that affective response plays an essential role in leading children to moral objectivism. For that proposal leaves us with a broadly sentimentalist account of the commitment to moral objectivity. If it is right, then we can explain the basic belief in objectivity without assuming that morality really is objective. Children come to treat morality as objective not because they discover it, but rather because of an emotional response to actions of the proscribed type.

3.2. The Preservation of Objectivity

If objectivism is grounded in sentiment rather than reason, why does the belief in objectivism persist? While children might regard disgusting violations as objectively bad, adults pretty clearly do not.[10] Why then do most adults persist in believing that morality is objective? We might turn again to Mackie for a starting point. In the above discussion, I treated Mackie as offering proposals for the acquisition of the belief in moral objectivity. But Mackie introduces his discussion of the basis for the commitment to objectivity by asking "how this belief, if it is false, has become established and is so resistant to criticisms" (1977, 42). Mackie here seems to fuse at least two different questions:

1. How is the commitment to objectivity acquired?
2. How is the commitment to objectivity preserved?

The developmental data press for an acquisition story that explains how the child acquires the belief in moral objectivity before he darkens the grammar school door. The preceding section argues that Mackie's proposals are distinctly unpromising on this score and that a better acquisition story is available. But even if we have a story about acquisition, Mackie might well think that we still need a story about preservation. For on Mackie's view, the belief in objectivity is manifestly false. Why do even adults perseverate in the commitment to objectivity? We put away many of our childish views, why does the false presupposition of objectivity get preserved? Here his proposals are more promising.

---

10. Adults do treat disgusting violations as authority independent (Nichols 2002b), but they do not treat them as bad in a fully generalizable way. Adults (at least in our culture) tend to think that in other cultures, it might not be wrong to act in a way that violates our disgust-based prohibitions (Nichols 2004).

Although religious considerations do not seem to explain the acquisition of the belief in objectivity, religious beliefs might play an important role in shoring up the belief in objectivity. The relationship between religion and morality is complicated, of course. Perhaps most importantly many people regard voluntarism (or Divine Command Theory) as implausible—that is, at least many adults think that right and wrong are not decided by God, and Nucci's evidence suggests that even Amish teenagers share this view. Nonetheless, it is undoubtedly part of the doctrine surrounding many religions, including those in the Abrahamic tradition, that morality is objective. The moral truths, if not created by God, are certainly known by God. This would provide an important preservative role for the belief in objectivity.

More interestingly, Mackie's appeal to motivation becomes much more plausible as a proposal about the preservation of the belief in objectivity. The social psychology literature on theory-maintenance and theory-change reveals a number of biases that make us more likely to retain beliefs that are motivationally attractive. We are less likely to recall evidence that leads to an unwanted conclusion, we are less likely to believe evidence that leads to an unwanted conclusion, and we are more likely to use our critical resources to attack undesirable conclusions. For instance in one experiment, men and women were presented with data that indicated at first glance that women tend to have inferior leadership skills, but on more careful inspection, it is clear that the data do not support this conclusion. Women, who are motivated to reject the conclusion, were significantly more likely than men to notice that the data did not really indicate that women had inferior leadership skills (Schaller 1992). This is just one study in a large and fascinating literature that indicates that motivation greatly affects which beliefs we are likely to retain (for reviews, see Nisbett and Ross 1980 and Kunda 1999).

If it is true that the belief in moral objectivity is motivationally attractive, as Mackie suggests, that would go some distance to explaining why the belief in moral objectivity persists in so many people. For the social psychological evidence indicates that in general, beliefs that are motivationally attractive are less likely to get overturned. That does not, of course, mean that we're incapable of challenging the belief in objectivity. There have been moral skeptics for a *very* long time. But it does mean that the belief in moral objectivity would be less likely to come under scrutiny simply because it is motivationally satisfying for us.[11]

11. The discussion in this section has rested on the assumption that the belief in objectivity is a default setting on folk metaethics, in which case the belief in moral objectivity should be cross-culturally universal in young children. If it turns out that the belief in objectivity is culturally variable, then we

The previous section made the case that moral objectivism is a default feature of commonsense metaethics. We now need to turn to the substantive question of whether commonsense is right to embrace moral objectivism. Philosophical debates about the truth of moral objectivism, because of their manifest importance, are extremely well trod, and the literature is forbiddingly subtle. Nonetheless, it will be important to have at least a sketch of how a sentiment-based account of moral judgment might contribute to an argument against objectivism. Sentimentalism, as the tradition flows from Hume, is associated with a distinctive argument against moral objectivism. That argument draws on the claims that our moral judgments depend on our emotional responses, and that our emotional responses themselves have no externally privileged status. Here I want to explore whether this kind of argument can be elaborated by the account of moral judgment developed in this volume.

The basic thesis of moral objectivism, stipulated in section 2, is that the moral status of an action is constituted by the action "as it is in itself" and accordingly, true moral judgments are nonrelativistically true. Humean sentimentalism is often regarded as directly opposed to moral objectivity in this sense. Inevitably, scholars disagree about Hume's actual position on moral objectivity (cf. Blackburn 1993; Mackie 1980; Norton 1982; Sturgeon 2001). I lack the exegetical talents to enter the debate, so I will adopt the dodge of calling the argument "Humean," without actually saddling Hume with it. According to Humean sentimentalism, morality hangs entirely on the particular emotional repertoire of humans. Here is one place where Hume seems to be making this point: "If we can depend upon any principle, which we learn from philosophy, this, I think, may be considered as certain and undoubted, that there is nothing, in itself, valuable or despicable, desirable or hateful, beautiful or deformed; but that these attributes arise from the particular constitution and fabric of human sentiment and affection" (1742 [1987], 162). Norman Kemp Smith paraphrases Hume's view using much the same language: "Moral judgments, in marking out the good and the evil, have their source not in the eternal nature of any independent reality, but solely in the particular fabric and constitution of the human species" (Kemp Smith 1941, 199). There are different ways to read Hume's passage. But on one reading, the passage claims exactly what objectivity denies—that moral properties

---

might set to work on developing a story about the cultural transmission of the belief in objectivity. Motivation would likely play a key role here too. The fact that moral objectivity is motivationally attractive makes it more likely to survive culturally.

are constituted by relations to populations such that the same particular action can have different moral properties for different populations. No thing is vile "as it is in itself"; rather, something might be vile for one group and not vile for another group.

This Humean case against objectivism can be cast broadly as a two-step argument. Morality is not objective because:

1. Rational creatures who lack certain emotions would not make the moral judgments that we do.
2. There is no principled basis for maintaining that these certain emotions (on which our moral judgments depend) are the *right* emotions. That is, there is no externally privileged basis for maintaining that all rational creatures *should* have the emotions.

In brief, moral judgment depends on certain emotions, and these emotions themselves are rationally arbitrary, so moral judgment, as we know it, is not objective. No action is wrong simpliciter. At best, an action is only wrong relative to a population—the population of individuals that share a certain emotional repertoire. A more careful way to frame the Humean conclusion here is that the commonsense commitment to objectivity is unwarranted. Given the emotional basis of moral judgment, we are not justified in our belief that morality is objective.

This Humean threat to objectivism is hard to develop without stepping outside of the human species, since Hume explicitly maintains that the sentiments are species general. Thus, one fanciful way to illustrate the point is to resort to that philosophical perennial, the Martian. On the Humean account, Martians who lacked analogues of human sentiment and affection would not make the moral judgments that we do. We think it is wrong to torture puppies, but the Martians might not believe anything like this. Furthermore, the argument continues, this need not be because the Martians are ignorant of any facts or because they are obtuse or too busy to do the calculations. Rather, the Martians might be as smart, well-informed, and have as much intellectual leisure as you please. The Martians might be exceptional (if solitary and back-stabbing) mathematicians and scientists. They fail to condemn puppy torture because they lack analogues of the human sentiments (though the Martians do experience a wide range of pains and pleasures). They recognize that humans oppose the torture of puppies. But they do not share this opposition because they do not share the emotional repertoire that leads us to revile puppy torture. The next step in the broad argument is to maintain that there is no externally privileged basis for saying that we have the right emotions and the Martians are emotionally defective. That is, there is no independent basis for saying that our emotional repertoire is the right one to have. Our moral convictions flow from our emotions, and those emotions themselves have no externally privileged status. As a result, the moral convictions themselves have no privileged status, no claim to objective truth.

As noted in section 2, it is likely that most people (at least in our culture) would maintain that puppy torture really is objectively wrong and the Martians' insouciance on the matter is simply a mistake. Thus, I think that the Humean conclusion does threaten commonsense moral objectivity. But the first step in the broad argument claims that our moral judgments have their source in the fabric of human sentiment. The Humean arguments for this have been widely attacked over the centuries. It is at that point that I think the empirical work exploited in this volume might make a contribution. For the account of moral judgment that has emerged from the empirical work suggests that our emotional responses play a critical role both in the character of individual normative judgment and in the cultural viability of norms. Affect seems to play a crucial role in leading individuals to distinguish harm norms and other Sentimental Rules from merely conventional norms. Further, as argued in chapter 7, harm norms, like other affect-backed norms, plausibly gain an advantage in cultural evolution through their resonance with our affective systems. As a result, it becomes plausible, though not certain, that Martians who lacked entirely an affective response to suffering would not share our harm norms. For instance, they might maintain that it is perfectly permissible to harm individuals that pose no threat to one's own well being. Furthermore, if the affect-based account is right, their disagreement with us would not be due to any defects in reason or to the lack of ideal circumstances. Rather, their disagreement with us would flow from basic, arational differences in emotional response. For, on this account, affective mechanisms have cascading effects on the character and cultural survival of normative judgments.

The case here is cleanest to make by appealing to the alien thought experiments. But of course, there are individuals that approximate these Martians even in our midst. Psychopaths show significantly diminished response to others' suffering, and, as we have seen, psychopaths display abnormal moral judgment. They disagree with us about authority contingency (Blair 1997) and about why moral violations are wrong (Blair 1995; Blair et al. 1995). In chapter 3, I argued that these differences between psychopaths and the rest of us apparently cannot be attributed to any differences in rational capacities. Rather, the psychopath's atypical performance on moral judgment tasks seems to be traced to their atypical emotional response. This account of moral judgment in psychopathy is corroborated by the findings on disgust-backed transgressions recounted in chapter 1. Disgusting violations are treated much like moral violations—as quite serious and wrong independent of authority. Furthermore, subjects with low disgust-sensitivity tended to regard disgusting violations as less serious and more authority contingent than subjects with high disgust-sensitivity. Thus, important differences and disagreements in normative judgments seem to follow from different levels of sensitivity. In addition, the etiquette norms that would evolve in a group of low-disgust-sensitivity individuals are likely to differ significantly from the etiquette norms that would evolve in a group of high-disgust-sensitivity individuals. In particular, one would expect that norms governing spitting and nose-blowing would be less restrictive in a culture made up of individuals with low disgust sensitivity to phlegm and saliva. Similarly, it is to be expected that a significantly different pattern of cultural evolution of harm norms would be found in a group of individuals with low emotional sensitivity to others' suffering. On the account of moral judgment I have suggested, if we had lacked sentiments such as reactive distress and concern, we would likely have exhibited a much different pattern of judgment about what we currently regard as the moral domain.[12]

Thus, there is some empirical support for the first Humean premise, that creatures who lacked certain emotions would not make the moral judgments we do. Let us turn to the second premise, that there is no externally privileged basis for saying that the operative emotions are the right emotions to have. On the account of moral judgment developed here, the emotions of reactive distress and concern play an especially important role in moral judgment. We can accordingly fill out the second premise somewhat: there is no principled basis for maintaining that all rational creatures should have emotional responses like reactive distress and concern. There is no independent reason to think that this emotional repertoire is the right one to have.

12. This suggests that on the Sentimental Rules account, moral judgment is, to some extent, subject-relative. But it is important to be clear that the sense in which moral judgment is subject relative is much different from traditional proposals of simple subjectivism. According to the textbook version of simple subjectivism, to say "X is wrong" is merely to report one's own subjective state of disapproval (see Rachels 2002). The model of moral judgment developed here suggests a much more complex relationship between moral judgment and the emotions. For when we say "X is wrong" we are reporting not our current feeling, but rather a norm. Emotions come into play in crucial but less direct ways. Emotions affect the way in which those transgressions are treated, and emotions affect the likelihood that the norms will continue into future generations. This means, among other things, that the account is not susceptible to the familiar antisubjectivist objection that if we are merely reporting our subjective states, it is impossible for us to disagree about morality. According to textbook subjectivism, when Joe says "Capital punishment is wrong" and Bill says "Capital punishment is not wrong," each is merely reporting his own subjective state (of disapproval and approval), so each is correct in his assertion, and thus they are not disagreeing. That, many think, is an intolerable consequence, because it seems obvious in such cases that the individuals are disagreeing. The Sentimental Rules account is not wedded to any such simplistic account of the relation between subjective states and moral judgment.

Another, perhaps less immodest, way to put the point is as a challenge: if moral judgment really does pivot on the emotions, then to defend objectivism, the objectivist needs to provide some principled reason to think that the emotions that drive moral judgment are the right emotions to have. That is, the objectivist needs to show that all rational creatures *should* have such emotional responses (or perhaps some other responses that would lead those creatures to share our moral norms). The difficulty is that it is not at all clear how to argue for such a claim. The objectivist cannot simply help himself to a moral intuition that rational creatures should have these emotions, because the Humean point is that our moral intuitions depend on the emotions we happen to have. It is manifestly circular to use these moral intuitions to underwrite the claim that rational creatures "should" have the emotions we do. One might, however, try to appeal to other kinds of considerations to mount a more principled argument that all rational creatures should have the responses. But the challenge here is considerable.[13] It is safe to say that Humeans do not expect the challenge to be met.

13. One might try to claim, for instance, that creatures who lack emotional responses to suffering are broken and malfunctioning in some deep way. One familiar way to develop accounts of malfunction is by appeal to proper evolutionary function (e.g., Casebeer 2003). So, one might try to argue that all rational creatures ought to have affective mechanisms with proper functions such that the mechanisms will lead the creatures to have the kinds of moral norms that we do. It is not at all clear that such a proposal would offer succor to the objectivist, for it is a familiar worry that a mechanism can serve a proper evolutionary function while delivering false beliefs. But in any case, the proposal is itself problematic. The fact that we have mechanisms that are responsive to suffering is presumably a function of our evolutionary history. To be sure, we have a limited understanding of this history, but it seems plausible that a radically different evolutionary history could result in radically different emotional systems. It seems nomologically possible for there to be aliens with evolutionary histories so radically different from ours that they function perfectly well to fit their environment yet they lack the sort of emotional mechanisms that would lead to norms like ours. If that is right, then the appeal to proper function itself has to be relativized—creatures with evolutionary histories relevantly similar to ours should have affective mechanisms that will lead those creatures to have norms like ours. But at that point the appeal to proper function no longer rescues commonsense objectivism. For commonsense objectivism says that the aliens are wrong to condone puppy torture, not that the aliens are wrong provided that they share a relevantly similar evolutionary history with us. (I am indebted to Bill Casebeer for helpful discussions of this topic.)

Indeed, even in our own species, it turns out to be a matter of debate whether psychopathy is a malfunction. In some important, disturbing work, Linda Mealey has suggested that one form of psychopathy ("primary sociopathy") might actually be a kind of genetic evolutionary adaptation (1995, 1997). Mealey exploits the game theoretic notion of "evolutionary stable strategy," the idea that what will maximize fitness for an individual depends on the traits of the other members of the population. This idea can be illustrated by considering a toy example of two genetically determined types: "hawks," who fight viciously in all conflicts over resources (and the losers in such conflicts suffer grave injuries) and "doves," who retreat immediately (and therefore without injury) from all conflicts. In a population comprised entirely of hawks, being a dove will give one an advantage, because in that population, every conflict leads to a vicious fight. Of course, in a population comprised entirely of doves, being a hawk will give one an advantage, because one will win every conflict. Hence, the population will evolve to include both hawks and doves in some more stable state (see Sober 1993, 136–42 for a summary). Now, Mealey's

The foregoing provides a sketch of how the account of moral judgment developed here might contribute to an argument against moral objectivity. According to the Sentimental Rules account, both the character and the evolution of moral judgment depend on our emotional repertoire. As a result, a group of individuals who shared our rational capacities but lacked our responsiveness to suffering would likely not develop the harm norms to which we are so committed. Unless the objectivist can provide some independent reason to think that rational creatures *should* have these emotions on which moral judgment depends, that it is a defect *not* to have the emotions, then the Humean argument suggests that the most plausible view is that morality is not objective. Puppy torture is not wrong simpliciter. At best, puppy torture is wrong for certain populations. This argument is only strengthened if, as suggested in section 3, there is a deflationary sentimentalist explanation for the origin of the commonsense belief in objectivity itself. Nonetheless, what I have sketched is clearly not a definitive and complete argument against objectivism.[14] But I hope it is enough to suggest that if moral judgment does depend on the emotions in the ways outlined here, then the moral objectivist inherits a considerable worry.

5. AFTER OBJECTIVITY: THE PERSISTENCE OF MORAL JUDGMENT

In the previous section, I argued that the account of moral judgment developed here might contribute to an argument against moral objectivity. However, in section 2, I argued that moral objectivity is a default setting on commonsense metaethics. As a result, the rejection of moral objectivity would demand a substantial revision of commonsense metaethics. In

---

suggestion is that primary psychopathy is a real example of a genetically based evolutionary stable strategy. Hence, she suggests that there will always be a "small, cross-culturally similar, and unchanging baseline frequency of sociopaths ... Those individuals will display chronic, pathologically emotionless, antisocial behavior throughout most of their lifespan and across a variety of situations" (Mealey 1995, 536). If this is right, then being a primary psychopath is not a developmental defect or a product of brain damage or a disadvantaged childhood. Rather, primary psychopathy is an evolved response to exploit a niche in the population. Repugnant though this thought is, if it is right, it becomes much more difficult to dismiss psychopathy as a malfunction.

14. The resolute moral objectivist might claim, for instance, that it does not matter if commonsense moral judgments do not issue from objective moral facts. For, the reply goes, the case for moral objectivism does not depend on folk moral judgments, which we might have expected to have spurious origins. Rather the proof of objectivism depends on some other kind of access to the moral realm. Obviously this position cannot be refuted. Perhaps there is some occult proof that central moral claims are nonrelativistically true. However, if philosophers truly eschew commonsense moral judgment, it will be incumbent on them to explain the nature of their special access to the moral realm.

this section, I will begin to explore the nature of "postobjectivist" moral judgment.

If we become convinced that morality lacks objective moorings, what will the consequences be for our commonsense moral judgment? Would a rejection of moral objectivism engender rampant nihilism? Or would the rejection of moral objectivism leave our normative lives relatively unfazed? Even at a popular level, these questions have real currency. People worry that the abandonment of moral objectivity threatens to unravel the moral tissue of society.

Meanwhile, professional philosophers debate the implications of non-objectivism for the status of commonsense moral claims. Mackie's error theory is perhaps the most notorious proposal in contemporary analytic philosophy. According to error theory, ordinary moral judgments are so infused with the commitment to objectivity that the falsity of objectivism renders all ordinary moral judgments false. Mackie maintains that the presupposition that moral values are objective "is part of what our ordinary moral statements mean: the traditional moral concepts of the ordinary man . . . are concepts of objective value" (Mackie 1977, 35). He goes on to say:

> I do not think it is going too far to say that this assumption has been incorporated in the basic, conventional meanings of moral terms . . . The claim to objectivity, however ingrained in our language and thought, is not self-validating. It can and should be questioned. But the denial of objective values will have to be put forward not as the result of an analytic approach, but as an 'error theory,' a theory that although most people in making moral judgements implicitly claim, among other things, to be pointing to something objectively prescriptive, these claims are all false. (Mackie 1977, 35)

Hence, on Mackie's view, once one comes to reject moral objectivism, one should regard common moral judgments, even one's own earlier moral judgments, as uniformly false. For all of those judgments are infected by the objectivist presupposition. The "traditional moral concepts" employed in lay moral judgments are, like the concept "witch," empty.

One might reject objectivism and try to resist error theory by maintaining that the belief in moral objectivity is simply not essential to lay moral concepts. On this "inessentialist" view, lay moral concepts might not be empty even if morality is not objective. Gilbert Harman defends moral relativism in a way that suggests an inessentialist account. According to Harman, when people make moral claims, the claims are best regarded as statements that have tacit restrictive quantification. As a result, even though objectivity is rejected, common moral judgments can often be true, because they are best read as implicitly relativized to a group or a framework. Harman intimates that it would be "mean-spirited" to suggest that common moral judgments are all false (Harman and Thomson 1996, 4). Although lay people might not intend their moral proclamations to be elliptical for relativized statements, it is best to interpret them thus. So, Harman writes, "a judgment of the form, *P ought morally to D*, has to be understood as elliptical for a judgment of the form, *in relation to moral framework M, P ought morally to D*" (Harman and Thomson 1996, 4, fn 2; emphasis in original). Now, then, when the Hopi say "it was okay for Fred to hurt that bird" and we say "it was not okay for Fred to hurt that bird," we might both be saying something true. The Hopi's claim is indexed to one moral framework and our claim is indexed to a different moral framework. Again, Harman takes pains to explain that he is not saying that this is what people intend (e.g., Harman and Thomson 1996, 17). But after one has relinquished objectivism, this may be the best way to interpret them.

Thus, according to error theorists, common moral judgments are all false. According to inessentialists, common moral judgments need not all be false; rather, commonsense moral judgments might be true judgments that are relativized to some moral framework. How do we decide who is right in this debate? Are lay moral concepts so infected with the metaethical claim of objectivity that the rejection of objectivity is tantamount to denying that lay moral concepts apply to anything? The question can take on a more concrete shape in light of the discussion in section 2, where I suggested both that moral objectivism is a default setting on commonsense metaethics and also that many college students apparently reject objectivism. If, as seems possible, some of these college students fully reject moral objectivism, it generates the longitudinal result that, at some point in their development, a number of individuals convert from objectivism to nonobjectivism. Such individuals still use terms like "morally wrong," and let us charitably assume that their postobjectivist uses of "morally wrong" are sometimes true. For such individuals who reject moral objectivity but still claim that certain actions are "morally wrong" do we want to say (1) or (2)?

1. Their term "morally wrong" expresses a different concept after the rejection of objectivity.
2. Their term "morally wrong" expresses the same concept that it did before the rejection of objectivity.

The error theorist will maintain (1). According to the error theorist, the traditional moral concepts are empty, so if postobjectivist uses of "morally wrong" accurately apply to certain actions (under certain conditions), the term "morally wrong" must express a concept different from the old concept. The inessentialist, on the other hand, can embrace (2). For according to the inessentialist, even if objectivity is false, the moral concepts of moral objectivists are not empty. As a result, according to the inessentialist, objectivists and nonobjectivists might well deploy the same moral concepts when they assert such things as "it is morally wrong to hit people."

To resolve this dispute between error theorists and inessentialists, we want to know the extent to which abandoning objectivity affects one's moral cognition. But there is a prior and more fundamental issue. To determine whether an individual deploys the same moral concepts before and after the rejection of objectivism, we need to know the answer to a longstanding problem in philosophy of mind: how are concepts individuated? In particular, to know whether "morally wrong" expresses the same concept before and after the rejection of objectivity, one needs to know the basic criteria for what makes one concept the same concept across changes in the cognitive economy. To see why, we need to pause to review recent debates on concepts and concept individuation (for a review, see Laurence and Margolis 1999).[15] Most theorists agree that two concept tokens are of the same type only if they have the same content; however, there is radical division about the conditions under which two concepts have the same content. Some theorists maintain that the content of a concept is partly determined by the concept's "conceptual role," that is, its pattern of causal interactions with other mental states (e.g., Block 1986; Murphy and Medin 1985). On these accounts, two concepts have the same content only if they have the same (or roughly the same) conceptual roles. As a result, if two concept tokens have even minor differences in their conceptual roles, then they are, on a fine-grained conceptual role theory, not tokens of the same type of concept. Hence, on such an account of concept individuation, when the objectivist and nonobjectivist each says "hitting is morally wrong," they would almost certainly be expressing different concepts, because there will at least be minor differences in the conceptual roles of their respective "moral" concepts. At the other end of the spectrum, there are accounts on which conceptual role plays no part whatsoever in determining the content of a concept (e.g. Fodor 1998). If some such account is right, and if content identity determines concept identity, then two concept tokens with radically different conceptual roles can still be instances of the same type. So two people might be deploying the same concept even though they hold drastically different beliefs that

15. The following treatment is shaped by the discussion of a related point in Nichols and Stich (2003).

involve the concept. As a result, on some theories of concept individuation, nonobjectivists and objectivists might be exploiting tokens of the same moral concepts even if those tokens have radically different conceptual roles.

On some accounts of concept individuation, then, even if nonobjectivists have radically different moral cognition than objectivists, it might still be the case that they are all using the same moral concepts. On other accounts of concept individuation, even if nonobjectivists have only minimally different moral cognition from objectivists, it might still be the case that uses of "morally wrong" express concepts of different types in objectivists and nonobjectivists. Roughly speaking, fine-grained conceptual role theories tend to be biased towards error theory, and anti-conceptual-role theories tend to be biased against error theory. These are just a couple of locations in the sophisticated and highly contentious theoretical landscape on concept individuation. However, they serve to indicate that, without settling fundamental issues about concepts and their individuation, we will be unable to determine whether error theory is right.

This is hardly the place to try to arrive at a considered view of concept individuation. Yet, one needs a theory of concept individuation to assess whether lay moral concepts get preserved as the same concepts after a nonobjectivist epiphany. As a result, it seems premature to pronounce on whether nonobjectivism entails error theory or inessentialism. While we await the resolution of how to individuate concepts (it may be awhile), we can, however, consider the subsequent issue about the extent to which rejecting objectivity impacts moral cognition. It is some consolation that this subsequent issue is the issue of central interest for non-philosophers—would a rejection of moral objectivity lead to moral chaos?[16]

As noted in section 3, there are a number of different psychological models for how the judgment that morality is objective gets secured. I have maintained throughout that for our broad philosophical purposes, once one has settled on an account that implicates both norms and affect, deciding among the detailed psychological models is less important. But in the current case, it is useful to chart one psychological model that, if true, would entail that the rejection of objectivity would have devastating effects on moral judgment. Among the available on-line processing mod-

---

16. Presumably there will be individual differences here. That is, presumably for some people the rejection of objectivity will have little effect and for some people it will have a significant effect (see Gill 1996 for a nice discussion of this). In some cases, postobjectivists might exhibit drastic normative changes because the rejection of objectivism is coupled with the rejection of God or with an enthusiasm for the transvaluation of values. The question posed in the text does not intend to exclude individual variation, but focuses instead on typical responses. That is, in general, does the rejection of objectivity lead to dramatic differences in normative judgments?

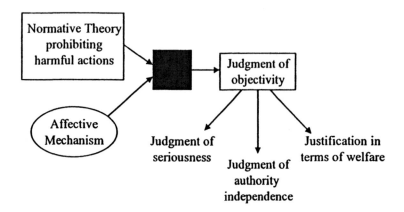

FIGURE 8.2 An on-line model of moral judgment on which judgments of objectivity are essential to generating the characteristic responses to moral violations

els of moral judgment, one possibility is that judgments of objectivity actually play a vital role in generating the other features of moral judgment. In particular, it is possible that it is because subjects explicitly judge a given moral violation as objectively wrong (i.e., wrong simpliciter) that they judge the violation as especially serious, authority independent and as having extra-conventional justification. This kind of model is depicted in figure 8.2. If this model is right, then the rejection of objectivity might have cascading effects on whether the subject regards moral violations as especially serious, authority independent and as prohibited because of welfare considerations.[17]

The work on disgusting transgressions goes some distance to addressing this worry and to supporting the idea that central characteristics of Sentimental Rules are preserved even without a belief in objectivity. For adults do not regard disgusting violations as objectively wrong. Yet they do treat disgusting violations as especially serious, independent of authority, and as having extraconventional justification (Nichols 2002b). Thus, it would seem that norms can be treated as nonconventional even if they are not treated as objective. Of course, it is possible that this does

17. The processing details here would be rather important. One possibility is that a tacit representation that the action is objectively wrong plays a crucial wrong in generating the suite of responses and that the explicit rejection of objectivity occurs downstream of all this core moral processing. On this model, the rejection of objectivity might come too late in the process to change the core set of responses, so this version does not entail that nonobjectivists will have radically different moral cognition. However, if the suite of distinctive moral responses depends on the explicit judgment that the action is objectively wrong, and if this explicit judgment is absent in nonobjectivists, then that would have profoundly deflating effects on the suite of distinctive responses to moral violations.

not hold for moral norms. But at this juncture, a nice experimental question emerges. A significant population of college students respond as moral nonobjectivists about canonical moral violations. And we know that moral judgments carry a typical suite of responses, probed by the moral/conventional task. Hence we might investigate whether students who respond as nonobjectivists about canonical moral violations continue to distinguish such moral violations from conventional violations on the classic dimensions.

I undertook this straightforward task in four studies (Nichols 2004). In each study, students were given a moral/conventional task together with a questionnaire on judgments about objectivity. The studies focused on students who responded as nonobjectivists about canonical moral violations (e.g., hitting others because you feel like it, puppy torture).[18] There were no systematic differences between these "nonobjectivists" and the "objectivists" on the moral/conventional task. That is, nonobjectivists responded in ways that could not be distinguished from objectivists. In some of the experiments, the moral objectivity question was about the *same violations* as the moral cases in the moral/conventional task. Still there were no systematic differences between the objectivist and nonobjectivist groups. Moreover, in each study, the group that endorsed the nonobjectivist claim drew a clear distinction between conventional violations (e.g., talking in class, leaving class without permission) and moral violations (e.g., hitting, shoving). Each group treated moral violations as more serious and less authority contingent than conventional violations. They also offered standard welfare-based justifications for why the moral violations were wrong, but they offered standard social-conventional explanations for why the conventional violations were wrong. Just like moral objectivists, nonobjectivists maintain that hitting other people is very serious, and it does not matter if the teacher says it is okay to hit other people. Further, just like moral objectivists, nonobjectivists maintain that the reason it is wrong to hit other people is because it hurts the other person. Apparently, then, people can be nonobjectivists about canonical moral transgressions while still treating such transgressions otherwise very much like moral violations, and very much in the way that objectivists treat them.[19]

18. Participants who responded as nonobjectivists about whether the earth is flat were excluded from the analyses. For details on the questions used to determine nonobjectivist responses, see chapter 8, footnote 2.

19. It is worth noting that these experiments are insulated from the familiar complaint (charted in chapter 8, footnote 3) that no undergraduates are *global* moral nonobjectivists (since it is expected that virtually no undergraduates will give nonobjectivist responses to cases of racist murder). The current experiments largely bypass this objection because the participants need not be global nonobjectivists for

The foregoing provides preliminary evidence that a person can be a nonobjectivist about certain moral transgressions (e.g., hitting) and yet still distinguish cases of such transgressions from conventional transgressions along the standard dimensions in the moral/conventional task. But if these subjects are really nonobjectivists, one might worry that their performance on the moral/conventional task shows them to be deeply confused.[20] That is, one might maintain that the patterns of the nonobjectivists' responses reveal that they hold an inconsistent normative view because nonobjectivists cannot be justified in drawing the moral/conventional distinction. If they do not think morality is objective, they have no business distinguishing morality from convention.

To address this objection, it is important to pull apart two different claims about the moral/conventional distinction. One might view the moral/conventional distinction as a sharp analytic distinction on which morality is entirely nonconventional. Alternatively, one might view the moral/conventional distinction as a measure of moral cognition in terms of a cluster of differential responses to moral and conventional violations. On the first, analytic, view of the moral/conventional distinction, the objection is that it is inconsistent to view morality as entirely nonconventional while judging it to be nonobjective. Although there is room to dispute this claim there is no need. For even if it is true that nonobjectivists cannot be thoroughgoing nonconventionalists, that does not affect the argument developed here. The moral/conventional experiments in these studies were not intended to show that the participants draw an analytic distinction between morality and convention. Rather the moral/conventional distinction was used as a measure of moral cognition.

Now then, is it inconsistent for moral nonobjectivists to make differential responses to moral and conventional violations? Are nonobjectivists unjustified in giving the normal responses to the moral/conventional task? It is hard to see why. It seems presumptuous to say that giving up objectivity means that I should not judge harmful violations to be more serious, that I should not judge the wrongfulness of hitting another as independent of the teacher's authority, or that I should not think that the actions are wrong because they are harmful. As philosophical sentimentalists have long maintained, you do not have to believe that an action is objectively wrong to have a deep and abiding opposition to such actions.

---

the point to go through. The key point is that people can be nonobjectivists about certain types of transgressions while still treating such transgressions otherwise very much like moral violations, and very much in the way they are treated by people who are objectivists about such violations.

20. This objection was made by an anonymous referee.

The philosophical quagmire over concept individuation prevents us from deciding between error theory and inessentialism. Until the issue of concept individuation issue is settled, we cannot determine whether nonobjectivists are using the same moral concepts as objectivists. Nonetheless, we do have the beginnings of an answer to perhaps a more important issue. One popular fear about anti-objectivism is that the rejection of moral objectivism will usher in a dangerous nihilism. Nonobjectivists, the worry goes, will only follow moral rules opportunistically, like Hume's sensible knave. Although the studies reported here are preliminary, they point in exactly the opposite direction from this worry. The rejection of moral objectivity apparently does not lead to flagrant nihilism. Nonobjectivists treat moral violations much the same way that objectivists do on the standard measure. They treat moral violations as especially serious, independent of authority, and grounded in welfare considerations. In addition, relinquishing objectivity would not mean that we rid ourselves of the emotions that generate much moral motivation. Even after we reject objectivity, we still have the emotions that motivate us to help others who are hurt and to prevent people from causing harm. Much this point was made by Hume in the context of his apparent nonobjectivism:

> Vice and virtue . . . may be compar'd to sounds, colours, heat and cold, which, according to modern philosophy, are not qualities in objects, but perceptions in the mind: And this discovery in morals, like that other in physics, is to be regarded as a considerable advancement of the speculative sciences; tho,' like that too, it has little or no influence on practice. Nothing can be more real, or concern us more, than our own sentiments of pleasure and uneasiness; and if these be favourable to virtue, and unfavourable to vice, no more can be requisite to the regulation of our conduct and behaviour. (*Treatise*, 469)

One need not agree with the details of Hume's moral theory to appreciate his insight that the rejection of objectivity will not radically alter our moral lives. The experiments on the moral/conventional distinction in nonobjectivists provide some empirical corroboration for Hume's characteristically insightful speculation.

6. CONCLUSION

The burden of this chapter has been to explore whether empirical work illuminates issues surrounding moral objectivism. Although I have tried to sketch a broad view on these matters, the empirical evidence is still shallow. Such as it is, the evidence suggests that moral objectivity is a default presupposition of commonsense metaethics. However, this commonsense view is threatened by a familiar Humean argument, and I have suggested that the account of moral judgment developed in this volume supplies the Humean with a new way to elaborate the argument against objectivism. For both the character and the cultural evolution of moral judgment depend on the emotions that we happen to have. Thus there is some reason to think that we should turn away from our commonsense commitment to moral objectivity. Such a move away from objectivity appears to be less disruptive than some have feared. The evidence recounted in the last section suggests that spurning objectivity by no means eradicates the power and authority of harm norms. This is hardly surprising if, as I have argued, harm norms acquire their distinctive status because of their connection with powerful emotional responses. Those emotional responses are not extirpated by coming to reject moral objectivity. The emotions that make moral judgment distinctive continue to burn even in people who abandon the lay metaphysics of morality.

References

American Psychiatric Association. (1994). *Diagnostic and statistical manual of mental disorders*. 4th ed. Washington, D.C.: American Psychiatric Association.

Alexander, R. (1987). *The biology of moral systems*. New York: Aldine.

Allestree, R. (1684). *The works of the learned and pious author of the whole duty of man*. Oxford: The Theatre.

Atran, S. (1998). Folk biology and the anthropology of science: Cognitive universals and cultural particulars. *Behavioral and Brain Sciences* 21:547–609.

Ayala, F. (1987). The biological roots of morality. *Biology and Philosophy* 2: 235–52.

Ayala, F. (1995). The difference of being human: Ethical behavior as an evolutionary byproduct. In *Biology, ethics, and the origins of life*, edited by H. Rolston. Boston: Jones and Bartlett, 113–35.

Ayer, A. (1936). *Language, truth, and logic*. London: Gollancz.

Axelrod, R. (1986). An evolutionary approach to norms. *American Political Science Review* 80:1095–111.

Bacon, A., D. Fein, R. Morris, L. Waterhouse, and D. Allen. (1998). The responses of autistic children to the distress of others. *Journal of Autism and Developmental Disorders* 28:129–42.

Baier, K. (1958). *The moral point of view*. Ithaca, N.Y.: Cornell University Press.

Baron-Cohen, S., A. M. Leslie, and U. Frith. (1985). Does the autistic child have a "theory of mind"? *Cognition* 21:37–46.

Baron-Cohen, S. (1995). *Mindblindness*. Cambridge, Mass.: MIT Press.

Barsalou, L. (1987). The instability of graded structure: Implications for the nature of concepts. In *Concepts and conceptual development: Ecological and intellectual factors in categorization*, edited by U. Neisser. New York: Cambridge University Press, 101–40.

Bartsch, K., and Wellman, H. (1995). *Children talk about the mind*. New York: Oxford University Press.

Batson, C. (1990). How social an animal? The human capacity for caring. *American Psychologist* 45:336–46.

Batson, C. (1991). *The altruism question*. Hillsdale, N.J.: Lawrence Erlbaum.

Batson, C., B. Duncan, P. Ackerman, T. Buckley, and K. Birch. (1981). Is empathic emotion a source of altruistic motivation? *Journal of Personality and Social Psychology* 40:290–302.

Batson, C., K. O'Quin, J. Fultz, M. Vanderplas, and A. Isen. (1983). Self-reported distress and empathy and egoistic versus altruistic motivation for helping. *Journal of Personality and Social Psychology* 45:706–18.

Benedict, R. (1934). *Patterns of culture*. New York: Penguin Books.

Blackburn, S. (1984). *Spreading the word: Groundings in the philosophy of language*. Oxford: Oxford University Press.

Blackburn, S. (1985). Errors and the phenomenology of value. In *Morality and objectivity*, edited by T. Honderich. London: Routledge and Kegan Paul.

Blackburn, S. (1993). Hume on the mezzanine level. *Hume Studies* 19: 273–88.

Blackburn, S. (1998). *Ruling passions: A theory of practical reason*. Oxford: Oxford University Press.

Blair, R. (1993). The development of morality. Ph.D. diss. University of London.

Blair, R. (1995). A cognitive developmental approach to morality: Investigating the psychopath. *Cognition* 57:1–29.

Blair, R. (1996). Brief report: Morality in the autistic child. *Journal of Autism and Developmental Disorders* 26:571–79.

Blair, R. (1997). Moral reasoning and the child with psychopathic tendencies. *Personality and Individual Differences* 26:731–39.

Blair, R. (1999a). Psychophysiological responsiveness to the distress of others in children with autism. *Personality and Individual Differences* 26: 477–85.

Blair, R. (1999b). Responsiveness to distress cues in the child with psychopathic tendencies. *Personality and Individual Differences* 27:135–45.

Blair, R., L. Jones, F. Clark, and M. Smith. (1995). Is the psychopath "morally insane"? *Personality and Individual Differences* 19:741–52.

Blair, R., L. Jones, F. Clark, and M. Smith. (1997). The psychopathic individual: A lack of responsiveness to distress cues? *Psychophysiology* 34: 192–98.

Blair, R., J. Monson, and N. Frederickson. (2001). Moral reasoning and conduct problems in children with emotional and behavioural difficulties. *Personality and Individual Differences* 31:799–811.

Blair, R., C. Sellars, I. Strickland, F. Clark, A. Williams, M. Smith, and L. Jones. (1996). Theory of mind in the psychopath. *Journal of Forensic Psychiatry* 7:15–25.

Block, N. (1986). Advertisement for a semantics for psychology. *Midwest Studies in Philosophy*, Volume X, edited by P. French, T. Uehling, and H. Wettstein. Minneapolis: University of Minnesota Press, 615–678.

Bloom, L. (1970). *Language development: Form and function in emerging grammars.* Cambridge, Mass.: MIT Press.

Bloom, L. (1973). *One word at a time: The use of single word utterances before syntax.* The Hague, Netherlands: Mouton.

Blum, L. (1994). Moral development and conceptions of morality. In *Moral perception and particularity*, edited by L. Blum. Cambridge: Cambridge University Press.

Boehm, C. (1999). *Hierarchy in the forest: The evolution of egalitarian behavior.* Cambridge, Mass.: Harvard University Press.

Bower, G. (1994). Some relations between emotion and memory. In *The nature of emotion*, edited by P. Ekman and R. Davidson. New York: Oxford University Press, 303–5.

Boyd, R. (1988). How to be a moral realist. In *Essays on moral realism*, edited by G. Sayre-McCord. Ithaca, N.Y.: Cornell University Press, 181–228.

Boyd, R., and P. Richerson. (1985). *Culture and the evolutionary process.* Chicago: University of Chicago Press.

Boyd, R., and P. Richerson. (1992). Punishment allows the evolution of cooperation (or anything else) in sizeable groups. *Ethology and Sociobiology* 13:171–95.

Boyer, P. (1994). Cognitive constraints on cultural representations: Natural ontologies and religious ideas. In *Mapping the mind*, edited by L. Hirshfeld and S. Gelman. Cambridge: Cambridge University Press, 391–411.

Boyer, P. (1999). Cognitive tracks of cultural inheritance: How evolved intuitive ontology governs cultural transmission. *American Anthropologist* 100:876–89.

Boyer, P. (2000). Evolution of the modern mind and the origins of culture: Religious concepts as a limiting case. In *Evolution and the human mind*, edited by P. Carruthers and A. Chamberlain. Cambridge: Cambridge University Press, 93–113.

Boyer, P. (2001). *Religion explained.* New York: Basic Books.

Brandt, R. (1946). Moral valuation. *Ethics* 56:106–21.

Brandt, R. (1950). The emotive theory of ethics. *Philosophical Review* 59: 305–18.

Brandt, R. (1954). *Hopi ethics.* Chicago: University of Chicago Press.

Brandt, R. (1959). *Ethical theory.* Englewood Cliffs, N.J.: Prentice Hall.

Brink, D. (1989). *Moral realism and the foundation of ethics.* Cambridge: Cambridge University Press.

Brink, D. (1997). Moral motivation. *Ethics* 56:108.

Byrne, D. (1971). *The attraction paradigm.* New York: Academic Press.

Call, J., and M. Tomasello. (1998). Distinguishing intentional from accidental actions in orangutans, chimpanzees, and human children. *Journal of Comparative Psychology* 112:192–206.

Campbell, J. (1999). Can philosophical accounts of altruism accommodate experimental data on helping behavior? *Australasian Journal of Philosophy* 77:26–45.

Capps, L., N. Yirmiya, and M. Sigman. (1992). Understanding of simple and complex emotions in non-retarded children with autism. *Journal of Child Psychology and Psychiatry and Allied Disciplines* 33:1169–82.

Carey, S. (1985). *Conceptual change in childhood.* Cambridge, Mass.: MIT Press.

Carey, S., and E. Spelke. (1996). Science and core knowledge. *Philosophy of Science* 63:515–33.

Casebeer, W. (2003). *Natural ethical facts: Evolution, connectionism, and moral cognition.* Cambridge, Mass.: MIT Press.

Chagnon, N. (1992). *Yanomamö.* 4th ed. New York: Harcourt Brace Jovanovich.

Cheng, P., and K. Holyoak. (1985). Pragmatic reasoning schemas. *Cognitive Psychology* 17:391–416.

Christianson, S. (1997). On emotional stress and memory. In *Intersections in basic and applied memory research,* edited by D. Payne and F. Conrad. Mahwah, N.J.: Lawrence Erlbaum.

Christianson, S., and E. Engelberg. (1999). Organization of emotional memories. In *Handbook of cognition and emotion,* edited by T. Dalgleish and M. Power. New York: Wiley.

Christianson, S., and E. Loftus. (1991). Remembering emotional events. *Cognition and Emotion* 5:81–108.

Clark, R., and L. Word. (1974). Where is the apathetic bystander? Situational characteristics of the emergency. *Journal of Personality and Social Psychology* 29:279–87.

Cohen, J. (forthcoming). Color properties and color ascriptions: A relationalist manifesto.

Cosmides, L. (1989). The logic of social exchange: Has natural selection shaped how humans reason? Studies with the Wason selection task. *Cognition* 31:187–276.

Cummings, E., B. Hollenbeck, R. Iannotti, M. Radke-Yarrow, and C. Zahn-Waxler. (1986). Early organization of altruism and aggression: Developmental patterns and individual differences. In *Altruism and aggression: Biological and social origins,* edited by C. Zahn-Waxler, E. Cummings, and R. Iannotti. New York: Cambridge University Press.

Cummins, D. (1996). Evidence of deontic reasoning in 3- and 4-year old children. *Memory and Cognition* 24:823–29.

Cummins, D. (1998). Social norms and other minds. In *The Evolution of Mind*, edited by D. Cummins and C. Allen. Oxford: Oxford University Press.

Currie, G. (1995). The moral psychology of fiction. *Australasian Journal of Philosophy* 73:250–59.

Currie, G., and I. Ravenscroft. (in press). *Recreative minds: Image and imagination in philosophy and psychology*. Oxford: Oxford University Press.

D'Arms, J., and D. Jacobson. (1994). Expressivism, morality, and the emotions. *Ethics* 104:739–63.

D'Arms, J., and D. Jacobson. (2000). Sentiment and value. *Ethics* 110:722–48.

Damon, W. (1988). *The moral child: Nurturing children's natural moral growth*. New York: Free Press.

Damon, W. (1977). *The social world of the child*. San Francisco: Jossey-Bass.

Dancy, J. (1999). Defending particularism. *Metaphilosophy* 30:25–32.

Darwall, S. (1983). *Impartial reason*. Ithaca, N.Y.: Cornell University Press.

Darwall, S. (1995). *The british moralists and the internal "ought:" 1640–1740*. New York: Cambridge University Press.

Darwall, S. (1998a). *Philosophical ethics*. Boulder, Colo.: Westview Press.

Darwall, S. (1998b). Empathy, sympathy, care. *Philosophical Studies* 89: 261–82.

Darwall, S., A. Gibbard, and P. Railton, eds. (1997). *Moral discourse and practice*. Oxford: Oxford University Press.

Darwall, S., A. Gibbard, and P. Railton. [1992] (1997). Toward fin de siecle ethics: Some trends. *Philosophical Review* 115–89. Reprinted in *Moral discourse and practice*, edited by S. Darwall, A. Gibbard, and P. Railton. Oxford: Oxford University Press.

Darwin, C. [1871] (1981). *The descent of man and selection in relation to sex*. Princeton, N.J.: Princeton University Press.

Darwin, C. [1872] (1965). *The expression of the emotions in man and animals*. Chicago: University of Chicago Press.

Davidson, P. E. Turiel, and A. Black. (1983). The effect of stimulus familiarity on the use of criteria and justifications in children's social reasoning. *British Journal of Developmental Psychology* 1:49–65.

Davis, M. (1980). A multidimensional approach to individual differences in empathy. *JSAS Catalog of Selected Documents in Psychology* 10:85.

Dawkins, R. (1976). *The selfish gene*. Oxford: Oxford University Press.

Dawson, G., and M. Fernald. (1987). Perspective-taking ability and its relationship to the social behavior of autistic children. *Journal of Autism and Developmental Disorders* 17:487–98.

Dawson, G., A. Meltzoff, J. Osterling, and J. Rinaldi. (1998). Children with autism fail to orient to naturally occurring social stimuli. *Journal of Autism and Developmental Disorders* 28:479–85.

Deigh, J. (1995). Empathy and universalizability. *Ethics* 105:743–63.

Dennett, D. (1995). *Darwin's dangerous idea*. New York: Simon and Schuster.

Dershowitz, A. (2002). *Why terrorism works*. New Haven, Conn.: Yale University Press.

De Sahagun, B. [1578–79] (1981). *Florentine codex: General history of the things of new spain. Book 2: The ceremonies*. Translated by A. Anderson and C. Dibble. Santa Fe, N.M.: School of American Research.

de Waal, F. (1996). *Good natured*. Cambridge, Mass.: Harvard University Press.

Doris, J. (2002). *Lack of character: Personality and moral behavior*. Cambridge: Cambridge University Press.

Doris, J., and S. Stich. (in press). As a matter of fact: Empirical perspectives on ethics. In *The oxford handbook of contemporary analytic philosophy*, edited by F. Jackson and M. Smith. Oxford: Oxford University Press.

Dulman, R. van. (1990). *Theatre of horror: Crime and punishment in early modern Germany*. Translated by E. Neu. Cambridge: Polity Press.

Duncker, K. (1939). Ethical relativity? (An inquiry into the psychology of ethics). *Mind* 48:39–57.

Dunn, J. (1988). *The beginnings of social understanding*. Cambridge, Mass.: Harvard University Press.

Dunn, J., and P. Munn. (1987). Development of justification in disputes with mother and sibling. *Developmental Psychology* 23:791–98.

Durham, W. (1991). *Coevolution: Genes, culture and human diversity*. Stanford, Calif.: Stanford University Press.

Edel, M., and A. Edel. (1968). *Anthropology and ethics*. New Brunswick, N.J.: Transaction Press.

Edwards, K., and E. Smith. (1996). A disconfirmation bias in the evaluation of arguments. *Journal of Personality and Social Psychology* 71:5–24.

Eisenberg, N. (1992). *The caring child*. Cambridge, Mass.: Harvard University Press.

Eisenberg, N., and J. Strayer. (1987). Critical issues in the study of empathy. In *Empathy and its development*, edited by N. Eisenberg and J. Straayer. New York: Cambridge University Press.

Eisenberg, N., and R. Fabes. (1990). Empathy: Conceptualization, measurement, and relation to prosocial behavior. *Motivation and Emotion* 14: 131–49.

Eisenberg, N., R. Fabes, P. Miller, J. Fultz, R. Shell, R. Mathy, and R. Reno. (1989). Relation of sympathy and personal distress to prosocial behavior: A multimethod study. *Journal of Personality and Social Psychology* 57: 55–66.

Eisenberg-Berg, N., and M. Hand. (1979). The relationship of preschoolers' reasoning about prosocial moral conflicts to prosocial behavior. *Child Development* 50:356–63.

Ekman, P. (1992). An argument for basic emotions. In *Basic emotions*, edited by N. Stein and K. Oatley. Hillsdale, N.J.: Lawrence Erlbaum.

Ekman, P. (1994). All emotions are basic. In *The nature of emotion*, edited by P. Ekman and R. Davidson. New York: Oxford University Press, 15–19.

Elias, N. [1939] (2000). *The civilizing process.* Translated by E. Jephcott. Malden, Mass.: Blackwell.

Emsley, C. (1987). *Crime and society in England, 1750–1900.* London: Longman.

Erasmus, D. [1530] (1985). *On good manners for boys.* Translated by B. McGregor, in *Collected works of erasmus,* Vol. 25, edited by J. Sowards. Toronto: University of Toronto Press.

Falk, W. D. (1953). Goading and guiding, *Mind* 62.

Ewing, A. (1947). *The definition of good.* New York: Macmillan.

Faucher, L., R. Mallon, D. Nazer, S. Nichols, A. Ruby, S. Stich, and J. Weinberg. (2002). The baby in the lab-coat: Why child development is an inadequate model for understanding the development of science. In *The cognitive basis of science,* edited by P. Carruthers, M. Siegal, and S. Stich, 335–62. Cambridge: Cambridge University Press.

Flanagan, O. (1991). *Varieties of moral personality: Ethics and psychological realism.* Cambridge, Mass.: Harvard University Press.

Flavell, J., Flavell, E., Green, F., and Moses, L. (1990). Young children's understanding of fact beliefs versus value beliefs. *Child Development* 61: 915–28.

Fodor, J. (1983). *Modularity of mind.* Cambridge, Mass.: MIT Press.

Fodor, J. (1998). *Concepts.* Oxford: Oxford University Press.

Fodor, J. (2000). *The mind doesn't work that way.* Cambridge, Mass.: MIT Press.

Foot, P. (1972). Morality as a system of hypothetical imperatives. *The Philosophical Review* 81: 305–316.

Foucault, M. (1977). *Discipline and punish.* Translated by A. Sheridan. New York: Random House.

Frank, R. (1988). *Passions within reason.* New York: Norton.

Frith, U. (1989). *Autism: Explaining the enigma.* Oxford: Blackwell.

Furnivall, F., ed. (1869). *Queene Elizabethes achademy, A booke of precedence, &c.* London: Kegan Paul, Trench, Trubner.

Garcia, J. (1990). Learning without memory. *Journal of Cognitive Neuroscience.* 2:298–305.

Geach, P. (1965). Assertion. *Philosophical Review* 74:449–65.

Gergely, G., Z. Nadasdy, G. Csibra, and S. Biro. (1995). Taking the intentional stance at 12 months of age. *Cognition* 56:165–93.

German, T. (1999). Children's causal reasoning: Counterfactual thinking occurs for "negative" outcomes only. *Developmental Science* 2:442–47.

German, T., and S. Nichols. (2003). Children's counterfactual inferences about long and short causal chains. *Developmental Science* 6:514–23.

Gewirth, A. (1978). *Reason and morality.* Chicago: University of Chicago Press.

Gibbard, A. (1990). *Wise choices, apt feelings.* Cambridge, Mass.: Harvard University Press.

Gill, M. (1996). A philosopher in his closet: Reflexivity and justification in Hume's moral theory. *Canadian Journal of Philosophy* 26:231–56.

Gill, M. (1999). The religious rationalism of Benjamin Whichcote. *Journal of the History of Philosophy* 37:271–300.

Goldman, A. (1989). Interpretation psychologized. *Mind and Language* 4: 161–85.

Goldman, A. (1992). Empathy, mind, and morals. *Proceedings and Addresses of the American Philosophical Association* 66(3):17–41.

Goldman, A. (1993). Ethics and cognitive science. *Ethics* 103:337–60.

Gopnik, A., and A. Meltzoff. (1997). *Words, thoughts and theories.* Cambridge, Mass.: MIT Press.

Gopnik, A., and H. Wellman. (1994). The theory-theory. In *Mapping the mind: Domain specificity in cognition and culture,* edited by L. Hirschfeld and S. Gelman. Cambridge: Cambridge University Press, 257–93.

Gordon, R. (1986). Folk psychology as simulation. *Mind and Language* 1: 158–71.

Gordon, R. (1995). Sympathy, simulation, and the impartial spectator. *Ethics* 105:727–42.

Grandin, T. (1995). *Thinking in pictures.* New York: Doubleday.

Grantham, T., and S. Nichols. (1999). Evolutionary psychology: Ultimate explanations and panglossian predictions. In *Where biology meets psychology: Philosophical essays,* edited by V. Hardcastle, 47–66. Cambridge, Mass.: MIT Press.

Grice, H. (1975). Logic and conversation. In *Syntax and semantics,* vol. 3, edited by P. Cole and J. Morgan. New York: Academic Press.

Haidt, J., F. Bjorklund, and S. Murphy. (forthcoming). Moral dumbfounding: When intuition finds no reason.

Haidt, J., S. Koller, and M. Dias. (1993). Affect, culture, and morality, or is it wrong to eat your dog? *Journal of Personality and Social Psychology* 65: 613–28.

Haidt, J., C. McCauley, and P. Rozin. (1994). Individual differences in sensitivity to disgust: A scale sampling seven domains of disgust elicitors. *Personality and Individual Differences* 16:701–13.

Halsall, G., ed. (1998). *Violence and society in the early medieval west.* Rochester, N.Y.: Boydell and Brewer.

Hare, R. (1952). *The language of morals.* Oxford: Oxford University Press.

Hare, R. (1991). *The Hare-psychopathy checklist-revised.* Toronto: Multi-Health Systems.

Hare, R.D. (1993). *Without conscience: The disturbing world of the psychopaths among us.* New York: Pocket Books.

Harman, G. (1985). Is there a single true morality? In *Morality, reason and truth: New essays on the foundations of ethics,* edited by D. Copp and D. Zimmerman. Totowa, N.J.: Rowman and Allanheld.

Harman, G., and J. Thomson. (1996). *Moral relativism and moral objectivity.* Oxford: Blackwell.

Harris, P. (1989). *Children and emotion: The development of psychological understanding.* Oxford: Blackwell.

Harris, P. (1992). From simulation to folk psychology: The case for development. *Mind and Language* 7:120–44.

Harris, P. (1993). Understanding emotion," In *Handbook of emotions,* edited by M. Lewis and J. Haviland, 237–46. New York: Guilford Press.

Harris, P. (2000). *The work of the imagination.* Oxford: Blackwell Publishers.

Harris, P. (2002). What do children learn from testimony? In *The Cognitive Basis of Science,* edited by P. Carruthers, S. Stich, and M. Siegal, 316–34. Cambridge: Cambridge University Press.

Harris, P., T. German, and P. Mills. (1996). Children's use of counterfactual thinking in causal reasoning. *Cognition* 61:233–59.

Harris, P., and M. Núñez. (1996). Understanding of permission rules by preschool children. *Child Development* 67:1572–91.

Harris, P., T. Olthof, M. Meerum Terwogt, and C. Hardman. (1987). Children's knowledge of the situations that provoke emotions. *International Journal of Behavioral Development* 10:319–44.

Heine, B. (1985). The mountain people: Some notes on the Ik of north-eastern Uganda. *Africa* 55:3–16.

Henrich J., and R. Boyd. (1998). The evolution of conformist transmission and the emergence of between group differences. *Evolution and Human Behavior* 19:215–41.

Henrich J., and F. Gil-White. (2001). The evolution of prestige: Freely conferred deference as a mechanism for enhancing the benefits of cultural transmission. *Evolution and Human Behavior* 22:165–96.

Heuer, F., and D. Reisberg. (1992). Emotion, arousal, and memory for detail. In *The handbook of emotion and memory,* edited by S. Christianson. Hillsdale, N.J.: Lawrence Erlbaum.

Hirschfeld, L., and S. Gelman. (1994). *Mapping the mind: Domain specificity in cognition and culture.* New York: Cambridge University Press.

Hoffman, M. (1981). The development of empathy. In *Altruism and helping behavior: Social, personality, and developmental perspectives,* edited by J. Rushton and R. Sorrentino, 41–63. Hillsdale, N.J.: Lawrence Erlbaum.

Hoffman, M. (1982). Development of prosocial motivation: Empathy and guilt. In *Development of prosocial behavior,* edited by N. Eisenberg, 281–313. New York: Academic Press.

Hoffman, M. (1976). Empathy, role-taking, guilt and development of altruistic motives. In *Moral development and behavior: Theory, research and social issues,* edited by T. Lickona. New York: Holt, Rinehart and Winston.

Hoffman, M. (1991). Empathy, social cognition, and moral action. In *Handbook of moral behavior and development,* edited by W. Kurtines and J. Gewirtz. Hillsdale, N.J.: Lawrence Erlbaum.

Hollos, M., P. Leis, and E. Turiel. (1986). Social reasoning in Ijo children and adolescents in Nigerian communities. *Journal of Cross-Cultural Psychology* 17:352–74.

Hooker, B., and M. Little, eds. (2000). *Moral particularism*. Oxford: Oxford University Press.

Hume, D. [1739] (1964). *A treatise of human nature*. Oxford: Clarendon Press.

Hume, D. (1742/1987). The sceptic. In Hume's *Essays: Moral, political, and literary*, edited by E. Miller. Indianapolis: Liberty Classics.

Hume, D. [1777] (1975). *Enquiry concerning the principles of morals*. Oxford: Clarendon Press.

Ignatieff, M. (1978). *A just measure of pain: The penitentiary in the industrial revolution, 1750–1850*. New York: Pantheon Books.

Izard, C. (1991). *The psychology of emotions*. New York: Plenum Press.

Jackson, F. (1998). *From metaphysics to ethics: A defence of conceptual analysis*. Oxford: Oxford University Press.

Johnston, M. (1989). Dispositional theories of value. *Proceedings of the Aristotelian Society* Supplementary Volume 63:139–74.

Kebeck, G., and A. Lohaus. (1986). Effect of emotional arousal on free recall of complex material. *Perceptual and Motor Skills* 63:461–62.

Kemp Smith, N. (1941). *The philosophy of David Hume*. London: Macmillan.

Kitcher, P. (1990). Developmental decomposition and the future of human behavioral ecology. *Philosophy of Science* 57:96–117.

Kitcher, P. (1994). Four ways of "biologicizing" ethics. In *Conceptual issues in evolutionary biology*, edited by E. Sober. Cambridge, Mass.: MIT Press.

Kleinsmith, L., and S. Kaplan. (1963). Paired-associate learning as a function of arousal and interpolated interval. *Journal of Experimental Psychology* 65:190–93.

Klimes-Dougan, B. and J. Kistner. (1990). Physically abused preschoolers' responses to peers' distress. *Developmental Psychology* 26:599–602.

Kluckhorn, C. (1953). Universal categories of culture. In *Anthropology Today: An Encyclopedic Inventory*, edited by A. Kroeber, 507–23. Chicago: University of Chicago Press.

Kohlberg, L. (1984). *The psychology of moral development: The nature and validity of moral stages*. New York: Harper and Row.

Korsgaard, C. (1986). Skepticism about practical reason. *Journal of Philosophy* 83:5–25.

Krebs, D. (1975). Empathy and altruism. *Journal of Personality and Social Psychology* 32:1134–46.

Kunda, Z. (1987). Motivated inference. *Journal of Personality and Social Psychology* 53:636–47.

Kunda, Z. (1999). *Social cognition: Making sense of people*. Cambridge, Mass.: MIT Press.

Kurdek, L. (1980). Developmental relations among children's perspective taking, moral judgement, and parent-rated behaviors. *Merrill-Palmer Quarterly* 26:103–21.

Langbein, J. (1974). *Prosecuting crime in the Renaissance: England, Germany, France*. Cambridge, Mass.: Harvard University Press.

Langbein, J. (1977). *Torture and the law of proof: Europe and England in the ancien régime*. Chicago: University of Chicago Press.

Lapsley, D. (1996). *Moral psychology*. Boulder, Colo.: Westview Press.

Latané, B., and Darley, J. (1968). Group inhibition of bystander intervention in emergencies. *Journal of Personality and Social Psychology* 10:215–21.

Laurence, S., and E. Margolis. (1999). Concepts and cognitive science. In *Concepts: Core readings*, edited by E. Margolis and S. Laurence. Cambridge, Mass.: MIT Press.

Leslie, A. (1994). ToMM, ToBY and agency: Core architecture and domain specificity. In *Mapping the mind: Domain specificity in cognition and culture*, edited by L. Hirschfeld and S. Gelman, 119–48. Cambridge: Cambridge University Press.

Leslie, A., and L. Thaiss (1992). Domain specificity in conceptual development: Neuropsychological evidence from autism. *Cognition* 43:225–51.

Lewis, D. (1970). How to define theoretical terms. *Journal of Philosophy* 67: 427–46.

Lewis, D. (1972). Psychophysical and theoretical identifications. *Australasian Journal of Philosophy* 50:249–58.

Lord, C., L. Ross, and M. Lepper. (1979). Biased assimilation and attitude polarization: The effects of prior theories on subsequently considered evidence. *Journal of Personality and Social Psychology* 37:2098–109.

Lorenz, K. (1966). *On aggression*. New York: Harcourt Brace Jovanovich.

Lycan, W. (1988). *Judgement and justification*. Cambridge: Cambridge University Press.

Macaulay, T. (1913). *History of England from the accession of James the Second*. London: Macmillan.

Machery, E., R. Mallon, S. Nichols, and S. Stich. (2004). Semantics, cross-cultural style. *Cognition*.

MacIntyre, A. (1984). *After virtue*. Notre Dame, Ind.: University of Notre Dame Press.

MacIntyre, A. (1998). *A short history of ethics*, 2d ed. Notre Dame, Ind.: University of Notre Dame Press.

Mackie, J. (1977). *Ethics: Inventing right and wrong*. London: Penguin.

Mackie, J. (1980). *Hume's moral theory*. Boston: Routledge and Kegan Paul.

Macklin, R. (1999). *Against relativism*. New York: Oxford University Press.

MacWhinney, B., and C. Snow. (1990). The child language data exchange system: An update. *Journal of Child Language* 17:457–72.

Maehle, A. H. (1994). Cruelty and kindness to the brute creation: Stability and change in the ethics of the man-animal relationship, 1600–1850. In *Animals and Human Society*, edited by A. Manning and J. Serpell. London: Routledge.

Mallon, R., and S. Stich. (2000). The odd couple: The compatibility of social construction and evolutionary psychology. *Philosophy of Science* 67: 133–54.

Mandler, G. (1984). *Mind and body*. New York: Norton.

Manning, C., J. Hall, and P. Gold. (1990). Glucose effects on memory and other neuropsychological tests in elderly humans. *Psychological Science* 1: 307–11.

Marshall, L. (1976). *The !Kung of Nyae Nyae.* Cambridge, Mass.: Harvard University Press.

Martin, G. B., and R. D. Clark (1982). Distress crying in neonates: Species and peer specificity. *Developmental psychology* 18:3–9.

Masserman, J., S. Wechkin, and W. Terris. (1964). "Altruistic" behavior in rhesus monkeys. *American Journal of Psychiatry* 121:584–85.

McDowell, J. [1985] (1997). Values and secondary qualities. Reprinted in *Moral discourse and practice,* edited by S. Darwall, A. Gibbard, and P. Railton. Oxford: Oxford University Press.

McKnight, B. (1992). *Law and order in Sung China.* Cambridge: Cambridge University Press.

McLynn, F. (1991). *Crime and punishment in eighteenth-century England.* Oxford: Oxford University Press.

Mealey, L. (1995). The sociobiology of sociopathy: An integrated evolutionary model. *Behavioral and Brain Sciences* 18:523–41.

Mealey, L. (1997). Heritability, theory of mind, and the nature of normality. *Behavioral and Brain Sciences* 20:527–32.

Michaud, S., and H. Aynesworth. (1989). *Ted Bundy: Conversations with a killer.* New York: New American Library.

Milgram, S. (1963). Behavioral study of obedience. *Journal of Abnormal and Social Psychology* 67:371–78.

Milgram, S. (1974). *Obedience to authority.* New York: Harper and Row.

Miller, A. (1996). An objection to Smith's argument for internalism. *Analysis* 56:169–74.

Miller, J. (in press). Culture and moral development. In *The handbook of culture and psychology,* edited by D. Matsumoto. New York: Oxford University Press.

Miller, J., D. Bersoff, and L. Harwood. (1990). Perceptions of social responsibilities in India and the United States: Moral imperatives or personal decisions? *Journal of Personality and Social Psychology* 58:33–47.

Miller, P., N. Eisenberg, R. Fabes, and R. Shell. (1996). Relations of moral reasoning and vicarious emotion to young children's prosocial behavior toward peers and adults. *Developmental Psychology* 32:210–19.

Miller, R., J. Banks, and N. Ogawa. (1963). Role of facial expression in "cooperative-avoidance conditioning" in monkeys. *Journal of Abnormal and Social Psychology* 67:24–30.

Moody-Adams, M. (1997). *Fieldwork in familiar places.* Cambridge, Mass.: Harvard University Press.

Morton, J. (1986). Developmental contingency modeling. In *Theory building in developmental psychology,* edited by P. van Geert. Amsterdam: Elsevier.

Murdock, G. (1945). The common denominator of cultures. In *The science of man in the world crisis,* edited by R. Linton, 123–42. New York: Columbia University Press.

Murphy, G., and D. Medin. (1985). The role of theories in conceptual coherence. *Psychological Review* 92:289–316.

Nagel, T. (1970). *The possibility of altruism.* Princeton, N.J.: Princeton University Press.

Nagel, T. (1986). *The view from nowhere.* Oxford: Oxford University Press.

Nagel, T. (1997). *The last word.* Oxford: Oxford University Press.

Nelson-Le Gall, S. (1985). Motive-outcome matching and outcome foreseeability: Effects on attribution of intentionality and moral judgments. *Developmental Psychology* 21:332–37.

Newcombe, T. (1961). *The acquaintance process.* New York: Holt, Rinehart and Winston.

Nichols, S. (2001). Mindreading and the cognitive architecture underlying altruistic motivation. *Mind and Language* 16:425–55.

Nichols, S. (2002a). Is it irrational to be amoral? How psychopaths threaten moral rationalism. *The Monist* 85:285–304.

Nichols, S. (2002b). Norms with feeling: Towards a psychological account of moral judgment. *Cognition* 84:221–36.

Nichols, S. (2002c). On the genealogy of norms: A case for the role of emotion in cultural evolution. *Philosophy of Science* 69:234–55.

Nichols, S. (2004). After objectivity: An empirical study of moral judgment. *Philosophical Psychology* 17.

Nichols, S. (in press a). Innateness and moral psychology. In *The Innate Mind: Structure and Content,* edited by P. Carruthers, S. Laurence, and S. Stich. New York: Oxford University Press.

Nichols, S. (in press b). Is religion what we want? Motivation and the cultural transmission of religious representations. *Journal of Cognition and Culture.*

Nichols, S., and T. Folds-Bennett. (2003). Are children moral objectivists? Children's judgments about moral and response-dependent properties. *Cognition* 90:B23 – B32.

Nichols, S., and T. Grantham. (2000). Adaptive complexity and phenomenal consciousness. *Philosophy of Science* 67:648–70.

Nichols, S., and S. Stich. (2000). A cognitive theory of pretense. *Cognition* 74:115–47.

Nichols, S., and S. Stich. (2003). *Mindreading.* Oxford: Oxford University Press.

Nichols, S., S. Stich, A. Leslie, and D. Klein. (1996). Varieties of off-line simulation. In *Theories of theories of mind,* edited by P. Carruthers and P. Smith. Cambridge: Cambridge University Press.

Nietzsche, F. (1887). *On the genealogy of morals.* Translated by W. Kaufman and R. Hollingdale. New York: Vintage Books.

Nisbett, R., K. Peng, I. Choi, and A. Norenzayan. (2001). Culture and systems of thought: Holistic vs. analytic cognition. *Psychological Review* 108: 291–310.

Nisbett, R., and L. Ross. (1980). *Human inference: Strategies and shortcomings of social judgment.* Englewood Cliffs, N.J.: Prentice-Hall.

Norton, D. (1982). *David Hume: Common-sense moralist, sceptical metaphysician.* Princeton, N.J.: Princeton University Press.

Nucci, L. (1986). Children's conceptions of morality, social conventions and religious prescription. In *Moral dilemmas: Philosophical and psychological reconsiderations of the development of moral reasoning,* edited by C. Harding. Chicago: Precedent Press.

Nucci, L. (2001). *Education in the moral domain.* Cambridge: Cambridge University Press.

Nucci, L., and S. Herman. (1982). Behavioral disordered children's conceptions of moral, conventional, and personal issues. *Journal of Abnormal Child Psychology* 10:411–25.

Nucci, L., E. Turiel, and G. Encarnacion-Gawrych. (1983). Children's social interactions and social concepts: Analyses of morality and convention in the Virgin Islands. *Journal of Cross-Cultural Psychology* 14:469–87.

Núñez, M., and P. Harris. (1998). Psychological and deontic concepts: Separate domains or intimate connection? *Mind and Language* 13:153–70.

Nunner-Winkler, G., and B. Sodian. (1988). Children's understanding of moral emotions. *Child Development* 59:1323–38.

Piaget, J. [1932] (1965). *The psychology of moral development: The nature and validity of moral stages.* Translated by M. Gabain. New York: Free Press.

Peter R. (1986). Moral realism. *Philosophical Review* 95:163–207.

Peters, E. (1985). *Torture.* Philadelphia: University of Pennsylvania Press.

Premack, D., and G. Woodruff. (1978). Does the chimpanzee have a theory of mind? *Behavioral and Brain Sciences* 1:516–26.

Preston, S., and F. de Waal. (2002). Empathy: Its ultimate and proximate bases. *Behavioral and Brain Sciences* 25:1–72.

Rachels, J. (1993). Subjectivism. In *A companion to ethics,* edited by P. Singer. Cambridge, Mass.: Blackwell.

Rachels, J. (2002). *Elements of moral philosophy.* 4th ed. New York: McGraw-Hill.

Radke-Yarrow, M., C. Zahn-Waxler, and M. Chapman. (1983). Children's prosocial dispositions and behavior. In *Socialization, personality, and social development,* vol. 4 of *Handbook of child psychology,* edited by P. Mussen. New York: Wiley.

Railton, P. (1986). Moral realism. *Philosophical Review* 95:163–207.

Rawls, J. (1971). *A theory of justice.* Cambridge, Mass.: Harvard University Press.

Repacholi, B., and A. Gopnik. (1997). Early understanding of desires: Evidence from 14- and 18-month-olds. *Developmental Psychology* 33: 12–21.

Revelle, W., and D. Loftus. (1992). The implications of arousal effects for the study of affect and memory. In *The handbook of emotion and memory: Research and theory*, edited by S. Christianson, 151–79. Hillsdale, N.J.: Lawrence Erlbaum.

Riggs, K., D. Peterson, E. Robinson, and P. Mitchell. (1998). Are errors in false belief tasks symptomatic of a broader difficulty with counterfactuality? *Cognitive Development* 13:73–91.

Roberts, W., and J. Strayer. (1996). Empathy, emotional expressiveness, and prosocial behavior. *Child Development* 67:449–70.

Rorty, R. (1998). Human rights, rationality, and sentimentality. In *Truth and progress: Philosophical papers*, vol. 3. Cambridge: Cambridge University Press.

Rosenbaum, M. (1986). The repulsion hypothesis: On the nondevelopment of relationships. *Journal of Personality and Social Psychology* 51:1156–66.

Roskies, A. (2003). Are ethical judgments intrinsically motivational? Lessons from "acquired sociopathy." *Philosophical Psychology* 16:51–66.

Rotenberg, K. (1980). Cognitive processes and young children's use of intention and consequence information in moral judgment. *Merrill-Palmer Quarterly* 26:359–70.

Rottschaefer, W., and D. Martinson. (1990). Really taking Darwin seriously: An alternative to Michael Ruse's Darwinian metaethics. *Biology and Philosophy* 5:149–73.

Rozin, Paul, J. Haidt, and C. McCauley. (2000). Disgust. *Handbook of emotions*, 2d ed., edited by M. Lewis and J. Havilland-Jones. New York: Guilford Press.

Ruse, M., and E. Wilson. (1986). Moral philosophy as applied science. *Philosophy* 61:173–92.

Russell, J. [1460] (1969). The boke of nurture. In *Early english meals and manners*, edited by F. Furnivall. Detroit, Mich.: Singing Tree.

Sachs, J. (1983). Talking about there and then: The emergence of displaced reference in parent-child discourse. In *Children's language*, vol. 4, edited by K. E. Nelson, 1–28. Hillsdale, N.J.: Lawrence Erlbaum.

Sacks, O. (1995). *An anthropologist on mars*. New York: Alfred A. Knopf.

Sagi, A., and Martin L. Hoffman. (1976). Empathic distress in the newborn. *Developmental Psychology* 12:(2):175–76.

Sayre-McCord, G. (1986). The many moral realisms. *Southern Journal of Philosophy* 24(Supplement):1–22.

Schaller, M. (1992). In-group favoritism and statistical reasoning in social inference. *Journal of Personality and Social Psychology* 63:61–74.

Scholl, B., and A. Leslie. (1999). Modularity, development, and "theory of mind." *Mind and language* 14:131–53.

Scott, G. (1959). *The history of corporal punishment: A survey of flagellation in its historical, anthropological, and sociological aspects*. London: Luxor Press.

Seligman, M. (1971). Phobias and preparedness. *Behavior Therapy* 2:307–20.

Selman, R. (1980). *The growth of interpersonal understanding*. New York: Academic Press.

Serpell, J., and E. Paul. (1994). Pets and the development of positive attitudes to animals. In *Animals and human society*, edited by A. Manning and J. Serpell. London: Routledge.

Sheridan, C., and R. King. (1972). Obedience to authority with an authentic victim. *Proceedings of the American Psychological Association* 2:165–66.

Sigman, M., and L. Capps. (1997). *Children with autism: A developmental perspective*. Cambridge, Mass.: Harvard University Press.

Sigman, M., C. Kasari, J. Kwon, and N. Yirmiya. (1992). Responses to the negative emotions of others by autistic, mentally retarded, and normal children. *Child Development* 63:796–807.

Simner, M. (1971). Newborn's response to the cry of another infant. *Developmental Psychology* 5:136–50.

Singer, P. (1981). *The expanding circle*. New York: Farrar, Straus and Giroux.

Singer, P. (1995). *How are we to live*. Amherst, N.Y.: Prometheus Books.

Sinnott-Armstrong, W. (1999). Some varieties of particularism. *Metaphilosophy* 30:1–12.

Slote, M. (1971). The rationality of aesthetic value judgments. *Journal of Philosophy* 68:821–39.

Slote, M. (1982). Is virtue possible? *Analysis* 42:70–76.

Smetana, J. (1985). Preschool children's conceptions of transgressions: Effects of varying moral and conventional domain-related attributes. *Developmental Psychology* 21:18–29.

Smetana, J. (1989). Toddler's social interactions in the context of moral and conventional transgressions in the home. *Developmental Psychology* 25: 499–508.

Smetana, J. (1993). Understanding of social rules. In *The development of social cognition: The child as psychologist*, edited by M. Bennett, 111–41. New York: Guilford Press.

Smetana, J., and J. Braeges. (1990). The development of toddlers' moral and conventional judgements. *Merrill-Palmer Quarterly* 36:329–46.

Smith, M. (1993). Realism. In *A companion to ethics*, edited by P. Singer, 399–410. Cambridge, Mass.: Blackwell.

Smith, M. (1994). *The moral problem*. Oxford: Blackwell.

Smith, M. (1996). The argument for internalism: Reply to Miller. *Analysis* 56:175–84.

Smith, M. (1997). In defense of *The moral problem:* A reply to Brink, Copp, and Sayre-McCord. *Ethics* 108:84–119.

Smith, M. (1998). Emotivism. In *Routledge encyclopedia of philosophy*, vol. 3, edited E. Craig, 291–93. New York: Routledge.

Smith, M., and D. Stoljar. (1998). Global response dependence and noumenal realism. *The Monist* 81:85–111.

Snarey, J. (1985). Cross-cultural universality of social-moral development: A critical review of Kohlbergian research. *Psychological Bulletin* 97:202–32.

Sober, E. (1994). *From a biological point of view: Essays in evolutionary philosophy.* New York: Cambridge University Press.

Sober, E., and D. Wilson. (1998). *Unto others.* Cambridge, Mass.: Harvard University Press.

Song, M., J. Smetana, and S. Kim. (1987). Korean children's conceptions of moral and conventional transgressions. *Developmental Psychology* 23: 577–82.

Spelke, E. (1994). Initial knowledge: Six suggestions. *Cognition* 50:431–45.

Sperber, D. (1996). *Explaining culture.* Cambridge, Mass.: Blackwell.

Spierenburg, P. (1991). *The broken spell: A cultural and anthropological history of preindustrial Europe.* New Brunswick, N.J.: Rutgers University Press.

Stevenson, C. (1944). *Ethics and language.* New Haven, Conn.: Yale University Press.

Stewart, R., and R. Marvin. (1984). Sibling relations: The role of conceptual perspective-taking in the ontogeny of sibling care-giving. *Child Development* 55:1322–32.

Stich, S. (1992). What is a theory of mental representation? *Mind* 101: 243–61.

Stich, S., and S. Nichols. (1992). Folk psychology: Simulation or tacit theory. *Mind and Language* 7(1):35–71.

Stich, S., and J. Weinberg. (2001). Jackson's empirical assumptions. *Philosophy and Phenomenological Research* 62:637–43.

Stotland, E. (1969). Exploratory investigations of empathy. In *Advances in experimental social psychology*, vol. 4, edited by L. Berkowitz. New York: Academic Press.

Stroud, B. (1977). *Hume.* Boston: Routledge and Kegan Paul.

Sturgeon, N. (1985). Moral explanations. In *Morality, reason, and truth*, edited by D. Copp and D. Zimmerman. Totowa, N.J.: Rowman and Allanheld.

Sturgeon, N. (2001). Moral skepticism and moral naturalism in Hume's "Treatise." *Hume Studies* 27:3–84.

Sumner, W. (1906). *Folkways: A study of the sociological importance of usages, manners, customs, mores, and morals.* Boston: Ginn.

Tager-Flusberg, H. (1993). What language reveals about the understanding of minds in children with autism. In *Understanding other minds: Perspectives from autism*, edited by S. Baron-Cohen, H. Tager-Flusberg, and D. Cohen, 138–57. Oxford: Oxford University Press.

Tajfel, H. (1981). *Human groups and social categories.* Cambridge: Cambridge University Press.

Tan, J., and P. Harris (1991). Autistic children understand seeing and wanting. *Development and Psychopathology* 3:163–74.

Thomas, K. (1983). *Man and the natural world: Changing attitudes in England 1500–1800.* London: Allen Lane.

Thompson, R. (1987). Empathy and emotional understanding: The early de-

velopment of empathy. In *Empathy and its development*, edited by N.
Eisenberg and J. Strayer. New York: Cambridge University Press.

Thompson, R., and M. Hoffman. (1980). Empathy and the arousal of guilt
in children. *Developmental Psychology* 15:155–56.

Tisak, M. (1995). Domains of social reasoning and beyond. In *Annals of
child development*, vol. 11, edited by R. Vasta, 95–130. London: Jessica
Kingsley.

Tomasello, M., and J. Call. (1997). *Primate cognition*. New York: Oxford University Press.

Toulmin, S. (1950). *An examination of the place of reason in ethics*. Cambridge: Cambridge University Press.

Trevelyan, G. (1942). *English social history: A survey of six centuries, Chaucer to
Queen Victoria*. London: Longmans, Green.

Trivers, R. (1971). The evolution of reciprocal altruism. *Quarterly Review of
Biology* 46:35–57.

Turiel, E. (1983). *The development of social knowledge: Morality and convention*,
Cambridge: Cambridge University Press.

Turiel, E., M. Killen, and C. Helwig. (1987). Morality: Its structure, functions, and vagaries. In *The emergence of morality in young children*, edited
by J. Kagan and S. Lamb, 155–244. Chicago: University of Chicago
Press.

Turnbull, C. (1972). *The mountain people*. New York: Simon and Schuster.

Wechkin, S., J. Masserman, and W. Terris, Jr. (1964). Shock to a conspecific
as an aversive stimulus. *Psychonomic Science* 1:47–48.

Wedgwood, R. (1998). The essence of response-dependence. *European Review of Philosophy* 3:331–54.

Weisser, R. (1979). *Crime and punishment in early modern Europe*. Atlantic
Highlands, N.J.: Humanities Press.

Weinberg, J., S. Nichols, and S. Stich. (2001). Normativity and epistemic intuitions. *Philosophical Topics* 29:429–60.

Wellman, Henry M. (1990–8). *The child's theory of mind*. Cambridge, Mass.:
MIT Press.

Wellman, H., D. Cross, and J. Watson. (2001). Meta-analysis of theory-of-
mind development: The truth about false belief. *Child Development* 72:
655–84.

Wellman, H., P. Harris, M. Banerjee, and A. Sinclair. (1995). Early understanding of emotion: Evidence from natural language. *Cognition and
Emotion* 9:117–79.

Westermarck, E. (1906–8). *The origin and development of the moral ideas*. London: MacMillan.

Wiggins, D. [1991] (1997). A sensible subjectivism. Reprinted in *Moral discourse and practice*, edited by S. Darwall, A. Gibbard, and P. Railton. Oxford: Oxford University Press.

Williams, B. (1981). Internal and external reasons. In *Moral luck*, edited by
B. Williams. Cambridge: Cambridge University Press.

Williams, G. (1966). *Adaptation and natural selection: A critique of some current evolutionary thought.* Princeton, N.J.: Princeton University Press.

Wimmer, H., and J. Perner. (1983). Beliefs about beliefs: Representation and constraining function of wrong beliefs in young children's understanding of deception. *Cognition* 13(1):103–28.

Wing, L., and J. Gould. (1979). Severe impairments of social interaction and associated abnormalities in children: Epidemiology and classification. *Journal of Autism and Developmental Disorders* 9:11–29.

Woodward, A. (1998). Infants selectively encode the goal object of an actor's reach. *Cognition* 69:1–34.

Yirmiya, N., M. Sigman, C. Kasari, and P. Mundy. (1992). Empathy and cognition in high-functioning children with autism. *Child Development* 63: 150–60.

Zahn-Waxler, C., and M. Radke-Yarrow. (1982). The development of altruism: Alternative research strategies. In *The development of prosocial behavior,* edited by N. Eisenberg-Berg. New York: Academic Press.

Zahn-Waxler, C., M. Radke-Yarrow, and R. King. (1979). Child rearing and children's prosocial initiations toward victims of distress. *Child Development* 50:319–30.

Zahn-Waxler, C., M. Radke-Yarrow, E. Wagner, and M. Chapman. (1992a). Development of concern for others. *Developmental Psychology* 28:126–36.

Zahn-Waxler, C., J. Robinson, and R. Emde. (1992b). The development of empathy in twins. *Developmental Psychology* 28:1038–47.

Zelazo, P., C. Helwig, and A. Lau. (1996). Intention, act, and outcome in behavioral prediction and moral judgment. *Child Development* 67: 2478–92.

Index

dissociation between normative theory and emotional response, 18–19
dissociation problem for neosentimentalism, 89–92
distress attribution, 57
   in children, 44
distributive justice, children's judgments about, 108–9
Doris, J., 149, 157n
dumbfounding, 20n
Duncker, K., 148
Dunn, J., 5, 10, 49, 90, 104, 114
Durham, W., 129

Edel, M., 143
Edel, A., 143
egocentricity in prosocial behavior, 49–51
Eisenberg, N., 17, 31, 32, 38, 49n, 52, 54, 55, 115
Ekman, P., 54, 125, 132, 155
Elias, N., 118, 130–32, 133, 158
emotion and memorability, 125–27
emotional contagion and altruistic motivation, 35–38, 42–43
   See also contagious distress
emotional response to suffering in nonhuman animals, 156–57
emotional response to suffering in others, 17–18, 30–64, 81–82, 154–55
   in nonhuman primates, 61
emotions, understanding of, 89–92
emotivism, 85–86
empathy, 9, 31, 38–39, 40–41, 55
Emsley, C., 146, 160
Engelberg, E., 127
Enlightenment, Western, 149–50
epidemiological approach to cultural transmission, 121–27
   and cultural variation, 123–24
   and emotion, 124–29
   and memorability, 123
Erasmus, D., 131, 133–34, 135, 136, 137

error theory, 178, 190–93
etiquette, 112–13, 116
etiquette manuals, 130–31
evolutionary ethics, 120, 150n
evolutionary function, 17, 61–62
   and moral objectivity, 188n
evolutionary psychology, 101, 122
Ewing, A., 85, 87

Fabes, R., 38, 49n, 54
false belief task, 10
Fernald, M., 11, 58
Flanagan, O., 171
Flavell, J., 172n
Fodor, J., 60n, 101, 192
Folds-Bennett, T., 173, 175, 180
Foucault, M., 146, 154
Frank, R., 120
Frege-Geach problem, 86, 106
Frith, U., 13, 58
Furnivall, F., 137n

Garcia, J., 132
Geach, P., 85, 86, 100, 106
Gergely, G., 39
German, T., 101
Gewirth, A., 65
Gibbard, A., 66, 83, 85, 87, 88, 89, 93, 98n, 117, 172
Gil-White, F., 121n
Gill, M., 66, 193n
Goldman, A., 8, 9, 35, 36, 40, 41, 52
Gopnik, A., 8, 50, 172n
Gordon, R., 8, 9, 40
Gould, J., 58
Grandin, T., 91
Grantham, T., 61
guilt, 88–95, 107

Haidt, J., 7, 20n, 23, 55n, 132, 142, 177n
Halsall, G., 145
Hare, R. M., 73, 98n, 112
Hare, R.D., 59, 77, 112
harm, 16

Wilson, E., 119
Wing, L., 58
Woodruff, G., 60
Woodward, A., 39
Word, L., 34–35, 37
wrong vs. bad, 14–16

Yanomamö, 142
Yirmiya, N., 14, 58, 59n, 81

Zahn-Waxler, C., 18, 25, 44–45, 55n, 49, 57
Zelazo, P., 15

Printed in the United States
202750BV00003B/69/A

9 780195 314205